ENCYCLOPEDIA OF

COUNTRY
FURNITURE

ENCYCLOPEDIA OF
COUNTRY
FURNITURE

SMITHMARK

A FRIEDMAN GROUP BOOK

This edition published in 1993 by SMITHMARK Publishers Inc.
16 East 32nd Street, New York NY 10016.

SMITHMARK Books are available for bulk purchase for sales promotion and premium use. For details write or call the manager of special sales, SMITHMARK Publishers Inc., 16 East 32nd Street, New York, NY 10016; (212) 532-6600.

ENCYCLOPEDIA OF COUNTRY FURNITURE
was prepared and produced by
Michael Friedman Publishing Group, Inc.
15 West 26th Street
New York, NY 10010

Editor: Sharyn Rosart
Art Director: Jeff Batzli
Designer: Edward Noriega
Photography Editor: Ede Rothaus
Photography Researcher: Emilya Naymark

Library of Congress Cataloging-in-Publication Data
Frankel, Candie.
    Encyclopedia of country furniture / by Candie Frankel.
        p. cm.
    Includes bibliographical references and index.
    ISBN 0-8317-2581-8 : $19.98
    1. Country furniture—Encyclopedia. I. Title.
NK2205.F69 1993
749.2—dc20

93-8272
CIP

Output by Bookworks
Color separations by Scantrans Pte. Ltd.
Printed in Hong Kong and bound in China by Leefung-Asco Printers Ltd.

10 9 8 7 6 5 4 3 2 1

FOR FRED

ACKNOWLEDGMENTS

THE AUTHOR WISHES TO THANK THE AUSTRALIAN CONSULATE, BRITISH INFORMATION SERVICES, THE CANADIAN CONSULATE GENERAL, THE CENTRAL RESEARCH LIBRARY OF THE NEW YORK PUBLIC LIBRARY, THE MUSEUM OF AMERICAN FOLK ART, THE NEW YORK PUBLIC LIBRARY, THE QUEENS BOROUGH PUBLIC LIBRARY, AND URSUS BOOKS, ALL IN NEW YORK CITY; AND THE AMERICAN ACADEMY OF PEDIATRICS, *EARLY AMERICAN LIFE* MAGAZINE, THE NATIONAL TRUST OF AUSTRALIA, AND THE POWERHOUSE MUSEUM OF APPLIED ARTS AND SCIENCES. SPECIAL APPRECIATION IS GIVEN TO JANET M. BACON, MELL COHEN, FRED FRANKEL, ROSEMARY GABRIEL, KENNETH HEISER, ALICE J. HOFFMAN, TRISHA MALCOLM, ANDREW F. MALONE, CANDACE ORD MANROE, JO MOTT, JUDY P. SOPRONYI, CAROL SPIER, JEAN VANDEWATER, LYNNE VANDEWATER, GREGORY VASILEFF, ANNE WATSON, EDITH C. WISE, AND LAST, BUT NOT LEAST, STEVE ARCELLA, EMILYA NAYMARK, ED NORIEGA, SHARYN ROSART, EDE ROTHAUS, AND LIZ SULLIVAN, WHO BROUGHT THESE PAGES TO FRUITION.

TABLE OF CONTENTS

INTRODUCTION

THERE IS NO DENYING THE MAGIC—YESTERYEAR'S COUNTRY FURNITURE HAS CHARMED OUR MODERN SOUL. COUNTRY AND CITY AUCTIONS, FLEA MARKETS, TAG SALES, SECONDHAND STORES, AND ANTIQUE SHOPS ARE AMONG THE SHOPPING MECCAS FOR VINTAGE FURNITURE. EXTRA-OLD OR RARE PIECES, OUT OF THE RANGE OF MOST PEOPLE'S POCKETBOOKS, CAN BE VIEWED IN "LIVING" MUSEUMS, HISTORIC HOUSES, AND VILLAGE RESTORATIONS. IF YOU REALLY LOVE THE LOOK AND AMBIANCE OF A PROHIBITIVELY EXPENSIVE ANTIQUE, YOU CAN SEEK OUT ITS LOOK-ALIKE AMONG MUSEUM-LICENSED REPRODUCTIONS OFFERED BY MANUFACTURERS OF QUALITY FURNITURE.

No longer strictly "colonial," today's country look is international and eclectic. The cozy homing instinct that once had us angling a colonial settle up to the fireplace might today find us on a grand tour of provincial country homes in Scandinavia, France, and England. In America, interest in a pioneer and immigrant past has uncovered regional and ethnic sources rich with decorative history— the Pennsylvania German, Midwest Norwegian, and Sante Fe Southwest among them. As our knowledge of these many furniture styles and construction techniques grows, the choices—and responsibilities—become staggering. That we can rediscover and preserve these styles in our own homes, oftentimes miles from their places of origin, is a tribute to the vision and imagination of all who work in the decorative arts.

Collectors are also discovering that many of today's most affordable pieces are neither handcrafted nor particularly old—nor originally intended for the country! During the Victorian era, new inventions, machines, and modes of transport made mass production and distribution of many different types of furniture possible. Steam-powered lathes, saws, and veneer cutters emphasized speed, symmetry, and quantity in production. Populations on the move responded to furniture that was attractive, lightweight, functional, and affordable.

Many nineteenth-century factory-produced pieces— such as pressed-back rockers, iron bedsteads, wicker settees, and Mission Oak chairs—were purchased by country and city dwellers alike, yet they are invariably considered "country" today. And in a surprising reverse move, Europe's once elegant rococo-style furniture has been stripped of its peeling veneer and dressed down as the newest country pine. The modern eye is also taking a closer look at yesteryear's business furniture. Store counters, apothecary cabinets, and old barrister's bookcases can do yeoman duty when it comes to solving modern storage dilemmas. Fortunately, not everyone discarded yesterday's sensation to make room for today's breakthrough, and affordable examples are still available.

It is perhaps ironic that the very industrial progress that blotted out the rural way of life makes us nostalgic for it today. But industry also brings us the means to explore our own and others' country roots beyond our wildest dreams. At this moment in history, we ordinary people, in our own homes, can learn about and actually live with the furniture of other times, other lands, and other traditions. This is an unprecedented privilege, and it is hoped that this encyclopedia will help the reader take advantage of it.

OPPOSITE PAGE: An eclectic mix of Canadian painted country furnishings includes a low cupboard, a child's chair, a side table, and a low stool.

HOW TO USE THIS BOOK

The straightforward A-to-Z format of this encyclopedia should help you find the information you need. If you are interested in reading about a particular piece of furniture that you own, are thinking of buying, or have admired in a museum or historic house, look it up directly by name or category. Examples include bentwood furniture, dressers, and rocking chairs. You can also look up different countries and regions by name. These entries will give you an appreciation of different furniture-making traditions, immigrant groups, and decorating styles. Many entries provide cross-references to related topics. To find out more about furniture construction or restoration, see the entries entitled Joining and Turning, Restoring Old Furniture, Stripped Pine, and Woods.

Throughout the encyclopedia, you will find Quality Checklist and Care Tips boxes. The Quality Checklists will help you know what features to look for—and to watch out for—when you are shopping for antiques. The Care Tips tell you how to safeguard your furniture for future generations. Technical words are defined in a glossary, and a source guide and bibliography will help you explore subjects of further interest.

Above all, have fun just browsing—and enjoy your country furniture!

ADIRONDACK CHAIR

THE ADIRONDACK CHAIR IS THE CLASSIC AMERICAN WOODEN LAWN CHAIR. THE LOW-SLUNG SEAT AND BACK ARE TILTED BACK IN A COMFORTABLE SEMIRECLINING POSITION, SIMILAR TO THAT OF A ROCKING CHAIR. ITS ORIGIN IS UNCERTAIN, BUT IT MAY HAVE SPRUNG FROM THE SOLID BOARD WESTPORT CHAIR FIRST MADE IN THE ADIRONDACK MOUNTAIN REGION AROUND 1904. CHAIR BUILDER THOMAS LEE REPORTEDLY HAD NEIGHBORS AND FAMILY TEST HIS DESIGN REPEATEDLY TO ACHIEVE JUST THE RIGHT ANGLE FOR EASY LOUNGING.

Considering its straight board construction, the Adirondack chair is surprisingly accommodating. Both seat and back are assembled from wood slats, which

allow rainwater to pass through. The back vertical slats are cut to rise up in a characteristic arch, and in some versions the horizontal seat slats form a soft roll at the front so that there are no sharp edges behind the knees. The rear legs slant back behind the chair to provide extra stability. The chair arms are flat, level, and broad enough to hold a drink tumbler or a sandwich plate. The Adirondack chair was popular throughout America from about 1920 to the beginning of World War II, and it is enjoying a revival today.

ARROW-BACK CHAIR

The arrow-back chair is a late development of the Windsor chair. It first appeared around 1810 and was most popular through 1835. Construction was the same as the Windsor chair, except that the back spindles were wider and slightly flattened, each one fanning out below the crest to resemble the feathered butt of an arrow. These flat arrows were a bit more comfortable than

---

OPPOSITE PAGE: A classic Adirondack lawn chair with rolled slat seat and flat, broad arms shows the wear and tear of outdoor life. *ABOVE:* Traces of decorative painting are visible on the crest of an antique arrow-back chair.

round spindles to lean against. They were usually worked from maple, though poplar and hickory were also used. Early versions had as many arrows as Windsor chairs had spindles, but by mid-century, only three large arrows remained.

Arrow-back chairs were decoratively painted and stenciled, imitating Sheraton-style fancy chairs. Dark green and rusty black with yellow striping appeared in Vermont, New York, and western Massachusetts; dark brown and solid yellow were used in eastern and southern New England; and bright blue, green, brown, and red were popular in Pennsylvania. Paint not only provided color and decoration but also concealed the variety of woods that made up a single chair.

See also Sheraton-Style Fancy Chairs, Windsor Chairs.

AUSTRALIA

Europeans learned of Australia through early seventeenth-century sea exploration, but it was not until the American colonies gained their independence that England began considering Australia as a new colonial outpost. The first Australian settlement, in 1788, was a colony of male and female convicts, their jailers, and some of the jailers' families. Subsequent settlements included both prisoners and free citizens. The hot, dry climate and dependence on cargo shipments from England made life especially difficult. Overland exploration over the next forty years would reveal a vast, remote, and largely inhospitable continent that called for tremendous resourcefulness, stamina, and courage to tame.

Almost all of the nineteenth-century Australian settlers were from England, Scotland, Wales, and Ireland. Their furniture traditions included Windsor-style stick chairs, settles, tables, chests, cupboards, kitchen dressers, and simple low-post beds. Most settlers could not duplicate this furniture, much less build permanent homes, when they first arrived. Instead, they made do with slab stools, stick chairs, and log-post bedframes. A trunk used on the sea voyage continued to hold personal clothing and valuables, and simple cupboards were fashioned from recycled wooden packing crates.

As a settlement prospered, more permanent furniture was built. Because new immigrants were constantly arriving throughout the 1800s, the cycle of first building basic stick furniture and then graduating to more traditional pieces repeated itself many times over. Because of this, it is very difficult to date Australian country pieces—they are chronological only within the life of an individual settlement. A crude stick chair from an outlying region may well be newer than a kitchen table with lathe-turned legs from an established coastal settlement.

Eventually, even newly arriving cabinetmakers could not meet the demand for furniture. The population grew so rapidly, through both birth and immigration, that cottage bedroom suites, bentwood chairs, iron bedsteads, and other factory-made pieces were shipped to Australia from England, continental Europe, and the United States.

ABOVE: Three broad arrow-shaped spindles form the backrest of this mid-nineteenth-century kitchen chair from Pennsylvania. *RIGHT:* A Jimmy Possum chair.

STICK AND SLAB FURNITURE

Early Australian settlers made "survival" furniture using sticks and slabs of wood. These pieces included crude benches, log stools, and slab tabletops resting on tree root pedestals. Norwegian sailors who jumped ship to join the gold rushes introduced the *kubbestol* log chair. Forked branches were used to support bedframes.

Stick chairs had joins designed to tighten when the person sat down. The Cootamundra Jack chair used two elegantly forked branches that divided into graceful front and back legs. The Jimmy Possum stick chair emerged as a distinct style in the Tasmanian Deloraine district during the late nineteenth and early twentieth centuries. This blackwood and hardwood chair was made in the Windsor stick tradition and had squared legs, stiles, and back spindles. The shearer's chair was a folding stick-style chair with a sling seat, something like a modern beach chair. The seat and back were angled and low to the ground and helped make the long hours in the shearing sheds more comfortable. Miners sometimes set up shearer's chairs right in the riverbeds, so they could sit while panning for gold.

COUNTRY CABINETMAKERS

Furniture making in Australia was much less formalized than in England. In England, joiners and turners were permitted to construct stick chairs, but only cabinetmakers were trained to make paneled furniture with mortise-and-tenon or dovetail joins. In Australia, the need for utilitarian furniture was too great and the territory too vast to be fussy about guild rules or restrictions. As a result, the country furniture made there between 1800 and 1940 represents many different skill levels and styles.

Settles and settees were used for indoor as well as verandah seating, and loose cushions were generally used to soften the hard wooden seats. Straight rectilinear furniture was very popular, as were heavy turned legs for tables. The Australians also had to become familiar with the new, native woods: dense, heavy eucalyptus jarrah, strong blackwood, aromatic cedars, and a variety of soft pines.

ABOVE: A settler-made slab table retains traces of bark on the underside, evidence of quick construction. *ABOVE RIGHT:* Triangular and diamond-shaped moldings dress up a home-crafted chiffonier from South Australia. *RIGHT:* Rather than discard the packing cases that brought goods to the frontier, resourceful carpenters used them as ready-made drawers.

German Influences

A significant German population also influenced Australian cabinetmaking. Often, entire villages would relocate from the continent and hold on to their old customs, language, religion, and furniture-making traditions. Most were from northern Germany and therefore did not practice decorative peasant alpine painting. But they did introduce the *Kleiderschrank,* the *Milchschrank,* the sawbuck table, and the dough box. German-made furniture also had playful touches, such as moustache pediments, wavy framing and aprons, and slightly curved, tapered legs in the Biedermeier style. In the late 1900s, spattric or spatterie work became popular. This paint craft was practiced mostly by women and involved using fern fronds and other plant leaves as reverse-stencils to decorate drawer fronts and tabletops.

Squatter's Furniture

In the early 1800s, merino sheep were introduced to Australia from Spain. They thrived in the Australian climate, and sheep ranching soon became a profitable enterprise. The sheep herders were called squatters. They ventured out into the government-owned wilderness in search of new grazing land and staked claims even though they had no legal title.

The furniture the squatters used reflected their hard and somewhat nomadic lifestyle. Zinc-plated mesh was necessary on all food safes to guard against blow flies, which are annoyingly present wherever sheep are grazing. It also became customary to fit the lower panels of dresser cupboards with mesh so that these too could be used for food storage.

The miner's, or shepherd's, couch provided comfortable seat furniture. This wooden couch bolted together and could be easily disassembled for moving. It was quite fashionable, with lathe-turned armrests and a "rolling pin" crest inspired by French Empire furniture. The loose seat cushions rested on wooden slats, and the entire piece stood on thick, low, turned legs. Many of these sturdy couches opened out into a full bedframe complete with extra sets of screw-on legs.

LEFT: Grain painting enhances the doors of this inexpensive, factory-produced cupboard front. *ABOVE:* A reproduction kangaroo-backed Federation chair.

The casual posture of sitting in a chair and dangling one's legs over the armrests led to the Australian squatter's chair. This unpretentious board chair had a backrest that adjusted at different angles and swing-out armrests designed just for leg dangling.

FACTORY-MADE FURNITURE

Australia's first factory-made furniture was imported from more industrialized countries, but by the late 1800s, homegrown manufacturing was well underway. The furniture made included Victorian pedestal tables, chiffoniers, bedroom furniture, upholstered parlor suites, and desks, chairs, and filing cabinets for government and business offices.

FEDERATION CHAIR

A particular favorite among collectors of Australiana is the kangaroo-backed Federation chair. Golden Oak

spindle-back chairs with steam-embossed designs in the crest rails were first introduced to Australia from the United States. Australia's Melbourne Chair Company adopted the steam-embossing technique and created its own cast dies featuring Australian motifs. In addition to the kangaroo, there were dies for emus, lyre-birds, and other native Australian wildlife. The chairs themselves were a sturdy kitchen type, featuring legs and spindles turned from Tasmanian blackwood, saddled or caned seats of kauri pine, and rails of hoop pine. Production continued through the 1930s, and reproductions made from dies newly cast from the original molds are quite popular today.

PEDDLE CHAIR

The Windsor-style Peddle chair is another factory-made chair with nostalgic appeal. Made of native blackwood, it appeared in railway stations throughout Australia into the early twentieth century. The Peddle chair is sturdy, serviceable, and built to last. It was named after an English furniture manufacturer who emigrated to Australia in 1884.

See also under Kitchen Furniture—Food Safes and Cupboards.

ABOVE: As Australian settlements prospered, the miner's couch grew more elegant in design, gaining Greek Revival features such as outwardly turned saber legs and a symmetrically curved backrest. Turned rails were more common as armrests than the gently shaped boards shown here.

BANISTER-BACK CHAIR

THE BANISTER-BACK CHAIR OF THE LATE SEVENTEENTH
AND EARLY EIGHTEENTH CENTURIES IS A MASTERPIECE OF
THE TURNER'S CRAFT. IT IS ALSO CALLED THE BALUSTER-
BACK CHAIR. IT IS RECOGNIZED MOST READILY BY THE
SPLIT HALF-BANISTERS THAT FORM THE CHAIR BACK AND
THE CONTRAST OF EBONIZED WOOD AGAINST THE HONEY-
COLORED RUSH SEAT.

The innovative feature of the banister-back chair is
its split banisters. Leaning back against turned spindles
was uncomfortable, so turners devised a way to make
these vertical spindles flat on one side. These half-banisters were joined into the crossrails flat side forward,
which was not only more comfortable but also put the
decorative turnings in striking silhouette. Occasionally,
the turned side appears forward, for a reverse-back banis-
ter chair.

Half-banisters were turned two at a time. Most banister-back chairs had four split banisters, but some had
three or five. An odd number of half-banisters on a chair
back may indicate it was made as one of a pair. The
chair is topped with a baroque crest imitating those used
on formal cane-seated chairs of the same period. Style
variations included Spanish feet and armchairs with

mushroom-shaped knobs as handholds (this feature was
revived in the nineteenth century by the Shakers). The
Dutch preferred two large bulbous turnings in the center
of the front stretcher. English banister-backs were generally black walnut, while American-made chairs were usually maple. Beech, hickory, and pine were also used, and
all were ebonized to a rich, dark black-brown. The chairs
were widely used in rural America from 1700 to 1725.

See also Joining and Turning, Rush Seats.

BEDS

Beds and private bedrooms are commonplace in modern homes, but less than three centuries ago, beds were
highly valued and a sign of prestige and wealth. Linens,
pillows, mattresses, and bed coverings were costly, well
cared for, and passed down to future generations
through dowries and wills. In seventeenth-century
homes, the bed was placed prominently in the main
room of the house, which also served for eating, cooking, reading, and receiving guests. Homes were typically
small, cold, drafty, and unevenly heated. The high-post
bed, with curtains to draw around on three sides (the

*ABOVE LEFT: A banister-back chair. The split half-banisters are positioned
flat side forward. ABOVE: Four banister-back chairs around a table show
the split banisters from several angles. OPPOSITE PAGE: A Jenny Lind
spool-turned bed.*

head of the bed backed against the wall), offered both privacy and warmth. Many yards of fabric were required, and the bed furnishings could easily be a household's single largest asset. A more affordable solution was to bundle up under the covers in a low-post bed, which could be pushed under the eaves or fit into cottages with low ceilings. In continental Europe, middle-class as well as peasant homes featured built-in cabinet beds.

In the eighteenth century, homes became larger and more comfortable, and an emerging sense of privacy led to separate bedrooms. By the end of the century, elaborate bed curtains were no longer a necessity, but the high-post bed continued to be in fashion, with decorative swags draped from the cornice. Since the bedposts were turned and the rails were plain, making a stylish high- or low-post bed for a country customer was within the range of the skilled joiner and turner. By the mid-nineteenth century, factory-made alternatives such as the spool-turned bed, brass and iron beds, and entire cottage bedroom suites were highly affordable and popular in all areas.

CUPBOARD BEDS

The European cupboard or cabinet bed is best thought of as a piece of architecture rather than a piece of furniture. Such beds were really small, platform rooms, with space for bedding and little else. Privacy was afforded by heavily paneled doors, curtains that drew closed, or a combination of both. An upper frieze was often grilled or fitted with turned spindles to let in air. Bedding could range from lowly straw to plump feather beds, depending on the prosperity of the household.

Pine and oak cupboard beds were built into peasant and middle-class homes in Holland, France, Switzerland, Scandinavia, and Central Europe. These were often carved or decoratively painted, and the interiors might be fitted with shelves or small secret closets. The French so appreciated coziness that in lieu of a cupboard bed, they fitted four-poster or box beds into snug alcoves. A common space-saving arrangement in Scandinavia was to build two beds along one wall, end to end, with storage cabinets underneath. For warmth, one bed was often built up against the stove or chimney flue and reserved for the elderly, the ill, or mothers with newborn infants.

What Is Provenance?

When museum curators or antiques specialists use the word provenance, *they are referring to specific information about the source or origin of a piece of furniture: where a piece of furniture originated, who made it, who the various owners were, and how and when the piece changed hands.*

The origins of country furniture are harder to establish than those of formal antiques. The opportune time to ask about a particular piece is at the point of sale. Especially in rural towns or at estate auctions, the seller may have an informal history to share. Details on who owned the piece, how long it was in the family, where it was made, and how much it cost are part of the piece's history and worth jotting down. If you buy a bed, find out who slept in it before you, and who was born in it. The serious antique hunter will be a bit of a history buff, perpetually reading, examining, and comparing in order to learn how to place interesting purchases into broader furniture history. The information and local color you collect now may be of unusual and unexpected interest sometime in the future.

In the British Isles, cabinet beds were much simpler and were associated with poorer households. Although the Dutch colonists used cabinet beds, they never really caught on in America. Today, cupboard beds are being rediscovered and used in vacation homes, ski lodges, and other dwellings where large groups of people gather and space is at a premium.

HIGH FOUR-POSTER BEDS

Four-poster bedframes were designed to be easily assembled and knocked down, a once-a-year job at minimum to eradicate the bedbugs living in the wood. Many people are surprised to find that the two headposts of old beds are plain stained pine. This is because the bed curtains hid them from view. The footposts, which were not hidden by curtains, can be quite decorative in comparison. Reproduction beds often ignore this distinction and cater to the modern customer's preference for four matching bedposts.

In addition to the four posts, the bed has four rails—two long rails at the sides and two short rails at the head and foot. They connect the posts with wedged mortise-and-tenon joins or, on newer beds, with a long bedscrew or bolt. Sometimes a sliding wooden panel or metal cover hid the bolt. Though it is no longer necessary, repro-

duction beds sometimes include this little ornament. On top of the posts were spikes to support the wood cornice. The cornice wrapped around the bed on three sides and concealed long metal rods with rings for hanging the curtains. On later high four-posters, the cornice was eliminated and the spikes were replaced with finials. One contemporary decorating trend is to bring back the bare metal rods and drape them with gauzy material.

The actual bedding—what is today called a mattress—was suspended on ropes laced from rail to rail. Some bedrails had holes bored through them for the ropes and others had knoblike pegs 6 to 8 inches (15 – 20cm) apart. A good bed included a straw or hair mattress topped by a feather bed filled with goose feathers and down. Making the bed took time and care. The feathers had to be coaxed into the middle of the bed and then evened out with a bed smoother, a wire mesh tool that resembles a large flyswatter. A bolster was placed at the headboard, followed by a bottom sheet, down pillows, a top sheet, blankets, and finally a whole cloth or pieced quilt. The bolster helped people sit up while sleeping, which was advised for pulmonary problems. A reminder upon retiring to "sleep tight" referred to the practice of tightening the bed ropes with a special key-like tool so the bed wouldn't sag during the night.

RIGHT: A reproduction pencil post bed has a contemporary tie-on canopy.

FIELD BED

The term "field bed" originally referred to a folding bed set up inside a military officer's tent near the field of battle. Eventually, the name came to mean a small bed with a tentlike canopy, which today is most often called a canopied bed. Rather than a high, rectangular tester, the field bed has an arched support that rises up from four low posts. A fabric canopy covers the top, but no curtains hang at the sides. The field bed first emerged in the eighteenth century and was popular through the early nineteenth century, when it was covered with a lacy openwork netting. Today, the style remains a special favorite of little girls.

PENCIL POST BED

The pencil post bed is a true country-style four-poster. It originated in late-eighteenth-century New England when country cabinetmakers began using designs that emulated the slender, tapering bedframes introduced by Hepplewhite and Sheraton. All four posts were six-sided, like a pencil, and tapered evenly toward the top.

LOW FOUR-POSTER BEDS

Low-post beds were a country favorite in North America, the British Isles, and Australia. The construction was basically the same as that of the high-post bed. The posts and rails were turned or cut from a strong hardwood such as ash, birch, or maple, and a simple headboard was cut from matching wood or pine.

Bedframes were smaller than those made today—a typical bed would be about 6½ feet (2m) long, 4 to 4½ feet (1.2 – 1.4m) wide, with rails 18 to 30 inches (46 – 76cm) high. The higher beds allowed a trundle bed to be rolled underneath. Ropes supported a mattress, which was stuffed with rushes, grass, straw, or corncobs, and the bedding, which was stuffed with down, flocks, or chopped wool. In the nineteenth

century, screws and nails eventually replaced the mortise-and-tenon joins and wooden slats replaced the ropes.

CANNONBALL BED

The cannonball bed is a low four-poster bed with large globe-shaped knobs on top of the posts, hence the name "cannonball." This massive turned style appeared in nineteenth-century America and was made from Louisiana to Ohio and north into Ontario, Canada.

EMPIRE LOW-POST BED

The Empire-inspired low-post bed features headposts and footposts equal in size, about 3½ to 4 feet (1 – 1.2m) high. The headboard is decoratively carved, and the posts are both turned and carved. Country furniture makers in Canada, New England, Ohio, Indiana, Tennessee, and many western states crafted beds of this style from 1820 to 1850 using cherry, maple, and birch, as well as the eighteenth-century favorite, mahogany. A footboard ending in a "blanket roll" was popular.

ABOVE: A nineteenth-century bedstead has a flat, scrolled headboard and massive mid-height posts with chunky, urnlike finials.

SWEDISH TRESTLE BED

This ingenious Swedish bed was popular in eighteenth- and nineteenth-century inns and servants' rooms as it could be disassembled quickly for cleaning or moving. It can also be spotted in Carl Larsson's charming watercolors of his children's bedrooms. The four posts were held upright by side planks secured in position with removable wedges. Hemp webbing supported the bedding.

THREE-SIDED CRIB

The three-sided infant's crib stood high off the floor so that its bedding was level with the parents' bed. It was built with four posts, but only three of the four sides were filled in with vertical turned spindles. The open side of the crib was pulled up alongside the mother's bed so she could easily reach over and tend to her child during the night. This practical crib seldom appeared outside the American South.

TRUNDLE BED

The trundle or truckle bed is a space-saving solution that proved especially valuable in early settler and frontier homes in Australia and North America. It is a low bed, no more than 15 inches (38cm) high, that was rolled under a four-poster bed during the day and rolled out at night for the children. A truckle is a wooden wheel and forerunner to the castor. Truckle also means to behave with servility. In England, truckle beds were first used for body servants, who slept close at hand to their master or mistress. Early trundle beds were simply boxes on wheels, padded with a straw mattress. By the mid-eighteenth century, however, they were built as "real" beds, with four-post construction and rope or slat supports for the mattress.

TOP: Ropes are laced through holes in the bed rails. *MIDDLE*: A three-sided infant's cot. *BOTTOM*: A trundle bed pulls out from underneath an imposing high-post bed. *OPPOSITE PAGE*: A brass bed featured in Montgomery Ward & Co.'s Catalogue No. 57, circa 1895.

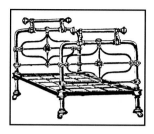

BRASS AND IRON BEDS

Brass and iron beds were a marvel of nineteenth-century industrialization. Never before in history were great populations able to sleep so comfortably at such an affordable price. Metal beds were hygienic, free of the bedbugs that infested wood bedsteads, easy to keep clean, and convenient to transport. The iron bedstead was first introduced by the French in the late 1700s. Manufacture of brass beds began in Birmingham, England, in 1830. By the mid-1870s, England alone was producing 6,000 beds per week, half of them for export to continental Europe, Australia, and the United States. Metal beds were made to suit every taste and pocketbook, from richly scrolled brass designs to the simple cast iron stump bed purchased for children, servants, hospitals, and sick wards.

The metal bedframe consisted of four basic parts: headboard, footboard, and two long side rails. The rails slotted into openings in the headboard and footboard, eliminating the need for separate corner posts. The mattress was supported on an open wire base suspended on a separate iron or wood frame. This frame was bolted to the bed, with appropriately placed brackets to prevent the mattress from slipping.

The styles of brass and iron beds were as varied as those of wooden beds. They included tent beds, half-tester or Italian beds, and high four-posters. The last could be draped with curtains and swags, which accounts for the more elaborate ornamentation being concentrated at the foot. Design motifs included vines, shells, and scrolls. To keep the pillows in place, a serpentine "pillow" bracket joined the headboard and side iron, for a sleigh bed look. Earlier styles were plainer, with perhaps just a wood or brass knob screwed into the top of each post. The bed could be solid brass, brass-coated iron, cast or wrought iron painted black or white, or a combination of these. More elaborate designs incorporated glass, mirrors, painted porcelain spindles, and mother-of-pearl inlay.

See also Cottage Furniture, Cradles, Sleigh Bed. See also under Settle—Settle-Bed; Spool Furniture—Jenny Lind Bed.

QUALITY CHECKLIST

- Check the mortises and tenons of old hand-built bedframes for roman numerals I–VIII. Woodworkers chiseled these numbers in pairs onto the posts and their corresponding rails to indicate how the pieces fit together. Buyers should compare all the numbers to make sure they were chiseled by the same person. If the styles look different, the bed parts may be replacements or the seller may have assembled them from several different beds.

- When choosing a pencil post bed, examine the posts carefully for even, uniform tapering. A general rule is: The thinner the posts, the better-crafted the bed.

- Vertical slots in wooden bedposts indicate that the bed was designed with a removable protective guard rail for the safety of children, the ill, or the elderly.

- Examine wooden bedposts and rails carefully for woodworm damage. These tiny holes are created when furniture beetle larvae hatch, mature, and bite their way out of the wood. Dark holes indicate past infestation that has most probably been successfully treated. Fresh holes will appear clean and lighter in color. To treat new infestations, squirt commercial insecticide into the holes every 2 inches (5cm) or so. The fluid will spread through the tunnel network underneath to kill any remaining larvae. Old woodworm holes can be filled with wax and sealed. Avoid purchasing pieces with heavy damage as the wood may be severely weakened beneath the surface.

BENCHES

The shared seating implicit in the bench is certainly in the country spirit, and for centuries it was the only seating available to common people. The simplest benches are constructed like stools. A long, thick plank or split log forms the seat, and four sturdy legs are wedged into holes bored in the ends. This type of bench could be put together relatively quickly in frontier areas. More sophisticated benches were built like joint stools, with carved friezes and turned legs joined by chunky stretchers. European peasant benches are substantial and stocky, with thick board legs and decorative contouring and cutouts.

A BRIEF HISTORY

In the Middle Ages, benches were built in flush against the wall, and narrow trestle tables, or boards, were brought up in front of the diners, who were served their meals from the front. This arrangement kept the center of the room free for servants and entertainment and also prevented an enemy's unwelcome approach from behind.

By the seventeenth century, the board had widened and diners were seated on both sides of the table. A chair, if owned, was placed at the head of the table and reserved for the head of the household or a special visitor, such as the parson or a suitor. A smaller chair for the wife was added as the family prospered.

During the eighteenth century, chairs came to replace benches around the table, and the idea of a permanent dining table took hold. In the nineteenth century, the trestle table and benches continued to be used on the frontier and in the country. Built-in benches continued to be used in Central European peasant homes into the early twentieth century.

COLLECTING ANTIQUE BENCHES

Antique benches in good condition are challenging to collect because even though they were made in great number, they received heavy use and little special care. Pioneers were apt to replace their split log puncheon benches with milled board benches as soon as they could. Surviving farmhouse benches from the nineteenth century were just as likely used for bucket stands outside the dairy or scullery as for seating. Of more recent vintage are the plain backless benches with straight or chamfered legs that were manufactured in great numbers for late-nineteenth- and early twentieth-century schools, hospitals, depots, and libraries. Also of interest to the collector are benches with open slat seats made for Finnish saunas and open-air gardens. The open slats let moisture and rainwater wash through without collecting on the surface. Old church pews are another specialized bench form that can add ambiance to the country interior.

See also under Central Europe—The Peasant Home; New Mexico—Benches; Stools—Joint Stool.

ABOVE LEFT: A plank bench with a worn paint finish serves as a coffee table in a country interior. A side overhang, called an apron, runs the length of the bench, and notches cut into the supporting end boards form rudimentary legs. *LEFT:* Travelers waiting in a train depot could easily move this pivoting backrest to face in either direction—a handy feature for keeping an eye on the arrival and departure schedule or conversing with fellow travelers.

ABOVE: Original Thonet bentwood rocker and settee with cane seats.

BENTWOOD FURNITURE

The bentwood chair might well be called the Windsor chair of the modern age. Like the earlier Windsor, it was made using steam-bending techniques and became extremely popular and affordable. The original bentwood chair was developed by Austrian cabinetmaker and designer Michael Thonet (1796–1871). He turned long rods from beech, a strong, lightweight, highly flexible wood, then steam-bent the rods and fit them into iron molds. When dry, the curved pieces were sanded, stained, and packed flat for shipping, to be assembled on site. A basic side chair might consist of six or eight pieces of bentwood plus a molded plywood or cane seat. The cane was machine-woven separately and glued into the seat frame, rather than woven on by hand. All the pieces were easily screwed together. The furniture was lightweight, strong, and elegant, and factory production coupled with compact shipping helped keep down costs.

The bentwood chair was shown with tremendous success at the 1851 Great Exhibition in London and heralded a major modern movement in furniture design and production. Low-cost "Viennese cafe" chairs became popular all over the world—Thonet himself manufactured 100 million of one style alone, and it is estimated that three times that number were produced in imitation. When Thonet's patent ran out in the 1860s, it was taken up by Hewlett and Company of London. By the turn of the century, more than 1,000 different bentwood designs had been sold, among them hallstands, hall trees, tables, cots, and chairs of every description, including the well-known bentwood rocker.

Authentic bentwood designs were identified by number, following Thonet's original no-nonsense system. Company branch offices, established in every corner of the industrialized world, served as salesrooms and distributors. Many other companies, particularly in Central Europe where beech is abundant, imitated the bentwood designs and production methods and also sold their furniture worldwide. An original bentwood chair always had a paper trade label pasted to the inside seat rail before it left the factory.

Thonet's designs continued to be popular into the twentieth century. His children's chairs were revived for schools and nurseries in the 1920s. Unfortunately, many poorly constructed imitations came out in the 1920s and 1930s, giving bentwood a reputation for being flimsy. Today, well-made reproductions are again available, many from Taiwan and the Far East.

QUALITY CHECKLIST

- Some bentwood chairs have wood plugs covering the screws. If you are buying an antique, make sure none are missing.

- Check the inside of the chair frame to make sure the front legs are securely glued and screwed. The back legs should be firmly bolted. It is important to make repairs promptly because improper hardware puts stresses on the chair.

- Check all corresponding screws throughout the chair to make sure they match. Replacements of the wrong size or type may not hold properly.

RIGHT: Original Thonet bentwood café chairs with cane seats.

THE BRITISH ISLES

The country furniture of the British Isles developed along a different path from that of continental Europe. On the continent, peasant culture was rich with material ornament such as decorative carving and painting. This decorative instinct seemed to flow from and echo the fashions and furniture of the royal courts, which were highly embellished, ornate, and meant to impress. It is only natural that the country furniture makers in such societies evolved their own independent world of decoration, style, and status.

English country culture was somewhat different. Since there was no land-owning peasantry, country people furnished their homes simply, without the accumulation of richly embroidered textiles or other signs of material prosperity that characterized European peasant households. This is not to suggest that English furniture was uninteresting or devoid of ornament, but just that in relation to other country styles, it was more straightforward and practical. While the Swedish peasant made pleasantly curved rococo-style trestles to support a tabletop, his English counterpart created simple I-beam trestles.

During the eighteenth century, another factor came into play. While English Queen Anne and Chippendale furniture was based on the rococo furniture of Europe, it was more cautious in its ornamentation. England's city cabinetmakers were independent guildsmen, and they designed and built vast amounts of furniture for a new and fast-growing mercantile class, not for the court. The country cabinetmakers who copied them were the first

ABOVE: Comfortably cushioned fireside chairs from a twentieth-century manufacturer trace their origin to upholstered easy chairs and Windsor chairs of the eighteenth century.

to introduce furniture that represented literacy and a more comfortable domestic life—desks, tables, chairs, bookcases—to the ordinary person.

Much of the country furniture that appeared in Great Britain during the seventeenth, eighteenth, and early nineteenth centuries developed concurrently throughout western Europe—chests of drawers, cupboards, and ladderback chairs. The English-Dutch exchange was especially strong during the 1600s. These and later styles were carried to America and Australia and with the rise of the British Empire became familiar around the world. Three distinctly English developments—the dresser, the kitchen work table, and the Windsor chair—are discussed under individual entries.

ENGLISH COUNTRY FAVORITES

Beehive Chair

This inviting barrel-shaped chair was woven of straw or wicker. The base of the chair resembled a bee skep (a somewhat conical hive made of straw), and the curved backrest arched up in a style similar to the Norwegian *kubbestol.* The beehive chair was springy, flexible, and offered considerably more comfort than the wood chairs

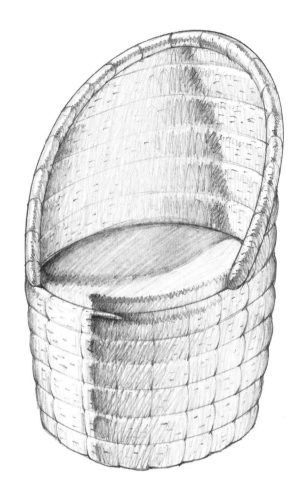

The English Country House

Decorating in the style of England's great country houses is one of today's most popular looks. The success of the style comes from the mix of well-worn furniture, textiles, and mementos that have been assembled by a family over many generations. No one really minds that an elegant mahogany breakfront cabinet appears alongside a simple fruitwood table made by the estate carpenter. In fact, much of the furniture needn't have country origins at all—except in the kitchen, where the oversized dresser and central worktable are a must.

The main attraction of the country house is its comfort. Couches and chairs are soft and overstuffed, with lots of needlepoint pillows layered on. A love of the outdoors and natural materials is represented by wood furniture and wool upholstery. Chintz slipcovers and drapes are printed with huge pink or yellow cabbage roses. In England's cold, damp climate, these floral prints are especially inviting and help cheer up rooms year-round.

The British love of world travel is reflected in the many porcelains, objets d'art, and Oriental rugs placed about the house. These accents represent the far-flung corners of the British Empire, and family members are sure to have stories to share concerning the travels that resulted in their acquisition. Guests are welcome to admire these family treasures but it is quite un-British to inquire about the price.

used by the upper classes. It was popular in the seventeenth and eighteenth centuries, and English colonists continued the style in America. Unfortunately, few examples have survived because the material is so fragile, but historians have confirmed their existence from old household inventories and wills. In the mid-nineteenth century, the base evolved into an openwork skirt and back, with the wicker spokes forming a diamond pattern.

CANDLESTAND

Candlestands brought a touch of refinement to eighteenth- and nineteenth-century English interiors. Wax candles were expensive, subject to taxation, and evoked a certain luxury, so it made sense to set the candle on its own high stand and make the most of the precious light shed about the room. Candlestands stood about 4 feet (1.2m) high and were constructed with a tripod or cross-shaped base. In America, Yankee ingenuity developed adjustable screw or ratchet candlestands, which allowed the user to direct the light more closely on the work or reading at hand. Hard maple was often chosen for use with these large screws, as it did not split or crack. Shaker candlestands were beautifully constructed with tapered posts and shaped legs. In the latter part of the nineteenth century, candlestands were used to hold oil lamps.

CRICKET TABLE

The English cricket table has a circular top and stands on three splayed legs. The name "cricket" most probably derives from the northern English *cracket*, which means a three-legged stool. Another theory as to the word's origin is premised on the three-legged wicket used in the

game of cricket. In Australia and Tasmania, the name "wicket" table has stuck.

Cricket tables can be constructed in different sizes in any of several ways. Usually, the legs are evenly spaced, forming an equilateral triangle. Another arrangement, easier for the carpenter to figure out, is a right-triangle arrangement, which gives a quirky skew to the legs. The legs can be joined by stretchers all around, or two stretchers can connect the three legs in a T shape. Niceties include a lower shelf, a drawer in the undercarriage, or tabletops with hinged wings that flip up and are supported by lopers. Cricket tables make excellent occasional tables and are stable on uneven stone and wood floors.

EASY CHAIR

The upholstered easy chair, or wing chair, appeared in England during the William and Mary period and was introduced to America around 1700. It descended from upholstered court furniture, and since it required much padding and stuffing inside and yards of fabric outside, it was an expensive and challenging chair to make. Country farmers copied the high back and wing extensions in wood (the form was something like a settle for one person) and then tacked on padding and fabric as best they could.

The professional upholsterer had a painstaking job. He was called an upholsterer because the layers of cushioning that he built "upheld" the sitter. First, strips of webbing were nailed to the chair frame, building support for the seat. The webbing provided a degree of give to the seat cushion that a wooden base could not. Stuffing materials, which included horsehair, straw, chaff, wool, and feathers, were sandwiched between linen fabric. These materials had to be evenly distributed, then stitched into place to prevent shifting and lumping. The outer covering could be leather, damask, velvet, wool, haircloth, or hand-

OPPOSITE PAGE, TOP: An artist's interpretation of the English beehive chair. *OPPOSITE PAGE BOTTOM:* A captain's chair (left), an Arts and Crafts style chair (right), and a Chesterfield in an English country living room. *ABOVE:* A reproduction cricket table.

stitched Turkey work, crewel embroidery, or needlepoint. The type of covering played a large part in determining the overall cost of the chair. It was held in place by rows of brass nails, called garnishing. Other trims, such as ribbon, tape, and welting, were also added.

Expensive as wing chairs were, they were not considered parlor furniture, but were placed in the bedroom, where they offered a comfortable draft-free seat where a person might doze during the day or read before retiring. They were often acquired to provide comfort to the infirm and elderly, who spent a great part of their day sitting and resting. Country easy chairs were most probably used in open family areas as well. The cushioning would have been lumpier, and the hard wood seat would have been felt no matter how much stuffing was mounded on to it.

MENDLESHAM CHAIR

The Mendlesham chair is a delightful example of country furniture that developed into a distinct style, but never ventured far beyond its place of origin. Mendlesham is a village in East Anglia, and the chair was made there and in nearby villages by the Day family

and other cabinetmakers during the late-eighteenth and early nineteenth centuries. The Days based their design on formal Hepplewhite and Sheraton chairs, but retained the decorative splat, turned legs, and shaped seat of the English Windsor. The chairs were made of elm or fruitwood with an elm seat. As far as descendants of the original owners can account, the chairs were specially ordered and used only on special occasions.

THE TEA-DRINKING ENGLISH

Country furniture devoted to the custom of taking afternoon tea is decidedly British. In the early part of the eighteenth century, tea was expensive, but by the 1740s, prices had come down, and tea drinking became popular throughout England and the American colonies. Tea drinking was a social occasion, and special furniture was developed to enhance the ritual.

TEA SERVICE CABINET

In English country homes, the china tea service was stored in a hanging corner cabinet. The cabinet was mounted in the living room where the tea was served,

LEFT: This Irish press of paneled pine has protruding shoe feet. *ABOVE:* Tiny leaves dance across the frieze of this Irish dresser. *OPPOSITE PAGE:* A pine table and chairs, a glazed hanging cupboard, and a wicker chair blend comfortably in an English country kitchen.

not in the kitchen. Country oak cabinets were made with fielded panels and perhaps a modest inlaid banding of walnut or mahogany. Later versions would be solid pine. These cabinets had one blind door (glazed panels would have been too expensive) or two side-by-side doors, depending on the width. A spoon drawer at the bottom could appear below the doors or inside them, accessible only when the doors were open. The English painted the inside walls blue, to show off the china. The Welsh wallpapered the interior to match the room.

TEA TABLE AND KETTLE STAND

Charming country tea tables were made in oak and fruitwood in England and were copied in maple, ash, and other native woods in America. Tea tables stood about 2 ½ feet (76cm) high and were supported by a single turned column on a tripod base. This allowed the tea drinkers to pull their chairs up close around the table for intimate conversation. The three legs were gracefully curved in the Queen Anne or Chippendale styles popular during this period. The round tabletop had a raised edge called a piecrust, which prevented porcelain sugar bowls and teacups from tumbling to the floor during accidental bumps and knocks. Country versions were made with a swivel base, called a birdcage, which allowed the tabletop to revolve. When tea was over, the tabletop tilted down and the table was placed up against the wall.

The kettle stand was an adjunct to the eighteenth-century tea table. It was similarly made, but smaller, and was used to hold a silver tea kettle filled with hot water. It allowed the gracious hostess to pour hot water without leaving her seat.

IRELAND

Irish country furniture occupies a unique niche in the British Isles tradition. English tenant farmers clustered their cottages in small villages and towns and went to work in the estate lands surrounding them. In Ireland, the tenants were scattered through-

out vast estates. Their cottages were isolated from one another and distant from roads and nearby neighbors. The lack of easy social contact and village life is reflected in Irish country-made furniture. Decoration, when it was added, had an unself-conscious primitive quality that many collectors today eagerly seek out.

Typical Irish country furnishings were plain and unpretentious. The settle-bed and chair-table are two dual-purpose pieces that were quite common in Ireland's tiny cottages. Both styles were carried by Irish settlers who emigrated to North America, especially Canada. Ireland's oak forests had been largely destroyed by 1750, so most Irish dressers were made of pine. Since the wood is soft, it was thickly cut. An upper frieze provided a lighthearted contrast, with decoratively cut heart, clover, pinwheel, or rosette motifs. Frequently, the shelves were given thin rails so that the plates could be tilted forward. Drawers were rarely dovetailed but rather had rabbeted nailed edges. Irish dressers and tables can often be recognized by two parallel, closely spaced stretchers running the length of the piece.

The Irish stick Windsor chair is especially collectible. The rough-hewn seat is angled toward the back in a semitriangular shape. The backrest is tall and ends in a crest which sometimes inexplicably slants up at a jaunty angle. The backrest's two outermost spindles pass through the side armrests, which are socketed to the seat with shorter sticks. The entire chair has a unique, quirky asymmetry—on some chairs, the armrests are not even the same height.

Note: Many of the individual encyclopedia entries describe furniture made or originating in the British Isles. See especially Banister-Back Chair, Beds, Chair-Table, Chests of Drawers, Country Chippendale Chairs, Desks, Dressers, Drop-Leaf Tables, Kitchen Work Table, Ladderback Chairs, Plate Racks, Presses, Settles, Trestle Table, and Windsor Chairs.

ABOVE: A reproduction tea table with birdcage swivel base.

C

CANADA

CANADA, LIKE ITS SOUTHERN NEIGHBOR, THE UNITED
STATES, OFFERED A VAST RICH TERRITORY FOR
EXPLORATION AND SETTLEMENT. THE FIRST EUROPEANS
TO ENTER CANADA WERE FRENCH TRAPPERS, FUR
TRADERS, AND PRIESTS. THE HARSH WILDERNESS WAS
DIFFICULT TO TAME, AND DURING FRENCH RULE FROM
1667 TO 1765, DEATHS EQUALED OR EXCEEDED LIVE
BIRTHS. SETTLEMENTS WERE MORE SUCCESSFUL DURING
THE NEXT ONE HUNDRED YEARS UNDER BRITISH RULE.
IRISH, SCOTTISH, AND ENGLISH SETTLERS EMIGRATED
FROM THE BRITISH ISLES, AND LOYALISTS FROM THE
AMERICAN COLONIES MOVED NORTH. THE AMERICANS
ESPECIALLY WERE ACQUAINTED WITH FRONTIER
HARDSHIPS AND HAD EXPERIENCE ESTABLISHING
FARMSTEADS. GERMAN-SPEAKING SETTLERS WERE THE
THIRD MAJOR GROUP TO ENTER CANADA DURING THIS
PERIOD. THEY CAME FROM BOTH EUROPE AND
PENNSYLVANIA AND INTRODUCED TRADITIONAL GERMAN
AS WELL AS ANGLO FURNITURE BUILDING TECHNIQUES.

The major difference between the development of
Canada and the United States is that the Canadian
immigrant groups retained their individual identities,
customs, and furniture-making traditions far longer than
American groups. From its first settlements, Canada has
been a mosaic of cultures, languages, and ethnic
traditions. French-speaking Quebec is evidence of this
today. The waves of immigrants entering the United
States during the nineteenth century were generally
eager to assimilate, and they formed a ready mass market
for factory-produced goods and furniture. In America,
wages were good and land was cheap. In Canada, by
contrast, the eastern frontier was virtually closed by

ABOVE: This French-Canadian chair made in the ladderback tradition
has wavy salamander slats, turned legs, stiles, and stretchers, and
gracefully shaped armrests.

1860, and it wasn't until the late 1800s, with the
opening of the Canadian Pacific Railway, that immigration once again began in earnest.

A slower-growing population, the reluctance to give
up ethnic traditions, and the more gradual transition to
factory-made furniture make Canada especially fertile
ground for today's antiques enthusiasts. Here, furniture
made in the nineteenth century more closely follows
European traditions. It is possible to find in Canada, for
instance, a baroque-style peasant dresser made by a late
nineteenth-century Polish immigrant. It is unlikely that
the same cabinetmaker, thrown into the culture of the
United States, would have clung to this old form.

Most Canadian furniture dating from before the
mid-1800s was made by individual craftsman of varying
skills and backgrounds, including carpenters, joiners,
and well-trained cabinetmakers. Furniture basic to all

immigrant groups included trunks and chests, tables, benches, chairs, beds, cradles, and blind cupboards. More sophisticated homes had chests of drawers and desks. The British introduced the open rack dresser; the Germans built *Schränke*; the Irish brought the settle-bed; and the French contributed armoires, wavy-rail ladder-back chairs, and the open-backed Ile d'Orleans chair.

Gradual exposure to other traditions and lack of strict guild rules encouraged woodworkers to stretch their skills and borrow from other groups. French immigrants would have used oak and fruitwood in their native Brittany, but in Canada they made the switch to pine and painted it red, blue, gray, yellow, or green in the Anglo settler style. The combination of French cornices and panels with colored surfaces created a unique French-Canadian style. German-made furniture shows evidence of Biedermeier pediments, scrolled armrests, "pie shelf" dressers with scalloped framing, and sturdy pegged construction throughout.

The presence of ethnic styles in Canadian country furniture is a subject for rich study that is sure to attract collectors' and historians' attention in years to come.

Note: Many of the individual encyclopedia entries describe furniture traditions present in Canada. See The British Isles; Chests; Chests of Drawers; Cupboards; Dressers; France; and Germany, Austria, and Switzerland.

CANE SEATS

Cane seats appear on many types of country furniture, including Sheraton-style fancy chairs, Hitchcock chairs, rocking chairs, wicker chairs, bentwood chairs, and pressed-wood spindle-back chairs. Cane is softer and more resilient than wood, stays cooler in hot weather, and requires little maintenance and no painting. There are two kinds of cane seats: those that are handwoven directly onto the seat frame and those that are woven by machine in large sheets and tapped into the seat frame.

A BRIEF HISTORY

The cane used for chair seats and backs is the thin glossy shell stripped from the rattan stem, a tall bamboolike plant that grows in southeast Asia. (One important difference between bamboo and rattan is that bamboo is hollow.) Cane was first introduced to Europe in the seventeenth century from India and China. Despite its advantages of being lightweight, resilient, and durable, cane was at first snubbed by society's elite because it was so inexpensive. Slowly but surely, cane began its social climb. By the end of the Baroque era, it was appearing on Europe's grandest furniture and was considered exotic, luxurious, and highly fashionable. Originally, the weaving was very simple and open, but over time tighter, more complex patterns were developed.

Since it was associated with the wealthy, caning did not appear on chairs used by ordinary people until the early nineteenth century, when furniture manufacture

ABOVE LEFT: The use of pine distinguishes this Canadian two-tiered Louis XV buffet, made in Quebec in the late eighteenth century, from its French hardwood cousins. *OPPOSITE PAGE:* Handwoven cane fills the seat and shaped back of this rocking chair.

for the masses began in earnest. It was a favorite throughout the Empire and Victorian periods, and its popularity has continued into the twentieth century. Cane seats contribute a light, airy, casual look to the country interior.

WHAT CANE LOOKS LIKE

Cane is stripped from the rattan reed in long, narrow pieces. At first, cane was stripped and split by hand. It is the nature of the plant fiber to separate evenly once a split is begun. By the middle of the nineteenth century, machines were invented to strip and split the cane into widths specified to the fraction of an inch. The outer surface of the cane is convex, and it is this slightly arched, shiny surface that faces up in the woven chair seat. The typical cane weaving pattern combines horizontal, vertical, and diagonal lines that create tiny octagon-shaped openings.

HANDWOVEN CANE

A handwoven cane seat can be recognized by the tiny holes bored all around the edge of the seat opening. If the cane joins into them, then the cane was handwoven onto the chair.

Six courses of cane make up the seat, but only the last three are woven. Each course—horizontal, vertical, or diagonal—is worked one at a time. The cane crosses the seat opening from hole to hole, then passes down under the seat frame and comes up in an adjacent hole for the

return pass. To help hold the cane strips taut while the work is in progress, tiny wood pegs are used to temporarily plug the holes. The cane is kept moist throughout to keep it more pliable. When all six courses are added and the entire seat is filled, the chair caner plugs alternate holes, then lashes on a wider cane all around the seat edge. This finish is called beading.

QUALITY CHECKLIST

- Generally speaking, chairs with handwoven cane seats predate those with set-in cane seats. Both the cane-weaving machine and the machine to cut the channel in the chair seat were invented in the 1860s by Gardner A. Watkins of the American firm Heywood Brothers and Company.

- If a cane seat is damaged in a small area, it can be repaired. Caning instruction manuals can show you how to proceed.

- If a chair is rare or valuable, consult a specialist before you recane. An original Hitchcock or Thonet bentwood chair may be more valuable with its slightly damaged original seat than with a replacement.

MACHINE-WOVEN CANE

A machine-woven cane seat can be recognized by the narrow channel running clear around the top of the seat frame, close to the opening. Replacing a set-in cane seat is an easy process. A sheet of purchased machine-woven cane is cut several inches larger all around than the seat opening. The cane is tapped down into the channel, then held in place with a flexible spline edging (spline is a triangular-cut reed). Once the spline is glued in place, the excess cane sheeting can be trimmed away.

Both hand caning and sheet cane replacement are easy for beginners. Materials, tools, and instruction manuals can be readily obtained by those interested in this aspect of furniture restoration.

ABOVE: A cane-backed rocking chair. *BELOW LEFT:* The octagonal weave of cane on the seat of a Thonet café chair.

CARE TIPS

• To clean cane, use warm soapy water and a soft but densely woven cloth that won't snag on the tiny cane spurs. Wring out the cloth, then wipe the surface. It is important to rewipe with a fresh rag and clean water to remove any trace of soapy residue that can grow mold or mildew.

• Central heating will cause cane to dry out and become brittle. A humidifier will help maintain the proper moisture conditions.

• Never use a cane chair as a stool. Standing on the cane can puncture it, causing damage to the chair as well as personal injury.

CENTRAL EUROPE

In continental Europe, there was always a wider gap between town and country tastes than in England, North America, and Australia. This is particularly true in Central Europe, where peasant dwellings retained their painted and carved furniture and embroidered textiles well into the twentieth century. Unlike English tenant farmers, Central European peasants celebrated life's events with great ritual, color, and display of wealth. The well-tended home was a treasure to be shown off, not simply a shelter from the elements. A spirit of friendly competition encouraged the accumulation of decorative needlework, carved furniture and utensils, and embroidered clothing and household linens. This culture perpetuated baroque ornamentation and massive furniture long after the formal Baroque period had ended. Basic furnishings included richly decorated trestle tables, benches, beds, food cupboards, and storage chests. These items were part of daily life throughout Hungary, the Slavic countries, and the Balkans. A description of the furniture of Hungary and Poland follows and gives the overall flavor of the region.

ABOVE LEFT: This bridal chest is rich with painted decoration, moldings, and carving. *ABOVE RIGHT:* A Hungarian *székreny,* or hewn chest.

HUNGARY

As in all peasant cultures, Hungarian life was highly ritualized. Long-standing social customs were applied to every area of life. These customs governed everything from weddings to where the father sat at the family table. The Hungarian focus on the wedding is seen in the furniture. Every bride had a dower chest, filled with embroidered linens that represented hours of labor over many years. This chest was carried in procession through the town to the home of the groom on the wedding day. Since it was to be in such a public display, the chest was always highly decorative, with painting or carving and the bride's initials and wedding date. Chests with two sets of initials and dates indicate use by two generations.

DOWER CHESTS

Two types of dower chests were made: the *székreny,* or hewn chest, and the board chest. The *székreny* was hewn of oak or beech. It was made in forest regions by arkwrights or cottage cofferers. Wood details, rather than paint, supplied the decoration. These included compass-drawn geometric designs incised into the side panels and a gabled lid with "horns." The boards used for the lid were fluted and attached shingle-style. As a result, the entire surface of the chest had some sort of textural decoration.

The board chest, in contrast, was doweled or dovetailed together (the joined chest, with frame and panel construction, was virtually unknown). The sides extended down to form legs. The chest could also be made with a flat bottom and set in a free-standing base. It was painted with allover designs of flowers, vines, birds, stags, and, of course, the bride's initials and wedding date. This style of chest was also made for everyday use in the home and was called variously the bride's, tulip, or home chest.

HAND-CARVED SETTEES

The settee is another example of Hungarian peasant furniture that is closely tied to significant life events. Many settees are carved with names of husband and wife and the year of their wedding. In northern Hungary, benches with repeat openwork designs were made to commemorate the end of a young man's military service. His safe arrival home was a time of great rejoicing for the family and community—and often brought with it the promise of a future wedding. The most ornate carving on settees was done by herdsmen. The solid back panels were covered with flowers, birds, murals of village life,

hunting scenes, and Bible stories. Cutwork and lattice-work also appeared, and elaborately carved finials topped the corner posts.

THE PEASANT HOME

Even though the peasant home was small, it was divided into distinct sections. The corner first seen across the room upon entering was the most important area of the house. A built-in L-shaped bench hugged the corner and a table for dining was set up in front of it. The corner seat was always reserved for the father. Above his head hung a corner cabinet that held the family's Bible and other precious possessions. In the opposite corner, close to the door, was the stove. The area around the stove was the work and play section of the room, while the table and father's seat were in the "sacred" side of the room. These demarcations ruled the conduct of family life. Serious matters were always discussed at the table, and children's misconduct at the table was always viewed as a more serious offense than misbehavior near the door.

Other furniture included a built-in wall cupboard with curtained opening, a milk cupboard with sliding lower door, dressers, and beds. The "best" bed was piled with the family's feather beds, linens, duvets, and pillows during the day. In the mid-1800s, wardrobes with half-hexagon pediments began to replace the chest for storage of clothing. The doors were painted to look like panels, and the front corners were canted. Chests of drawers also were introduced, though these were rarely decoratively painted.

All the Hungarian peasant household furniture was made by professional joiners and painters. They worked exclusively at building the peasant furniture and moved in a separate sphere from cabinetmakers to the bourgeoisie and the nobility. Peasant families began to integrate factory-made furniture into their homes in the mid- to late 1800s. Still, dower chests were carried to brides' new homes right up to World War I.

ABOVE LEFT: Built-in and freestanding benches, a wall-mounted plate rack, and a rectangular table furnish the kitchen of this peasant log house. Crockery is stored on the rafters above. The "best" room beckons through an open doorway.

POLAND

Polish country furniture is characterized by vivid painted decoration and a naive interpretation of the baroque style. Cupboards and wardrobes rise up in arched pediments dripping with carved fans, shells, or leaves. An overabundance of elaborate finials seems to rise up out of the top of a piece. A favorite painted design for door panels is a basket with a bouquet. Flowers, stars, and vines appear as accents around them. All of the painting has a clear, stenciled quality that is quite distinct from the free brushstroke work of other regions. Colors contrast vividly, with surprising combinations that catch and hold the eye. Backgrounds are usually rich burgundy, Prussian blue, brown, or green.

The Polish *kredens*, or dresser, typifies the provincial Baroque style that continued in rural northeastern Europe throughout the eighteenth and nineteenth centuries. The *kredens* was heavy and massive, with a carved pediment that scrolled up toward the center. The corners of the lower cabinet are canted in the manner so often seen in Central Europe and Scandinavia. The upper section of the dresser abounds with carving. The shelves are supported by numerous bold turned columns and are fronted with fretwork galleries. For each supporting column, there is a corresponding finial rising up out of the top.

CHAIR-TABLE

The chair-table first appeared in the 1600s in the British Isles, Holland, and northern France and spread from there to North America. It was used widely in Ireland in the nineteenth century, and the United States Army introduced it to the American southwest, where it was copied by New Mexico *carpinteros.*

As its name implies, the chair-table was two pieces of furniture in one. The chair portion had an attached tabletop that pivoted up and down on removable wooden pegs. As a single chair, the piece was placed up against the wall, with the tabletop positioned vertically to double as a backrest. Pulled into the center of the room, the chair became a base for the tabletop, which pulled down on top of it. Construction was heavy, legs

were thick, and the unit was cumbersome to maneuver. Tabletops were round, oval, rectangular, or octagonal. A similar piece, called the hutch table, featured a small box instead of a chair and was used to store bread or tableware.

CHESTS

Chests were used in country households to store clothing, textiles, grain, flour, a bride's dowry, tools, and much more. On the frontier, the chest served as closet, suitcase, and bench all in one. Chests could be plain, carved, or painted. Despite their many uses, there were just two basic construction styles: framed chests with mortise-and-tenon joins and board chests with dovetailed or rabbeted joins.

TOP: A reproduction chair-table constructed by a twentieth-century cabinetmaker. Each trestle has two semicircular supports for bracing the tabletop from the underside. *ABOVE:* This convertible settee is a twentieth-century artist-cabinetmaker's interpretation of the eighteenth-century settle-table. The heavy tabletop pivots down and then pulls forward along shallow grooves that are visible on the inside armrests.

FRAMED CHESTS

The framed, or joined, chest had its origin in the strongbox or coffer, used since ancient times to safeguard gold, silver, jewels, and other valuables. Smaller sizes were made for valuable documents such as deeds and wills. During the Middle Ages, the nobility carried their possessions in trunks and strongboxes as they traveled from estate to estate, but merchant and professional households required more permanent storage, a need met by the chest.

Early joined chests had sturdy corner stiles and paneled sides. The stiles extended down to form feet, which lifted the chest up off damp stone floors and helped prevent the floor of the chest from rotting. Framed chests were constructed from many individual pieces of wood, and they were massive, solid, and heavy. The lid of the chest lifted up on strap hinges to reveal a deep storage space, filled with the household's clothing, linen, and valuables. The nuisance of having to unload the entire chest to reach an item at the bottom led to the development of lower drawers. The evolution into a full chest of drawers was complete by 1700, but the paneled chest continued to be made in rural and colonial areas for another century and a half.

BOARD CHESTS

The board chest was also called the six-board chest. It actually was made from five boards of equal length, one of which was sawn in half for the two sides. Board chests meant for travel were flat-bottomed, but those built for storage at home stood off the floor on legs that were simply extensions of the sides. A triangular notch cut into the bottom of the extensions gave the illusion of two separate legs. At first, the boards were butted and nailed together, but later versions were dovetailed. Wide solid boards—pine in North America, kauri pine or red cedar in Australia—almost always indicate a settler's chest, since the

virgin forests capable of producing wide boards had all but vanished from Europe by the eighteenth century.

The blanket chest was one of the most common board chests built. Blanket chests provided clean, dry storage for clothing, linens, and, of course, the blankets needed to ward off the chill in drafty houses with no central heating. Like paneled chests, they had locking lift-up tops and bottom drawers. This hybrid status, somewhere between a chest and a full chest of drawers, led to the English name mule chest. English mule chests built prior to 1830 contained a small box inside the lid to store candles. The tallow was believed to repel moths.

For settlers and pioneers, plain board blanket chests were certainly easier to construct and transport than heavy paneled chests. Once a family was settled, they might decorate a plain chest with painted folk motifs or incised compass-drawn geometric designs. Attempts to imitate more expensive framed chests were common.

Wood graining, painted trompe l'oeil panels and false drawers, and applied moldings and half-banisters were among the decorations used. Blanket chests continued to be made well into the nineteenth century. Their flat tops and roomy interiors make them versatile for seating, tables, and storage today.

See also under Central Europe—Dower Chests; Germany, Austria, and Switzerland—Dower Chest; New Mexico—Board Chest, Framed Chests.

OPPOSITE PAGE, TOP: Gracefully cut notches form the legs of a plain board blanket chest. The upper trunk portion has a keyhole lock, and the old wood has mellowed to a warm, golden patina. *OPPOSITE PAGE, BOTTOM:* A custom-made reproduction chest is painted with Pennsylvania German motifs. *ABOVE:* A William and Mary chest of drawers rests on a raised stand with turned legs.

CHESTS OF DRAWERS

The chest of drawers evolved from the framed chest with lift-up storage lid (see previous entry). Once the chest was given bottom drawers, it wasn't long before woodworkers figured they could fit the entire case with drawers. These early chests of drawers first appeared in the late 1600s. They were massive and clunky, with heavy mortised drawers sliding in and out on side runners. In the 1700s, the refinement of dovetailing combined with the strong cabriole leg ultimately led to a more lightweight construction. The result was taller, more elegant chests, such as highboys.

Chests of drawers were certainly more convenient to use than the trunks they replaced, and throughout the nineteenth century, country people associated them with economic prosperity and improved social status. Immigrants to America often used their old family trunks as luggage on the Atlantic crossing, hoping to acquire or make a modern chest of drawers in their new home. Norwegian-Americans built their own version of the four-drawer Empire-style chest, with cyma-curved upper drawers, recessed middle drawers, and columned sides. By the mid-1800s, producers of factory-made cottage furniture made chests of drawers available on both sides of the Atlantic and in Australia. Still, many peasant households in central and eastern Europe clung to their old-style chests.

HOW THE CHEST EVOLVED

The first chests of drawers were heavy, massive pieces built by traditional frame and panel methods. These construction methods limited their size—if the chests were built too tall, they would have been difficult, if not impossible, to move. One solution to this problem was to stack two chests—one on top of the other—which helped increase storage without taking up any more floor space. Unfortunately, the resulting drawer arrangement of narrow, deep, narrow, deep was not aesthetically pleasing. A refinement of the late 1600s, along with dovetailing, was to graduate the drawers, placing the deepest on the bottom and the narrowest on the top. The top level often was divided into two small drawers. Dovetailing made the drawers much lighter, so it was possible to build a larger chest in one unit. Bun or onion feet were fashionable during this time and continued to appear on country-made pieces, especially in Dutch and German areas, into the nineteenth century.

The Queen Anne period introduced the sturdy yet graceful cabriole leg and further dovetailing refinements. The new, lighter chest that resulted from these developments was exuberantly raised up on a frame and expanded to hold five or six levels of drawers, instead of the usual four. A country cabinetmaker might skip the high frame and cabriole legs and substitute bracket feet instead. He would use solid walnut drawer fronts with oak sides and top or possibly pine sides stained to resemble walnut. In the Connecticut Valley of the American colonies, a unique scalloped top with a deep overhang became the signature style. Graduated drawers helped prevent the chest from appearing top-heavy.

Thomas Chippendale's pattern books introduced the curved serpentine front, intricate cutout carving, and other details that would challenge the country cabinetmaker and certainly be out of the price range or needs of the settler on the frontier. But even away from city centers people made an effort to be up-to-date. A Chippendale-inspired country chest might have three or four dovetailed drawers, with edges protruding fashionably beyond the frame. Each drawer could be pulled open by ball-type handles and locked with a key. A typical finish on a pine chest would be black-over-red grain painting designed to resemble mahogany. In America, many fanciful painted finishes and designs were sponged, grained, or stippled onto the wood to dress up the chests and make them seem more special.

By the late eighteenth century, Hepplewhite and Sheraton furniture introduced straighter lines, tapered or outcurved French feet, and a lighter, simpler look that was more easily copied by country cabinetmakers in both Great Britain and America. The drawer fronts were flush and the top overhung the base. In England, country pine chests were given elongated onion feet and painted to imitate the bamboo carving popular on fine furniture. Later versions were painted more simply in a gray or stone-colored background color with green or brown decorative striping around the top and drawers. During the early to mid-nineteenth century, the straight lines gave way to Empire motifs such as half-banister side pilasters and protruding cyma-curved top drawers.

OPPOSITE PAGE: A high chest of drawers with decorative painting is a newly crafted custom interpretation of a New England colonial piece. The original, made between 1690 and 1710, is in the collection of a Massachusetts historical society.

THE ROCOCO PINE COMMODE

In England and North America, chests of drawers developed in a rectilinear shape, a form that was relatively easy for country cabinetmakers to copy. In continental Europe, though, case furniture was much more ornamental and developed rococo curves in the sides and front. This curved cabinet with drawers was called a commode, and the style was called *bombé*, meaning swollen. The shape was challenging for country woodworkers to copy. As a result, the traditional joined chest lingered longer in the country areas of Europe than in England and the American colonies. Bavarian Germans, for example, continued to make joined chests following their medieval construction techniques well into the 1700s.

In an ironic twist of history, many old *bombé* chests of the eighteenth and nineteenth centuries are reappearing today as elegant country furniture. The original carcases were well-constructed of soft, inexpensive pine, which was overlaid with marquetry, veneer, ormolu, paint, and gilding. As this style became outmoded, old commodes were relegated to poor storage conditions or ended up in less prosperous households as utilitarian furniture. Over time, the rich surface decorations chipped or peeled off.

Antique dealers saw through the irreparable surface damage to the good bones underneath. They stripped the pieces to the bare pine, pickled and waxed the surfaces, and offered them for sale. The warmth of the pine combined with the sophistication of the cabinetry has produced a distinctly European country style that is steeped in history yet totally fresh.

QUALITY CHECKLIST

- A locking chest with numerous small drawers in the bottom is an old carpenter's chest. The carpenter's tools were placed in the top section, and the small drawers were used to store different types of nails and screws.

- The dovetails on a board chest can give a clue to its origin. European-trained woodworkers cut the dovetails so that the angled portion showed on the front panel of the chest. American craftsmen traditionally positioned the angled cuts on the side panels.

CLOCKS

The appearance of a clock in a pioneer or peasant home was a sure sign of the family's rising prosperity. In the eighteenth century, two types of clocks were available: tall case clocks and small pocket watches. Both had expertly crafted mechanisms and were expensive to own. In the early nineteenth century, household clocks became smaller and more affordable, largely due to American entrepreneurship. Attractive wall and shelf clocks were manufactured in tremendous quantity during this period and were purchased eagerly by consumers in America, Canada, England, Australia, and other countries.

TALL CASE CLOCKS

Tall case clocks were made jointly by a clockmaker and a cabinetmaker. The case had to be long to accommodate the weights and pendulum. In England and North America, the cases were rectangular. Dials and faces could be brass, but a country customer more typically chose a painted face and decoration.

In France, tall clocks with plain wood cases and faces were popular throughout the countryside. The cases were always locally made, but the clockworks could come from as far away as Switzerland. The cases could be straight, as in the tall, narrow St. Nicholas clock from Normandy, or gently curved in the French hourglass shape called *la demoiselle*. The Swedish grandmother clock shows a similar hourglass shape that fans out into a wide skirtlike support. Another Swedish clock, the *moraklocka*, was popularly called the "bride's clock" because of its graceful curves. These shapes were necessary to allow for the movement of the pendulum.

AMERICAN CLOCKS

The American-made shelf clock first appeared in the early 1800s, due largely to the entrepreneurship of Connecticut clockmaker Eli Terry. By using mass-produced wooden clockworks, his factory was able to turn out sixty clocks per day by 1807. By 1815, shelf and mantel clocks could be had for $15, a much better buy for the average citizen than the tall case clock at $75. Clocks continued to change dramatically over the next decades. Brass works were introduced in 1840, and the modern spring mechanism, eliminating the need for weights, came in 1845.

Many of the early American shelf and wall clocks were decorated with reverse painting on glass. Later, color prints were mounted behind the glass to save on manufacturing time. Another popular style was the wall-mounted banjo clock, so named because its case resembled a banjo. It was invented by Simon Willard in the 1790s, patented around 1800, and remained popular through the mid-1800s.

ABOVE: A wall-mounted banjo clock. RIGHT: This mantel clock has a crisp roman numeral dial. The country estate scene is reverse-painted on glass. OPPOSITE PAGE: Small painted flowers decorate this gently bulging clock carcase.

The Act of Parliament Clock

The large octagonal Act of Parliament clock, up to 2 feet (61cm) across, appeared in England's hotels, stage stops, and inns during the eighteenth and early nineteenth centuries. These clocks were so ubiquitous that many people assumed the government had mandated their installation. The name actually refers to a 1797 act that levied a tax on personal clocks and watches, making them unaffordable for most people. According to popular lore, inns and stage lines responded by installing large, easy-to-read clocks as a public service to help travelers reach their destinations and appointments on time. The act was soon repealed, but the sensible practice of installing prominent clocks in public places continued.

ABOVE: A Swedish grandmother clock. RIGHT: An Australian parlor clock made in the late 1800s uses a "modern" spring mechanism.

UTILITARIAN CLOCKS

Beginning in the late eighteenth century, plain wall clocks were made for public places such as stage stops, hotels and inns, stores, offices, schools, factories, and hospitals, as well as servants' quarters. Their easy-to-read dials and warm wood casings make them well suited to country interiors today. Weights and pendulums may be exposed or encased behind glass panels. The alarm bells in old school or factory clocks can be earsplitting and are best disengaged for home use.

COTTAGE FURNITURE

Cottage furniture was the first widely marketed factory-made furniture in nineteenth-century America. It was affordable to working-class people and newly arrived immigrants, and the upper middle classes chose it for servants' and children's bedrooms and summer cottages. Production began around 1845 and continued through the 1920s. Many different types of furniture were made, with the emphasis on simple styles, pretty but economical decoration, and broad public appeal. For a European immigrant, the transition from a hand-decorated trunk to the simplest cottage chest of drawers represented an improved standard of living and a rise in status and economic prospects.

ABOVE: This period advertisement for cottage furniture invites the buyer to choose from among natural wood or painted finishes and a variety of styles and categories. Matching bedroom suites, such as the bedstead and dressing table depicted, were considered very stylish.

DESIGN AND CONSTRUCTION

Cottage furniture was built for the mass market, and compared to the pieces coming out of the nineteenth-century woodworker's shop, it was less sturdy. To keep costs down, for instance, manufacturers substituted glue and dowels for dovetail joins. When the glue dried out, the dowels loosened and the joins lost their strength. Nails and screws were also used, and as these did not shrink and expand with the wood, they eventually worked loose or caused the wood to split or crack. Back panels and drawer bottoms were cut thinner, so furniture was lightweight and prone to breakage.

On the plus side, precision power tools meant mechanically true joins and evenly planed surfaces that required little hand shaping. Drawer bottoms and carcase panels were easily slotted into machine-cut grooves. When dovetails were used, they could be cut quickly and precisely, and assembly was rapid. Many different kinds of woods appeared in cottage furniture. Pine, poplar, and birch were most popular, but maple, cherry, ash, hickory, and walnut were also used.

DECORATION

What cottage furniture lacked in craftsmanship was camouflaged by decoration. Surfaces were painted, grained, or stenciled in a variety of styles to mimic the machine-carved Victorian furniture of the period. Painted furniture was much less expensive than carved pieces, and many customers considered it just as stylish. Crests, medallions, and striping were used to imitate Empire furniture. Ornately painted scrolls and oaklike graining helped capture the flavor of rococo, gothic, and Renaissance revival styles. Freehand painting of vines, leaves, fruit, and flowers was rapidly done with suggestive rather than precise brushstrokes. Stock scenes and motifs were repeated dozens of times each day by factory artists and stencilers. Popular background colors were black, white, and light, muted hues such as lilac, mint green, powder blue, and gray. Split turnings were glued onto flat surfaces to suggest hand carving.

THE FURNITURE

The backbone of the cottage furniture industry was the bedroom suite, often sold by mail. Getting a customer to buy not simply a chest of drawers, but an entire matched suite including bed, chest, wardrobe, washstand, dressing table, and towel rack meant more business and bigger profits. Most cottage furniture was made for the bedroom, though kitchen table and chair sets were also popular. The furniture was on the small side, to fit more comfortably into the residences of the working class.

The kitchen cottage chair was widely distributed in the nineteenth and early twentieth centuries. Enormous quantities were exported to Australia, to meet the great need for inexpensive furniture among the young and fast-growing population. Although factory-assembled, the chair back could reflect any number of chairmaking traditions: spindles and arrow-backs from the Windsor, gently curved rails from the Sheraton-style fancy chair, elaborate crests from the Pennsylvania Germans, fiddleback splats from the Hudson Valley Dutch. High stiles, with the crest fitting between them, reflect New England origins. Yoke-shaped "angel-wing" crests that sit on top of the stiles show Pennsylvania German influence. Many distinctive variations were made, and chairs in good condition with their original painted finish are especially collectible.

QUALITY CHECKLIST

The straightforward design of cottage furniture can resemble settler furniture made more than a century before. Factory-made pieces that have been grained or stripped can be especially deceiving at first glance. Examine construction details carefully, being sure to check the following:

- Drawer dovetailing. Are the dovetails even and precise or slightly off? A dovetail cut by hand usually shows a bit of the saw mark beyond the chiseled-out section.

- Corner joins. Look for any sign of wooden pegs that could indicate a hand-worked mortise-and-tenon join. Be alert to wooden plugs glued into holes to hide screw heads; they may look like wooden pegs.

- Hardware. If the hinges and knobs look genuinely old, check the drawer back or framework to see if they are original to the piece. Extra screw holes or mismatched chiseling for a hinge plate could indicate a substitution.

- Circular saw marks. Examine drawer bottoms and other flat interior surfaces for circular saw marks. The circular saw first appeared around 1830 and left distinctive curved marks.

- Machine-planing marks. The shallow parallel ripples of machine planing always run against the wood grain. Hand-planing marks are more wavy to the touch and usually run with the grain.

COUNTRY CHIPPENDALE CHAIRS

THE FORMAL HISTORY

The Chippendale chair, with its signature ball-and-claw foot and delicately pierced splat, was the crowning achievement of the eighteenth-century "golden age" of furniture making. The style combined lavish baroque ornamentation, graceful Queen Anne symmetry, and the crest rail "ears" of Chinese chairs. Chippendale chairs were made of fine-grained mahogany imported from the West Indies, which could be carved with extraordinary precision and fragile, intricate detail.

Many British cabinetmakers contributed to the new style, but Thomas Chippendale was the one who undertook to publish a pattern book. *The Gentleman and Cabinetmaker's Director*, printed in 1754, was enthusiastically received by cabinetmakers in Europe and America, who went about adapting the patterns in their own workshops. European cities as well as colonial Philadelphia, Charleston, Boston, and Newport began turning out furniture that closely reproduced Chippendale's designs. In general, though, Americans found the style too ornamental, and cabinetmakers toned it down to a level that was still considered highly fashionable by colonial standards.

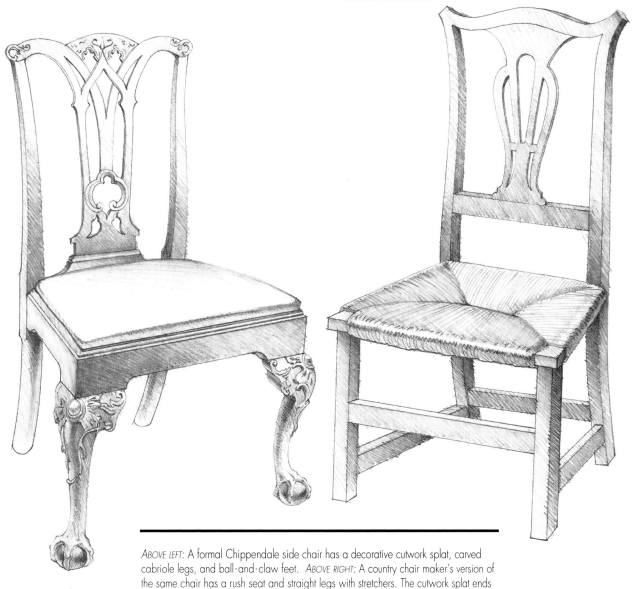

ABOVE LEFT: A formal Chippendale side chair has a decorative cutwork splat, carved cabriole legs, and ball-and-claw feet. *ABOVE RIGHT:* A country chair maker's version of the same chair has a rush seat and straight legs with stretchers. The cutwork splat ends in a crossrail above the seat.

QUALITY CHECKLIST

- Check the underside of the English drop-in seat and the inside chair frame for numbers. If the numbers match, the seat is original to the chair. If they don't match, the seat is a replacement. Closer examination will probably reveal their imperfect fit.

- Small holes showing up on the underside of the drop-in seat may actually be tack holes made when the seat was recovered, not wormholes.

THE COUNTRY VISION

Country furniture makers also referred to the Chippendale pattern book. They borrowed what design elements they could, interpreting the style to suit their own skills and tools as well as the needs and budgets of the buyers. Often, they were paid in eggs, grain, live-stock, or hours of service instead of cash. They rarely used imported mahogany, choosing instead to work with woods harvested locally—oak, elm, ash, birch, and yew. The use of local woods dramatically limited the level and intricacy of carving they could undertake.

Typically, country-made chairs had Chippendale features above the seat but smooth Queen Anne or even turned William and Mary legs, which were often strengthened with stretchers. While formal chairs had removable slip seats, which fitted into the molding and could be padded and covered with fabric, country versions were more likely to have permanent wood or rush seats. Hard wood seats were made by nailing planking to the chair underframe. They look more uncomfortable today than they actually were in the eighteenth century, consid-ering the petticoats, coattails, and other layers of padding built into people's clothing. Some chairs were made with drop-in seats of horsehair or rush.

Throughout England, Chippendale-style chairs were made in sets of twelve—huge by modern standards but essential for large households common then. American country chair makers who borrowed from the Chippen-dale style include the Dominy family of Long Island, the Dunlap family of New Hampshire, and Eliphalet Chapin of New Jersey. The Chippendale era ended in the 1790s, but country Chippendale lasted as a style in rural areas well into the nineteenth century.

CRADLES

The cradle has been the infant bed of many generations. Early cradles were hollowed-out tree trunks that could be rolled gently from side to side. The Scandinavians hung box cradles from the rafters. By installing several hooks around the room, they could move the baby closer to the fire for warmth or into a dark corner away from the noise of the family for sleeping. It is unclear when arc-shaped runners were added to the box bed, but it may have been as early as the fourteenth century.

ABOVE: This hanging cradle is made to sway gently from side to side in a stationary stand. Side boards stabilize the stand and guard against overzealous rocking.

DESIGN AND CONSTRUCTION

Wooden cradles were constructed in two ways. They could be framed with panels and mortise-and-tenon joins or made of boards that were dovetailed or nailed at the corners.

Framed cradles had four corner posts that extended below and above the cradle bed. The rockers were joined to the posts with wooden pegs, which simplified replacement when they wore out. The upper posts ended in small knobs or finials, which were used as handholds for rocking.

Board cradles were easier to construct and appeared more frequently in rural, frontier, and peasant communities. The end boards often were cut with angled sides, giving the finished cradle a trough shape. Sometimes corner posts were used and the board sides were slotted into them. Deep rockers were indented several inches from the end and pegged or screwed in place. Cradles were made of various woods, including pine, ash, elm, and fruitwood. Pine cradles were often grained and varnished to imitate oak.

Early cradles used pretty much the same linens as adult beds. There were tiny sheets and blankets. The rush bedding and straw mattress had to be renewed daily. Some cradles had a hinged door at the foot so that the damp rushes could be swept out.

REGIONAL VARIATIONS

Cradle styles differed from region to region and also from century to century, as child-rearing practices changed. In northern climates, many cradles were built with deep hoods or bonnets to protect the baby from drafts. German woodworkers added small knobs on the cradle sides. When the baby was laid in cradle, the "coverlid," or blanket, was made snug by wrapping lacing over it and securing it around the knobs. In Central Europe, the cradle sides were decorated with repeat geometric cutouts, and strips of fabric could be laced through these openings to secure the blanket. Scandinavian pine cradles were painted in two solid colors, different inside and out, then decorated outside with tiny flowers and other brushstroke designs. These cradles were usually smaller and more cozy than English-made cradles. In Sweden, an extra-long "rocking post" was sometimes built into the cradle. It could be rocked by hand or by pulling a scarf that was tied to it. Some

LEFT: This unusual child's cot was made in South Australia around 1900. The ends of the cot are actually two chair backs salvaged from a cedar dining set. They are joined by packing case boards, which form the cot bed and sides. *ABOVE:* A settler-made cradle is simple, but not crude. The headboard and footboard arc up, and the sides dip in near the center. All four pieces are mortised into corner posts topped by squared-off rocking knobs. The rocker blades join the posts underneath.

Scandinavian cradles had the rockers attached along the length of the cradle so that it rocked from front to back instead of side to side.

Tight bundling and deep bonnets sometimes caused infant suffocation, especially when the cradle was placed too close to the fireplace, and in the nineteenth century, a more open, less restrictive style came to be favored. These included Windsor-style stick cradles, wicker cradles, and rush cradles. All of these encouraged greater air circulation and allowed the baby to be more visible. By the late nineteenth century, the practice of rocking was universally frowned upon, and the stationary open-slat crib, still in use today, became the norm.

ABOVE: A board cradle is constructed with a high bonnet to keep out drafts. Extra-wide rocker blades guard against accidental tipping. *LEFT:* Gouge-carved flowers and baskets decorate this peasant cradle. The thick board sides are joined to the end boards by protruding tenons. Fabric strips could be laced through the cutout hearts to prevent a swaddled infant from falling out.

Using Old Cradles Today

Heirloom cradles can be charming to use, but should be examined carefully before an infant is placed in them. Be sure to avoid the following:

- *Any sign of splinters, rough wood, or damaged wicker.*

- *Splats or spindles further apart than 2 ⅜ inches (6cm) or any cutouts in the headboard or footboard that could trap the baby's head or limbs.*

- *Rockers that are not securely attached or that could allow the cradle to tip if knocked accidentally or rocked too vigorously.*

- *Any paint, stain, or sealer fumes lingering from a recent refinishing job.*

The mattress should fit the cradle snugly. You should be able to place no more than two fingers between the cradle sides and the mattress. If the mattress is too thick, the sides of the cradle may not be high enough to keep the baby from falling out. Never leave the baby unattended in the cradle. Once the infant begins to turn over or sit up by itself, it's best to start using a standard crib instead. Remember, yesteryear's children were bundled and laced into their cradles to prevent accidents. If in doubt about any of the above, do not use the cradle.

CUPBOARDS

The cupboard began as the cup board—a group of board shelves that held cups, dishes, and crockery. The shelves might stand on the floor, rest on a tabletop or low cabinet, or be mounted on the wall. In time, the frame supporting the shelves became more substantial, and it made sense to add doors.

Many different cupboard styles evolved. Open shelves without doors are called hutches or pewter cupboards. Those with doors are called blind cupboards, because the doors hid the contents from view. The glass-paned door, used in expensive cabinetry since the 1700s, became more affordable by the mid-1800s. Cupboards could be built-in, freestanding, or wall-mounted. Styles range from decoratively painted peasant cupboards to simple utilitarian board cupboards nailed together by pioneers.

CORNER CUPBOARDS

The corner cupboard descended from the old medieval custom of arranging furniture around the walls of the room. Building a triangular cupboard made the most of the hard-to-fill corner space and helped draw the eye around the room. Corner cupboards could be built-in or freestanding.

ENGLISH BUILT-IN CUPBOARD

The eighteenth-century Georgian cupboard appeared in both Great Britain and North America. The cabinet wood was oak or pine and could be left plain or painted to match the room. The cupboard was built in two sections, with the larger section on top. Depending on the size, each section had one or two doors. Architectural details included a split pediment crest, reeded pillars, and a domed interior carved to resemble a seashell. The interior shelves bowed out in front and had narrow grooved channels in the back to stand plates upright for display.

Early architectural corner cabinets featured doors that were solid or paneled. To display her treasured dishes and platters, the housewife left the top doors swung open. The interior was painted soft blue, green, or pink to show off the white dishes inside. The Welsh wallpapered the cupboard interior to match the room. Once glazed panels became more common, the doors were kept shut. Eventually, the built-in corner cupboard came to be viewed as provincial and old-fashioned, and newly built homes no longer included them. Freestanding cupboards, however, continued to feature the architectural elements.

PEASANT CORNER CUPBOARD

Freestanding corner cupboards were common in many European peasant traditions. The most impressive is the French Louis XV–style *encoignure à deux corps*. Like the

ABOVE: This unusual hanging cupboard has triangular drawers that pivot out from the wall. LEFT: Solid doors on corner cupboards were left open to display the crockery inside.

English version, it was massive and built in two sections with enclosed shelving above and below. Less formal cultures had a closed cabinet below and open shelves above. An open space between the upper and lower sections served as a work counter and serving area. In Sweden, the upper shelves were supported by turned spindles. The entire cupboard was painted in one or more solid colors, then further decorated with painted flowers. Central European peasant cupboards featured high baroque cornices, numerous ornate finials, decorative repeat carving, and door panels painted in contrasting colors to highlight the moldings.

HANGING CUPBOARDS

Hanging cupboards have a simplicity that belies their significance in the European peasant or immigrant home. Often, they held the family Bible, which was removed daily for readings. Others articles kept inside—

special dishes, silver spoons, needlework, or a newly arrived letter from a loved one—were equally precious. Such cupboards, mounted high on the wall so the children couldn't disturb them, assumed a shrinelike importance.

Hanging cupboards typically were made of a light-weight wood such as pine. They could be triangular, to fit into a corner, or rectangular, to mount flush on a wall. They were built simply but carefully, sometimes with decoratively scalloped edges. Finishes included decorative painting, staining, and wood graining.

FREESTANDING CUPBOARDS

Plain board cupboards were built by pioneers and settlers throughout North America and Australia to hold canned goods, preserves, and staples. Strictly utilitarian, they had straight sides, several interior shelves, and blind doors that latched closed with a turnbuckle—a small chunk of wood that turned on a nail or screw. The jelly cupboard of the American midwest is an example of this pioneer furniture. Some cupboards included exterior drawers, either at the top of the cupboard or in a center section between upper and lower cabinets. Examples with their original milk paint finish are highly collectible today.

OPPOSITE PAGE, TOP: The upper section of an Australian food cupboard has mesh inserts to promote ventilation. The interior shelves are specially shaped so that fowl or a joint of meat can be hung from a hook in the ceiling. *OPPOSITE PAGE, BOTTOM:* This utilitarian cupboard, perhaps once used for preserves in the kitchen, is fitted with interior shelves. The carpenter dressed up the plain design with a wavy floor-skimming apron. *ABOVE:* An ornamental backboard suggests that this Australian cupboard was intended for use in the dining room. A turnbuckle prevents the doors from swinging open.

QUALITY CHECKLIST

- Today, built-in corner cabinets are being rescued from old, crumbling houses and fitted with new sides and shelves to make them saleable as freestanding units. These conversions can be quite successful as long as the new backboards are firm, solidly joined, and in keeping with the character of the piece. The buyer should be made aware of any addition or restoration.

- Glazed doors are most attractive when the muntins (the wood strips holding the panes of glass) are level with the cupboard shelves inside. Careful woodworkers thought ahead so that the new muntins did not disrupt the line of vision and the items on the shelves were in full view behind the glass. Muntins that do not align with the shelves may indicate that the doors were added at a later date or that they were recycled from a totally different piece.

- If the tongue-and-groove joins on a plain board cupboard are wide and square, they were cut by hand. It they are rounded, they were cut by machine. To see the joins clearly, look for exposed board ends at the top of the backboard or at the top or bottom edges of doors. Hand-cut joins can indicate a settler-made piece.

DESKS

DESKS ARE RELATIVE NEWCOMERS TO THE COUNTRY HOME. IF A FARMER NEEDED A DESK, IT MEANT HE COULD READ AND WRITE, HAD TO KEEP TRACK OF PERSONAL ACCOUNTS, OR POSSIBLY WAS RUNNING A SMALL BUSINESS WITH PART-TIME WORKERS ON THE SIDE. A DESK WITH A LOCKING CABINET WAS A SIGN OF HIS RISING BUSINESS PROSPECTS AND PROSPERITY. INTERIOR CUBBYHOLES AND DRAWERS MADE IT EASIER TO KEEP TRACK OF RECEIPTS, ORDERS, LEDGERS, AND ACCOUNTS.

PORTABLE DESKS

The first desks were small portable boxes with locking lids. The box was set on a tabletop to use, and the hinged slanted lid formed the writing surface. The lid lifted up for access to the correspondence, documents, and fresh parchment stored inside, a design that still is used on desks for schoolchildren. Inside the desk, pigeonholes and small drawers stored quills, ink, and sealing wax. The inconvenience of having to open and close the writing surface lid to retrieve supplies and notes led to a new style with the hinges at the bottom, so that the lid opened out and down to rest on the tabletop. In this version, the inside of the lid became the writing surface, and the user had continuous access to the pigeonholes and cubbies during the course of the work. New developments followed, but the small portable desk continued to be made well into the nineteenth century and accompanied American and Australian settlers into the frontier.

FALL-FRONT DESKS

Construction of the fall-front desk followed on the heels of the chest of drawers, sometime in the late 1600s. At first, the portable desk (described above) was mounted on a low chest of drawers. The desk portion was larger

and overhung the chest slightly. The top drawer was pulled out to support the open lid. Later, special pull-out bars, called lopers, were built in, saving wear and tear on the drawer.

The Dutch called this new piece of furniture a "fall-flap bureau," but it is also called a fall-front desk, a drop-front desk, or simply a bureau. A strip of molding along the bottom of the sloping lid let the desk function as a music stand, bookrest, or easel when closed. The chest portion rested on bun or bracket feet. Each drawer was locked with and could be drawn open by a key. Many different woods were used, including walnut, oak, fruitwood, maple, and pine.

In the 1730s, yet a third piece was added—a bookcase with two side-by-side paneled doors. The bookcase also locked closed, making the entire unit a repository for important documents, records, and receipts. In the 1750s, the interior cubbies became more sophisticated, with a small locking cupboard in the center, stepped pigeonholes, "secret" drawers disguised as reeded and fluted columns, and other hiding places. Improvements

ABOVE: Empire-style legs, a wavy cornice, and attached candle holders lend elegance to this plantation desk with a drop-lid writing surface.
OPPPOSITE PAGE: Schoolhouse desks were lined up in rows as each desktop was attached to the bench of the pupils in front.

and additions like these reflected a growing public literacy as well as more permanent settlements. Over the course of the century, glazed panels became more common on the bookcase portion, but at first, only the wealthy could afford them. A variation on the slant-front desk-and-bookcase is the secretary, which had a vertical lid that dropped forward and a deeper cabinet above instead of the narrow bookcase.

OTHER DESK VARIATIONS

Country cabinetmakers continued to make fall-front and bookcase desks for their customers well into the nineteenth century. Most desks made for homes or family businesses had cubbyholes and drawers—along with secret hiding places—to sort and store important documents.

In the American South, the plantation desk became popular. The base was a plain table on turned legs, and a tall, narrow, locking cupboard was set on top. The front of this bookcaselike cupboard was hinged at the bottom so that it dropped forward and leaned on the table at a slight angle to form the writing surface. No lopers were needed. Inside were large and small cubbies for the papers and ledger books needed to manage a plantation.

Tall desks are another popular nineteenth-century form used widely in schools and academies, accounting and law offices, retail establishments, and other

businesses. In Australian shearing sheds, clerks stood behind tall pine desks to keep the tallies. In offices, workers using tall desks either stood or leaned back on high stools. Numerous variations were designed. The tall desk legs could be exposed, or the base of the desk could be enclosed and have low interior shelves for books or papers. The sloped writing surface might lift up on hinges for access to the storage compartment, or the front could fall forward with deep inside compartments for books and records. A drawer, inkwell, pencil tray, and other grooved compartments might also be included. A low spindled railing kept books on the top ledge from toppling off.

Yesteryear's schoolhouse desks are an affordable acquisition for collectors since they were made in such quantity. As a cost-saving measure, seats were built with desktops attached behind them, for use by pupils one row back. Today, these unusual two-tier pieces can function as hall benches, and the back shelf can hold plants, books, the telephone, or the day's mail.

See also under Scandinavia—"Natural Curve" Furniture.

Searching for Secret Drawers

Part of the romance of antique, hand-crafted desks is the possibility of secret drawers. To locate a secret drawer, conduct your search methodically, and keep a record of the possible locations you've tried. If you think you've found a secret drawer, don't force it—you may break a hidden spring. Gently work the drawer out, then rub the hidden parts with a candle or piece of dry soap for easier sliding the next time. Here's how to proceed.

- *Gently try pulling out any fluted or reeded pillars.*

- *Pull out a drawer all the way, then check to see if another drawer is hidden behind it. Look especially for a cloth tape or leather tab to pull on.*

- *If the interior of the desk has a built-in canopy, see if you can reach your fingers up under the canopy and pull it out or feel any tabs.*

- *If the interior has a central cubby or small cabinet, see if it will pull out in its entirety. There may be hidden space behind it.*

- *Measure the outside of the desk, then measure the inside of all the drawers and cubbies. Compare the figures, factoring in the wood thickness, and look for discrepancies.*

- *Compare corresponding drawers and cubbies. If a drawer on the right side of the desk is 7 inches (18cm) deep and its symmetric partner on the left side is only 5 inches (13cm) deep, check behind the shorter drawer to see if you've missed a clue, such as a flap of tape.*

- *Look for a section of molding and try pulling it straight out. Sometimes a shallow drawer, able to hold just a single document, is hidden behind a molding facade.*

OPPOSITE PAGE, TOP: This bureau is enhanced by a band of marquetry along the apron. The top drawer is flanked by lopers, which pull out to support the desktop when it is down. OPPOSITE PAGE, BOTTOM: An extra-long Shaker desk features a slanted writing surface and shelves with glass-paneled doors. ABOVE RIGHT: An oversized dresser rack displays crockery, glassware, and cups on hooks.

DRESSERS

No single piece of furniture says "country" better than the outsized kitchen dresser. Most often associated with the British Isles, the dresser may have originated in the Netherlands. Dutch homes had two kitchens, one for food preparation and messy chores and a second outer kitchen for dining. It was in this "best kitchen" that the dresser displayed the family's brass, pewter, and china.

HOW THE DRESSER EVOLVED

The forerunner of the dresser is a long narrow board that was placed on trestle legs. This "side board" was set up against the wall for serving food and was dismantled after each use. Eventually, four to six permanent legs replaced the knock-down trestles. A single row of drawers was fitted into the frieze in the late 1600s—about the same time drawers were appearing in the bottom of chests.

English oak side tables of the early eighteenth century were long enough to have three drawers running across the front. For easy access, plates were stored in a rack that hung above the table. In sophisticated homes, this hanging plate rack disappeared along with a change in dinnerware. Newly imported porcelain plates were too expensive to trust to a wall-mounted rack, so the wealthy turned to freestanding cabinets with glazed cupboards for showing off their collections. In country homes, earthenware and pewter plates were simply too heavy for the rack. As a result, the plate rack was moved down and mounted on the sideboard, and the dresser was born. The name "dresser" may have come about because the rack was "dressed" with pewter or because meats were dressed on the tabletop.

DESIGN AND CONSTRUCTION

Dressers were built with many variations to meet the needs of the people who used them. They ranged from 3 to 8 feet (0.9 to 2.4m) long. Six or eight legs were mandatory to support the additional weight of the rack. Low stretchers about 6 inches (15cm) off the floor joined the legs and provided a base for a low potboard, used to store big cookware and soup tureens. In farmhouse kitchens, this lower shelf was constructed of open laths, which allowed air to circulate around the cheeses curing there. In Irish kitchens, straw was placed on the potboard, encouraging the resident hen or goose to roost and lay her eggs there. The top work surface was 2-inch (5cm) -thick oak or pine, and it was scrubbed clean after every use. As country families became more prosperous, the middle frieze drawer was fitted with a lock for storing silver.

The dresser rack held dishes, platters, and cups. In England and New England, the shelves were graduated in size, becoming deeper toward the top. Although this arrangement looked top-heavy, it made sense for the cook, as it increased the work surface for preparing and serving food. The more frequently used smaller dishes were stored on the bottom shelf, where they were easily accessible, while large platters and crockery were kept on the top shelf. Jugs and cups were hung from hooks mounted in the underside of the shelves. In Ireland, Scotland, and continental Europe, the sides of the rack were much plainer. In some well-to-do Irish and Scottish homes, the dresser was used only to display the household's best pieces, and the everyday dishes were kept in a blind cupboard.

Dresser racks could be either open-backed or covered. Often very large racks were bolted to the wall as a precaution, and unfortunately, many have become separated from their bases. In England, the back interior

of the rack frequently was painted a blue-green color that showed off the plates.

WELSH DRESSER

The name "Welsh dresser" is loosely applied to any British-made dresser with an enclosed cupboard base instead of a potboard. Welsh dressers were made from the late 1700s through the late 1800s, and it is believed that the soot-laden air in the coal-mining regions of Wales first led to the enclosed cabinet style. The lower cabinet had two doors, one on each side of a plain center panel. Sometimes the lower area was designed as two separate cabinets, with a large, open space, called a "dog kennel," between them. The dog kennel was used to display a large, heavy soup tureen or the crocks used in dairying or making ginger beer. The plate rack above also was enclosed. Cabinets were built on either side of open shelving, and a deep overhanging canopy ran across the top.

LATER DRESSER STYLES

The dresser continued to serve country kitchens throughout the nineteenth and early twentieth centuries. During this period, many style changes occurred that were practical to the users but not as attractive to today's buyer of antiques. Dressers were built smaller, to fit into cottages and small residences, and glazed doors became common. An enclosed cabinet replaced the potboard, and some pieces were given clocks or built-in mirrors. In Australia, dressers were constructed in one piece, not two separate sections, beginning around 1860, and were often built in after 1890. In the mid to late 1800s, English painted pine dressers were fitted with deep drawers for baking tins, irons, and other housekeeping equipment. By 1900, housewives had given up their laborious scrubbing and were covering the dresser top with wipe-clean oilcloth—a sign of the modern kitchen on the horizon.

See also under Central Europe—Poland.

LEFT: An Australian utilitarian dresser from the mid-1800s has a deep rack, which served as general-use kitchen storage rather than as display shelving.

DROP-LEAF TABLES

Large tables that can fold down are a boon in small quarters. The idea of cutting a tabletop into sections and joining them with hinges originated in the seventeenth century. During this period and continuing into the early nineteenth century, furniture was arranged around the perimeter of the room. The center of the room was left open and when a piece of furniture, such as a table for dining, was needed, it was brought into the center of the room and set up. Trestle tables, in use since medieval times, were assembled and disassembled several times daily under this arrangement. The heavy board was set against the wall when the table was not in use.

The gateleg drop-leaf table was an aesthetic and practical improvement. A small, rectangular center section of the tabletop was permanently attached to the table base, and large extensions, called leaves, were hinged to it on each side. The leaves could be lifted up, level with the tabletop, and supported by swing-out legs. With the legs swung back in, the leaves could be folded down, and the table was placed back against the wall as a sideboard.

Over the years, various other designs developed. In addition to swing-out legs, the leaves could be held in place by sliding supports, swing-out brackets, or hinged legs. The first drop-leaf tables had turned legs and stretchers. A century later, Empire-influenced tapered legs were easy enough to construct in the home workshop, and painted drop-leaf tables appeared in many farmhouse kitchens.

THE DUTCH AND ENGLISH GATELEG

The oak or walnut gateleg table, the grandfather of the drop-leafs, originated in seventeenth-century Holland and spread from there to England and Spain. All had turned legs and stretchers, following the heavy baroque fashion of this period. Very large tables were made at first, but by the early eighteenth century, several smaller tables were used instead, and dining in intimate groups of six to eight became the fashion.

Dutch and English tables can be distinguished from one another by their legs. Dutch tables featured split legs. The legs were massively thick, allowing two of the

four legs to be turned by the split-banister method. The inner half of a split leg was connected to the table base, and the outer half formed the swing-out gate. When the leaves were folded down, the deception was complete—the table appeared to rest on four solid legs.

English tables, in contrast, featured all solid legs. The swing-out gatelegs were turned separately from the supporting legs and, as a result, did not have to be as massive in diameter to support the tabletop. Even though the legs were more slender, there were more of them. A small table had a minimum of six legs—four in the center support and two that swung out. Larger tables had six or eight legs supporting the base and two gatelegs supporting each leaf.

OTHER DROP-LEAF STYLES

BUTTERFLY TABLE

The round-topped butterfly table is an ingenious variation on the gateleg principle. Like the gateleg, the top has a rectangular center section supported by four solid legs. Two rounded leaves fall to each side. When a leaf is opened, a tall pivoting brace swings out on pintle hinges to support it. The brace is cut from a board and is gracefully shaped so that it is widest just under the leaf and tapered as it nears the floor.

The butterfly support is not as sturdy as a gateleg but has the advantage of clear floor space under the leaves. It was made in colonial New England, and simple carpenter-made versions were especially popular in Scandinavia.

HANDKERCHIEF TABLE

This small, single-leaf table hinges along the diagonal, for a tabletop that is triangular when closed, square when open. The table stands on four legs, one of which swings out to support the flap. It slips into a corner when closed, with the very pretty triangular leaf folded down in front.

OPPOSITE PAGE: A gateleg table is compact and space-saving when closed, large and accommodating when open. The center section and leaf extensions are supported by turned legs and stretchers, for a rich concentration of design under the table. *OPPOSITE PAGE, INSET:* The rule joint creates a neat finish when the table leaf is down.

Quality checklist

- Examine the hinged edges of the leaf and tabletop for a special curved fit called a rule joint. Before attaching the hinges, experienced woodworkers used a molding plane to contour the edges of the wood. First, the tabletop center was given a quarter-round edge, and then a corresponding concave shape was grooved into the edge of leaf. Tables without the rule joint edge are quickly recognized by their ugly "black hole" gaps when the leaves are down.

- Make sure that the leaf opens up freely, without binding or bruising the rule joint. If there is friction, a simple adjustment to the hinges may be all that's necessary.

- Make sure the gatelegs swing open freely, and check under the table to see that the pivots are secure.

- William and Mary–style gateleg tables were very popular during the American colonial revival period, from 1920 to about 1935. They were made of walnut, oak, or pine. Be aware that many of the gateleg tables available today are reproductions from this period.

The handkerchief table is said to have originated in England during the eighteenth century. A card game for three players, in fashion for a brief while, led to a three-sided table which was kept in a corner when not in use. The idea of attaching a matching leaf must have appeared as a logical next step.

SCANDINAVIAN GATELEG TABLES

The gateleg concept was used widely in Scandinavia in the eighteenth and nineteenth centuries. The enormous pine tabletops were rectangular or oval in shape, with transverse bracing strips on the underside to support the planks. Norwegian tables had leaves that extended nearly to the floor. A large drawer in one end of the base held the flat hard bread served with most meals. Leg styles changed along with the fashion in formal furniture: early legs were turned, but by the Empire period they were straight or tapered. The largest tables were given a protective coat of varnish, but smaller tables were painted.

YEOMAN TABLE

The seventeenth-century English yeoman table had a leaf and gateleg on one side only. It was meant to stand against the wall, with just the single leaf extending into the room. A long sliding drawer went clear through the middle section and could be opened at either end.

EUROPEAN FOLK CHAIR

FOLK OR PEASANT CHAIRS WITH FLAT BOARD SEATS ARE FOUND ALL OVER THE EUROPEAN CONTINENT. THEY BEGAN EMERGING IN THE LATE SEVENTEENTH CENTURY AS MILLED LUMBER AND FINER SAWS AND WOODWORKING TOOLS BECAME MORE COMMONPLACE. CONSTRUCTION WAS QUITE BASIC: LEGS AND BACK WERE STRAIGHT AND THE LEGS WERE JOINED BY STRETCHERS ALL AROUND. BOARDS WERE NAILED OR PEGGED ONTO THE OPEN FRAME TO FORM THE CHAIR SEAT. OFTEN, THE BACK CREST RAIL AND SEAT APRON WERE CUT WITH MATCHING CONTOURS.

Interest was provided through the many backrest variations, which included horizontal rails, vertical rails, and vertical turned spindles. A French version had an open-framed rectangular back, a style that reappeared in the Canadian Ile d'Orleans chair. Some folk chairs had a narrow board backrest with a cutout handhold at the top, similar to the German *Brettstuhl*. The New Mexico chair with chip carving is yet another variation. Folk chairs were most often painted in one or more solid colors, then decorated with striping, flowers, and other motifs. In general, they were not as widespread in the United States or Australia, where English-inspired Windsor-style chairs predominated.

OPPOSITE PAGE: Back view of a reproduction corner handkerchief table. *ABOVE RIGHT:* A flat plank seat, low stretchers, and a slightly canted backrest are hallmarks of folk chairs from many regions. This version shows through mortises in the legs. The stiles are chamfered just above the seat.

FIDDLEBACK CHAIR

THE EIGHTEENTH-CENTURY AMERICAN FIDDLEBACK CHAIR IS A HANDSOME EXAMPLE OF HOW OLD AND NEW CHAIRMAKING TECHNIQUES WERE COMBINED. THE FIDDLEBACK IS BASICALLY A TURNER'S CHAIR, BUT THE WOODWORKER HAD TO VENTURE INTO NEW TERRITORY TO CUT THE GRACEFUL VASE- OR FIDDLE-SHAPED SPLAT AND YOKE-SHAPED CREST SUCH AS THOSE FOUND ON QUEEN ANNE CHAIRS. TURNED TRUMPET LEGS ENDING IN PAD FEET ALSO BORROW FROM THE QUEEN ANNE VOCABULARY. OTHER CONSTRUCTION DETAILS WERE MORE FAMILIAR. BECAUSE THE SEAT WAS WOVEN OF RUSH, THE SPLAT DID NOT EXTEND ALL THE WAY TO THE SEAT BUT JOINED A LOW HORIZONTAL RAIL ABOVE IT.

ABOVE: An American colonial fiddleback chair features turned trumpet legs, a center stretcher with ball turnings, and a Queen Anne crest that descends into a vase-shaped splat.

Rush-seat fiddlebacks were made of hickory, maple, and pine throughout New York, New Jersey, and New England. They usually were painted black or reddish brown. Often associated with the Dutch, they actually reached a diverse ethnic and economic market along the northeast seaboard. Connecticut versions, called rush-bottom or York chairs after their New York origin, had flat, horizontally scrolled arms that were quite comfortable to grasp. Dutch and German makers might incorporate a single cutout heart or other motif into the splat, evidence of a lingering folk tradition. On better-made chairs, the seat corners are flat, and the front legs are joined into them on the underside. This feature is worth looking for in a reproduction as the chair will be more comfortable.

FRANCE

France's country provinces are renowned for their rich, elegant, hand-carved armoires, *dressoirs*, and buffets. These pieces are at once suited to gracious living yet are also perfectly at home in rural districts where agricultural seasons govern the rhythms of daily life. They succeed in combining the same qualities of luxury and humbleness in modern interiors, which explains their growing popularity today.

Of all Europe's eighteenth- and nineteenth-century peasantry, the French were the most aesthetically sophisticated. They were proud of their homes and their property and valued their furniture for its craftsmanship as well as its sentimental associations. They planned their estates and family succession of property carefully. Their provincial furniture (called *régional* in France) translated the outstanding styles of the French court into rich natural woods. Many people find that the warmth and charm of the hand carving far surpasses the gilded, heavily ornamented court furniture that originally inspired it.

A BRIEF HISTORY

The high court furniture of Louis XIII through Louis XVI was very elegant and was made only for the nobility. It was created by a complicated, multifaceted guild system. Unlike the English workshops, in which a single cabinetmaker might design and build a piece of furniture with the help of apprentices, the French system was a carefully controlled group effort. Distinct craftsmen were called in each step of the way, with separate guilds handling building, carving, veneering, marquetry, gilding, painting, and so on. A dozen or more craftsman could easily contribute their skills to the making of a single piece of furniture.

Knowledge of these high court styles filtered into the countryside by the usual channels—pattern books, city-trained artisans who relocated, travelers returning home with news, and so forth. But even with detailed pattern books, provincial cabinetmakers could not begin to provide the range of skills and expertise necessary to replicate the court styles—nor was there the need for such grand gilded furniture in a farmer's or fisherman's house. Instead, country cabinetmakers aspired to the new designs using locally available woods. This interpretation began in the early seventeenth century with the Louis XIII style and reached its full flowering with the Louis XV style of the eighteenth century. As is typical of provincial furniture, the new forms, once adopted, continued to flourish in the provinces long after they had been replaced by newer fashions in the cities. The Louis XV style, for instance, continued to be made well into the nineteenth century, and its popularity for repro-duction furniture has continued to this day.

A brief description of the court styles and the role they played in provincial furniture making follows:

Louis XIII (1610–1643). This seventeenth-century style featured sturdy, solid lines with geometric carved ornament, especially diamond points and star diamonds on paneled doors. The style was straightforward and easy for provincial cabinetmakers to copy. It continued in fashion for practically a century before being replaced by the Louis XV style.

Louis XIV (1643–1715). This style was largely bypassed by the provincial cabinetmaker. The style was sumptuous, bold, grand, massive, and somewhat overwhelming. It appealed to the city-dwelling bourgeoisie but rarely was seen in country pieces.

Louis XV (1715–1774). This style flourished throughout the eighteenth century and into the nineteenth century in provincial France. It is the style most people associate with French country furniture. Its graceful rococo curves, cabriole legs, and flexible,

Provençal Decorating

French country furniture has many moods. It can set the stage for an elegant dinner, but still feels welcoming and unpretentious after a day of gardening or household chores. Of all the provinces, Provence is the most informal and the most celebrated as a decorating style. Here, dressoirs are loaded with colored glassware and locally made faience pottery. Wire mesh doors recall the days when cooks kept poultry coops in the kitchen to fatten birds for the pot. A shallow stone sink in the kitchen adds a touch of authentic rusticity.

Throughout the house, shades of ochre, olive, and terra-cotta pop up. Provence is famed for its tiny hand-blocked printed cottons, and these charming floral and paisley patterns are a must. Many of the original patterns are still in production today (although by machine-printing methods) and can be made up into tablecloths, chair cushions, or bedspreads. A typically French alternative for the bedspread is lace. Lace is also used at windows and to edge shelving.

In the dining room, a faience lavabo can add a special touch. The reservoir on top has a spigot that lets the water run into the bowl below. Both are attached to a board for mounting on the wall. Most French country furniture shows its wood tones, but in Provence, rush-seated chairs are painted, striped, and even stenciled. If the chairs don't match exactly in size or design, so much the better—many French peasants acquired their furniture one piece at a time.

asymmetrical moldings create movement and pattern that is vibrant yet balanced. Paneled armoires and buffets, especially, gave cabinetmakers the opportunity to create fanciful arches and swirls.

Louis XVI (1774–1793). This late-eighteenth-century style introduced straighter, lighter lines and carved neoclassical ornament, an interest inspired by the successful archaeological excavations at the ancient sites of Herculaneum and Pompeii. Even though the Louis XVI forms would have been technically easier for the provincial craftsman to execute, the transition never fully occurred. The overwhelming preference was to continue the graceful contours of the Louis XV style and work in some of the newer neoclassical elements.

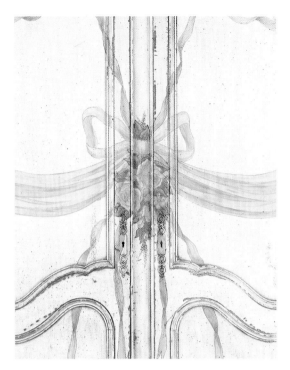

Germany and France, and cultural exchange occurred on both sides of the border. Alsatians, for instance, produced a low-backed plank chair, related to the German *Brettstuhl,* often carved with geometric motifs and emblems. Alsatian armoires and buffets featured wood inlays and painted flower motifs in the Germanic style. Bedsteads were placed in small alcoves that closed off with privacy curtains.

BRITTANY

Brittany is located in the northwest corner of France, where it juts out into the sea. Fishing and farming had long been its economic mainstays, and it was populated by peasants and wealthy landowners, but no real middle class, up until the nineteenth century. The rugged, rock-bound coastline and isolated farm life account for the region's massive, heavy Louis XIII style continuing so long. Armoires and buffets were solidly built, with broadly carved geometric designs, religious symbols, hearts, or birds. To stay warm on cold winter nights, families of four piled into huge cupboard beds with solid doors. Turned spindles and yellow-copper studs began appearing on chairs, benches, and garde-mangers in the nineteenth century. The fold-down hutch-table (like a chair-table) was used as a kneading platform and grain bin. Most of the furniture was oak, but the resourceful Bretons also used chestnut, walnut, wild cherry, pear, and wood salvaged from shipwrecks.

DISTINGUISHING THE PROVINCES

French country-made furniture does vary from province to province, and the distinctions can be exciting for the collector to pick out. Most of the regional variations emerged during the eighteenth century, a period when furniture was being produced in great quantity. Peasants and bourgeoisie alike were improving their homes and making them more comfortable. Furniture styles were influenced by climate, proximity to borders, and the economic livelihood and stability of a region. Areas closer to Paris were quicker to shed their distinctive regional color for more cosmopolitan fashions. Still, throughout France, the Louis XV style was the most popular and the variations were similar enough in look and function that the term "French Provincial" can be applied to them all.

ALSACE

Alsace is located near the German-Swiss border. Throughout history the region was claimed by both

OPPOSITE PAGE: French colonists in America's Mississippi valley brought many of their furniture styles with them. The ladderback chairs around the table feature decoratively cut slats, as does the salamander-slat ladderback against the wall. The open-backed chair under the window was made in Canada's St. Lawrence Valley, where it became known as the Ile d'Orleans chair. A spindled panetière, used for holding bread, is mounted on the wall. The armoire with diamond-paneled doors is in the Louis XIII style. ABOVE: Asymmetrical moldings on armoire doors crafted in the Louis XV style seem to undulate with movement .

BURGUNDY

Burgundy first rose to prominence during the Middle Ages as a center for culture and trade. During this time, its furniture was massive and heavy, with pronounced architectural detail and bold geometric designs carved in high relief. These style preferences persisted for centuries. When Burgundy's eighteenth- and nineteenth-century cabinetmakers created Louis XV–style furniture, they continued to incorporate these same qualities of mass, pronounced carving, and rich detail. They brought out the contrasting shapes by combining light and dark woods in the same piece.

LORRAINE

Lorraine is a border area just west of Alsace. Unlike German-influenced Alsace, it retained its full French identity. Here, the Louis XV style was marked by dignity and sobriety. Framework and moldings were simple and graceful rather than exuberant or flamboyant. Carving or marquetry work, usually of flowers in vases, decorated the panels. Chairs were slender and well proportioned. Beds were built into curtained alcoves. Oak, walnut, and cherry were typical woods.

NORMANDY

Normandy is a northern coastal province located just east of Brittany. It is closer to Paris than Brittany, and for centuries has been a favorite vacation spot for wealthy Parisians. This influence placed more wealth in the region and led to a rising middle class. As a result, Normandy's cabinetmaking became the most sophisticated of all the provinces. Richly carved decoration, upward-swelling cornices, good proportions, and carefully executed details are among the defining characteristics. The carving includes symbols of agriculture, such as cornucopias, grapes, and sheaves of wheat, and also symbols of love and marriage, such as hearts, quivers of arrows, and bird's nests. Other motifs include acanthus leaves, musical instruments, and anchors.

Normandy's cabinetmakers crafted many different kinds of furniture, including armoires, cabinets, tall case clocks, and wall shelves, for the wealthy peasant and middle-class residents. Most pieces were oak, though wild cherry, apple, elm, chestnut, and beech were also used. The Norman devotion to fine craftsmanship makes the region's furniture among the most desirable and expensive for collectors.

PROVENCE

Provence is located in southeastern France on the Mediterranean coast. It is one of the oldest and least formal of the provinces. The climate is sunny and windswept, and the terrain is hilly and picturesque. Provence's Louis XV–style furniture is full of life and vigor, displaying a wide variety of decorative shapes, curves, curls, and arcs that are gay and flirtatious. Even the hardware is fancy—the elaborately pierced steel escutcheons are extra-long, extending far above and below the keyhole. Moldings are always firm, clean-cut, and applied so as not to conceal the solidly built framework.

Decorative carving was not added until the late eighteenth century with the introduction of the Louis XVI style. It featured romantic garlands, doves, entwined hearts, and angels. In the northern provinces, oak was the wood of choice, but in the south of France, walnut was preferred. Provençal folklore suggests that a bride's marriage armoire be built from walnut trees planted by her parents on their wedding day.

THE FURNITURE

ARMOIRES

The armoire was the traditional wedding gift that a French bride brought to her new home. Armoires were used to store clothing, linens, silver, dinnerware, and even food. They were the pride of every French housewife and a visible emblem of successful household management. Even the most humble peasant homes had at least one.

Early armoires in the Louis XIII style featured strong, heavy lines and deep, heavily molded cornices. They were composed of two stacking sections, with the upper

unit recessed. Carvings featured geometric motifs and deep diamond points. This old style continued to be made in the provinces of Brittany, Gascogne, and Guienne into the late eighteenth century.

Louis XV is the style most often associated with armoires today. The cabinet is single-bodied, with two full-length doors. Each door is divided into two or three panels with asymmetrical curved framing. The cornice can be flat or it can arch up in the center. The entire armoire rests on short cabriole legs with a skirt between them. The later Louis XVI-style armoire was never fully adopted in the countryside, but it did contribute to the Louis XV style. Reeding, fluting, and cornice crests are Louis XVI features.

Both antique and reproduction armoires are very popular today. They can be used in any room in the house as storage for clothing, linens, food, cookware, office supplies, or coats and umbrellas. Old armoires can be fitted to hold televisions and other audio and video equipment, and reproductions are designed for just this

purpose. Another contemporary manufacturer's design is the armoire china cabinet. The asymmetrical top panels are filled in with glass, and the roomy interior is fitted with shelves and drawers to hold all the china, glassware, and silver a family could possibly accumulate.

BUFFETS

The buffet is a storage and serving cabinet used in the dining area, but it might hold other items as well. French peasant homes did not have a formal dining room, but rather a large table used for many purposes throughout the day. When it was time to eat, everyone pulled up a stool or chair. The buffet was located near this table. It typically featured two paneled doors, but the cabinet length could stretch to 9 feet (2.75m), with up to five or six doors opening onto the storage inside. Often a drawer was built in above each door. The usual Louis XV features— asymmetrical paneling, decoratively cut skirt, and short cabriole legs—were present.

Another type of buffet has a narrower, recessed section mounted on top. Instead of doors, this upper cabinet was fitted with two sliding panels at either end, giving rise to the name *buffet à glissants*. This style of buffet is identified with Provence, and many examples were made at Arles. All are finely carved and have large buttress hinges and fret-pierced steel escutcheons in the Provençal style.

CHAISE À CAPUCINE

This basic ladderback chair with rush seat was common throughout France during the 1700s and 1800s. Legs and stiles were straight or turned with simple balls and rings, and stretchers added stability. More ambitious chair makers worked in cabriole legs and curved stiles for a more sophisticated piece. The distinguishing feature is the back slats, two or three in number, which were cut in a Louis XV–style serpentine shape. Three-seat benches, called *banquettes* or *canapés*, were made in the same way.

ABOVE LEFT: Asymmetrical panels and lavish allover carving characterize this French-Canadian armoire made in the early to mid-nineteenth century.

Generally, they were positioned near the fire, much like the English settle. The Louis XVI style introduced flat slats and carving or fluting on the stiles and legs.

FAUTEUIL

Provincial versions of this open-armed easy chair were made well into the nineteenth century. The chair frame is wide and deep, with elegant, graceful, cabriole legs and carved scrolls as handrests. A network of webbing was stretched and nailed to the open seat frame to support a loose cushion. Two or three rails, often serpentine-shaped, crossed the back, and a loose cushion could be tied on to make leaning back more comfortable. Serviceable fabrics were chosen for the cushions; they included wool and silk blends, painted and printed cottons and linens, and needlework on canvas. Often, the wood arms are padded on top; the wood surface is scooped out and stuffed with horsehair and a fabric covering is nailed on top.

See also under Clocks—Tall Case Clock; Kitchen Furniture—Dough Boxes, Food Safes and Cupboards.

ABOVE LEFT: A modern manufacturer's reproductions of the *chaise à capucine* include an armchair and sidechair. The gouge carving is brought out by pickling but the originals would have been painted. *LEFT:* The fauteuil is typically broader than the chaise à capucine.

QUALITY CHECKLIST

- An armoire with plain or unfinished sides and back is from Brittany. The Breton peasants lined up their armoires against the wall at one end of the main living room. They didn't think it was necessary to embellish the parts that wouldn't show.

- A tiny alcove in a cupboard is a *niche de dévotion*. These alcoves held patron saints and were especially common in Lower Brittany.

- Deeply scrolled cutwork escutcheons, such as those on armoires and buffets from Provence and Normandy, should be applied mirror-image to one another. They are frequently applied "same-side up" on reproductions, but be suspicious if they appear this way on pieces posing as antiques.

- Armoires fitted with shelves make excellent displays for pottery, glassware, or quilts. Many people leave the armoire doors permanently open to show off their collections. To show off both the collection *and* the armoire doors, remount each door on the opposite side of the cabinet. That way, the lovely framing will show too.

GERMANY, AUSTRIA, AND SWITZERLAND

THE DEVELOPMENT OF PROVINCIAL FURNITURE IN THE GERMAN-SPEAKING REGIONS OF EUROPE—GERMANY, AUSTRIA, AND PARTS OF SWITZERLAND—HAS TRADITIONALLY LINGERED BEHIND THAT OF FRANCE AND ENGLAND. IN THE SEVENTEENTH CENTURY, ENGLISH JOINERS GRADUATED TO A NEW FURNITURE FORM, THE CHEST OF DRAWERS. WELL INTO THE EIGHTEENTH CENTURY, GERMAN-SPEAKING JOINERS CONTINUED TO MAKE THE PANELED CHEST WITH LIFT-UP LID THAT HAD BEEN IN USE SINCE MEDIEVAL TIMES.

The persistence of old forms was due to several factors. One is the degree of formal separation between the classes in continental Europe. The furniture-making guilds that served the wealthy were separate from those that served the yeoman farmers. Another reason is the extremely fine quality of country furniture that was made. German farmers were proud of their furniture and their homes, took good care of them, and were not readily motivated to change something that was so satisfying to them. Eighteenth-century German immigrants to Pennsylvania, for instance, did not adopt the chest of drawers until they were settled on America's shores.

GERMANY AND AUSTRIA

Most of the folk furniture associated with Germany and Austria comes from the Bavarian and Alpine regions. These areas remained agrarian and provincial during the 1800s and 1900s when northern Germany was undergoing industrialization. At the Alsace border, a French influence crept in, resulting in scalloped framework and aprons, fancy pediments, cabriole legs, and asymmetrical detail.

As in France, a carefully monitored guild system directed all furniture making. Joiners built the finer pieces, such as dower chests, while carpenters were called on for utilitarian jobs, such as kitchen shelves. German provincial furniture was soundly made, pegged rather than nailed. The peasant home was well furnished with a large draw-leaf table, chests, benches, a "best" bed, a dresser, *Schränke* (or cupboards), *Brettstühle* (board-backed side chairs), hanging corner cupboards, and even a clock. As in many peasant homes, there was one main room for living, eating, and sleeping. As families prospered, they extended their homes with extra rooms and lofts. The German kitchen was always separate, a practice which helped keep cooking fumes and smoke out of the rest of the house. The kitchen was well equipped. Besides a cast iron or ceramic stove, there would be a table for informal eating, a *Milchschrank* for dairy items, a butcher block, wall boxes for salt and other staples, a bucket bench, and a stone sink that drained outside.

German furniture was always carefully made, with attention to detail. Draw-leaf tables were especially prevalent during the middle of the nineteenth century. They were a boon for large extended families because they doubled in size when opened. Kitchen tables with

ABOVE: Swiss peasant chairs made in the seventeenth century.

Louis XV– or Louis XVI–style legs were made in all parts of central Europe. These tables had a wide overhang, which made it possible to pull up a chair or a stool to work. The open-top dresser was especially popular in German homes for displaying dishes. An open area underneath the rack was called the "pie shelf."

A number of bed styles appeared in German homes. Four-poster beds had high solid or paneled headboards. Cupboard beds also were used. Boxlike sleigh beds were homemade, with only one side cut out for entry. The Germans take the credit for the duvet—a feather- or down-filled coverlet that provides warmth without excess weight.

A discussion of some special articles of Germanic furniture follows.

BRETTSTUHL

The *Brettstuhl,* or board stool, is made in the chair tradition of medieval Europe. The backrest of the chair is a solid board that is wedged into the plank seat at a slightly backward-tilting angle. Eighteenth-century chair backs can be recognized by their evenly shaped outlines and surface carvings of pictures, dates, initials, and folk motifs. The backs of nineteenth-century chairs are noticeably different. They are decoratively cut in a distinctive silhouette that tapers in at the waist. The surface is planed smooth except for a small cutout handhold at the top.

DOWER CHEST

The German and Austrian dower chest, or *ausschteier kischt,* was an important cultural symbol of a young girl's hopes for marriage. Most dower chests were professionally constructed and were presented from father to daughter. Each chest was designed for the individual and showed the owner's name or initials and the year the chest was presented to her. Decorative symbols included hearts for love, pomegranates for fertility, doves for wedded bliss, lilies for virtue, and unicorns for chastity. Over the years, the girl and her family would fill the chest with the embroidered linens and other items that she would one day use in a home of her own.

Early dower chests were joined of oak and sat on bun or bracket feet. The panels were arched or rectangular, and decoration was by carving or incising. Around 1760, painting on pine was introduced. The chest lid overhung

LEFT: A Brettstuhl *has a cutout handhold in the shaped back. BELOW: Painted flowers, a date, and initials personalize this paneled German dower chest.*

the top and locked shut with a key. Inside was a sliding tray called a till that held small valuables. Some chests were built with drawers at the bottom, which eliminated the need for a till. Unfortunately, most old chests that once had tills are missing them today.

SCHRÄNKE

There were many specialized *Schränke*, or cupboards, in the German house. The *Kleiderschrank* held the family's clothing, the *Kuchenschrank* kept dry staples, dishes, and utensils in the kitchen, and the *Milchschrank* had wooden bars in the open panels to keep the cat away from the milk.

Kitchen *Schränke* were usually tall single-door units. Tall legs lifted them up off the stone floor, which was washed down daily. The *Kleiderschrank* was a massive cupboard, and it is this piece that is most often referred to as a *Schrank* today. It was the largest single item of furniture in the home, next to the bed, and by far the heaviest. It was built in stages that were joined with wooden pegs. To move the *Schrank* to another location, the pegs were removed and each section was moved separately. The base of the *Schrank* was low. It had two side-by-side drawers and rested on bun or bracket feet. A cupboard with two long doors rested on top. One side

was fitted with pegs to hang clothes and the other side had open shelves and drawers for smaller articles. The top was fitted with a large overhanging cornice. Like dower chests, the first *Schränke* were joined of oak and carved and incised for decoration. Later *Schränke* were made of pine and painted.

TYROLEAN MARRIAGE BED

The painted marriage bed is a custom from the Tyrol Alpine region of Austria. It was given to the couple, or presented from husband to wife, as a wedding gift. The bed is a four-poster type, with a high scrolled and scalloped headboard. The footboard is low. The entire bedstead is decoratively painted in bright colors with exciting contrasts. Designs include baskets of flowers, fruit, birds, and hunting scenes. The names of the bride and groom and the year of their wedding is painted across the center of the headboard.

ABOVE LEFT: A single-door *Schrank* from Austria is painted with bold geometric and floral repeat patterns. *MIDDLE:* The pie shelf of a German kitchen *Schrank* angles out, echoing the shape of the pediment above. *RIGHT:* A massive German *Schrank* with highly decorative folk painting.

SWITZERLAND

Switzerland is well known for its beautiful alpine scenery, but the mountains presented a challenge to those who lived in them year-round. Heavy snows could cause mountain passes to be closed off for months at a time. It was important for every chalet to be self-sufficient, able to provide at least cured cheeses and fresh-baked bread until the spring thaws.

The Swiss peasant chalet was generally built into a slope. The ground floor housed the animal stalls, hay, and feed. The animals stayed indoors during the winter, and the heat they generated rose up to warm the floor-boards of the rooms above, where the family lived, ate, cooked, and slept. An indoor staircase led down to the animals so they could be tended even during a blizzard.

Typically, furnishings were simple and practical. They included tables, plank chairs, cupboard beds, and cabinets. Large pieces, such as cabinets or beds, often were presented as wedding gifts. They were inscribed with the names of the husband and wife and the year of their wedding. Often, another message would be added as well, along with tiny flowers, vines, and geometric designs. Both carving and painted decoration were used, with painted decoration gaining favor over carving in the eighteenth and nineteenth centuries.

Above all, the furniture built for the chalet was practical. Cabinets often were constructed to fit a particular space. If the ceiling was vaulted, for instance, a cabinet could be built with a correspondingly curved top. Asymmetry was the rule rather than the exception. A multipurpose cabinet could include a section with a full-length door on one side and a recessed waist-high shelf with smaller cabinets above and below on the other.

One unusual piece of Swiss furniture is the board back chair in the "auricular" style. Auricular means "having to do with ears." Like the *Brettstuhl*, this chair featured a board back that was carved and had a decoratively cut edge. On the Swiss version, the carving showed grotesque faces and figures akin to the gargoyles on a Gothic cathedral. The top of the chair back was cut with two protruding sections that resembled human ears.

GERMAN MIGRATIONS
PENNSYLVANIA

A large German migration to the American colony of Pennsylvania took place during the eighteenth century. Most of the settlers were from the Palatinate, which included the Rhine Valley and adjacent regions. They represented many faiths, mostly Lutheran and German Reformed, but also Moravian, Amish, Mennonite, and Schwenkfelder. William Penn's colony promised good farming and religious freedom, and the new German settlers were not disappointed on either account.

The Pennsylvania Germans incorporated English furniture styles into their vocabulary, but they remained a distinctive group because of the way they held on to

symbols. The decorative painting was practiced by amateurs as well as professionals. Typical motifs included tulips, birds, hearts, and geometric designs that could be scribed with a compass. The resulting style was a brand new folk art that became recognizably distinct. A related folk art, called *fraktur*, also developed in Pennsylvania. *Fraktur* is decorative calligraphy on parchment, used to commemorate births, baptisms, school exercises, or weddings. The parchments often were pasted to the inside lids of dower chests.

TEXAS

In the mid-nineteenth-century, the influx of Germans to America was much larger than the stream of migration to Pennsylvania over a century earlier. Nineteenth-century German society was reeling from the Napoleonic wars, suffering from overpopulation, and undergoing industrial reorganization and political upheaval. Masses of people decided to resettle elsewhere, resulting in waves of migration to North and South America and also Australia.

their European traditions. They continued to make *Schränke*, dower chests, *Brettstühle*, hanging corner cupboards, and "pie shelf" dressers well into the nineteenth century. *Schränke* were especially practical since the Pennsylvania houses were built of fieldstone and had no interior framework for closets. From the English they borrowed presses, chests of drawers, blanket chests, and a variety of chairs, including the Windsor and the arrow-back.

Pennsylvania German furniture is appreciated today for its fine pegged construction, lively graining and painting, bright contrasting colors, and Old World

Texas is but one of many regions where farmers, small-town artisans, middle-class intelligentsia, and political refugees from all areas of Germany found themselves thrown together. The Texas German community stands out because of the fine quality of furniture it produced. The German immigrants quickly showed a preference (within one generation) for American furniture styles, but retained their own high standards of craftsmanship for re-creating it. For example, while other Americans were experimenting with steam power to operate their saws, Texas German cabinetmakers continued to rely on hand tools and small workshops. The demand for furniture was great, and these small shops turned out an enormous inventory. Examples of their work are highly sought after today.

For more on Austria, see Bentwood Furniture. See also under Australia—German Influences.

OPPOSITE PAGE: Decorative painting creates the illusion of inset panels on this Pennyslvania German blanket chest. *ABOVE:* This Texas-German paneled wardrobe is trimmed with split turnings. The two-drawer base and commodious closet are modeled after the German *Schrank,* but the painted surface decoration characteristic of Old World *Schränke* is conspicuously absent.

GOLDEN OAK

Golden Oak furniture was made between 1895 and 1910. It was widely manufactured and distributed and is purchased for country interiors today for its colonial American look. In contrast to the strictly rectilinear Eastlake style which preceded it, Golden Oak positively glowed with curved forms and surfaces. Typical pieces include deeply bowed chests, massive round tabletops on heavy scrolled legs, rolltop desks, curved-back rockers, and chairs with rolled arms. Decoratively pressed chair crests, which inspired the Australian Federation chair, are also from the Golden Oak period.

Golden Oak furniture was indeed made of oak, but many people do not know that it also was made of ash. Like oak, ash is a hard, durable wood, but it was cheaper and easier to work than oak, even by machine. Sometimes, chests combine both woods, using one for the drawer fronts and the other for the framework, for example. If these are restored to their natural colors, the result can be an interesting two-tone look.

QUALITY CHECKLIST

- Golden Oak furniture may look durable because of its imposing size, but construction was definitely not high-end. Dovetailing is conspicuously absent. Drawers and casework were machine-routed and joined with nails and glue. Backboards are thin plywood. When restoring Golden Oak furniture, check to make sure that all joins are secure and that no hardware is missing or defective.

- Some Golden Oak furniture is mounted on castors or wheels. When moving the furniture, it is best not to roll it. An accidental catch on a rug or door jam could cause a leg to split or come off. It is better to lift the furniture from underneath or use a professional mover's dolly.

H

HIGH CHAIRS

HIGH CHAIRS THAT HELPED A BABY SIT UP FOR EATING OR PLAYING WERE MADE IN ALL COUNTRY CULTURES AND ARE AN EXAMPLE OF THE ADAPTABILITY PEOPLE HAVE SHOWN WHEN IT COMES TO CARING FOR THEIR CHILDREN. HOME-BUILT HIGH CHAIRS OF THE LATE EIGHTEENTH CENTURY HAD HIGH BACKS, DRAFT-STOPPING SIDE WINGS, AND A REMOVABLE TRAY. THE WOOD FOOTREST MIGHT BE PIERCED, WITH ROOM FOR A WARMING BRICK UNDERNEATH. SOME CHAIRS HAD A SECOND SEAT WITH A HOLE CUT IN IT FOR TOILET TRAINING. THE WELSH MADE A CRUDE BOOSTER SEAT FROM A THICK SLAB OF WOOD. IT HAD A BACK AND ARMS BUT NO LEGS. IT COULD BE SET DIRECTLY ON THE FLOOR OR ON AN ADULT'S CHAIR OR BENCH.

OPPOSITE PAGE: This reproduction Golden Oak tabletop is planted on a broad, round pedestal supported by four extending legs. *LEFT:* A slat-back high chair with seat woven of wood splints. *ABOVE:* A mid-nineteenth-century high chair from Tasmania.

Most nineteenth-century high chairs had baby sitting right up to the table. The typical design had tall, deeply splayed legs for stability, a woven rush seat, and a simple splat back that might be softened with a tie-on pad. Windsor-style chairs, wicker, bentwood, and turned wood all were popular. By the end of the nineteenth century, factory-made high chairs began featuring a separate fold-up tray for food or toys.

Another style is the two-piece chair-table, used from the mid-1700s through the late 1800s. The chair mounted on top of the table for use as a high chair, or they could be separated and used as a child-sized chair and table on the floor. The two pieces were anchored together by a long screw that went through the chair's X-shaped stretcher directly into the tabletop. Country versions eliminated the need for the screw. The chair simply sat on top of the table and was held in place by a thick rim that went all the way around.

Children's furniture has always received hard use, and examples in good condition are excellent finds for the collector. If you plan to use an antique high chair, check all parts carefully to make sure the chair is solid-standing and free of splinters. Also make sure the old paint is not lead-based, as the baby is sure to gum it at some point.

HITCHCOCK CHAIR

The Hitchcock chair marks one of the first nineteenth-century attempts to produce a popular fancy painted chair using assembly line techniques. The chair is most readily recognized by its smooth black-painted surface with fruit and flower stenciling. Alternative surface treatments included imitation graining of mahogany, walnut, and rosewood. Lambert Hitchcock was by no means the originator of this look nor the designer of the stencil patterns, but he did have the business savvy to sign his chairs on the back, making the Hitchcock name synonymous with the style.

FACTORY MANUFACTURING

Lambert Hitchcock's two-story brick factory was sited at the junction of two rivers about thirty miles outside of Hartford, Connecticut. Nearby forests supplied ample hardwood and pine. The first floor had waterwheel-powered machinery for trimming and shaping the lumber, turning legs and spindles, cutting the seat rails, and steam-bending back slats and crests. Upstairs, these various chair parts were assembled, kiln-dried, painted, and stenciled. Old ledgers indicate that assembly and stenciling were also farmed out as piecework. The factory was able to turn out 15,000 chairs a year in many different styles, including Boston rockers. Prices ranged from 45 cents to $1.75.

Unfortunately, Hitchcock's vision was ahead of his time. His dreams for mass-marketing his chairs beyond local markets were hampered by the infant transportation and advertising networks of the early to mid-1800s. He declared bankruptcy in 1828, liquidated a 3,000-chair inventory, and ran his factory for three more years to pay off his creditors. His brother-in-law, Arba Alford, joined him in 1832 and they continued in partnership until 1840, then split to form two separate firms.

LEFT: A Texas-German craftsman designed this Windsor-style high chair with blocky handgrips at the ends of the armrests. They anchored under the tabletop to prevent the chair from tipping backwards.

Bronze Powder Stenciling

Stenciling with bronze powders is an easy way to decorate painted or natural wood furniture. Bronze powders are sold at art supply stores in many colors and are easy to apply. You can use purchased stencils or stencils you have traced and cut from Mylar.

First, apply a light coat of slow-drying varnish on the area to be stenciled. Wait about 30 minutes, or until the varnish is tacky but no longer wet. The stencil should adhere to the surface but also be easy to peel off. Slip a suede glove tip over your index finger and dip it in the bronze powder. Gently rub the powder over the stencil, working from the outside edges in. To shade fruit, use a heavier touch at one edge, making sure all shadows fall on the same side. Rub leaves darker toward the center, then add veining using a separate stencil and a different color powder. You can add color or deepen shadows by going over a stenciled area with transparent oil paint. For a longer-lasting "tacky period" (important for multiple-stencil designs), add a few drops of turpentine or linseed oil to the varnish before beginning.

ABOVE: A broad crossrail is the canvas for a handpainted winter scene on this limited edition Hitchcock Christmas chair. The remaining designs are stenciled. The armchair features a turtleback painted with a maritime scene. An eagle is stenciled on the crest rail above. Both chairs have handwoven rush seats.

The factory changed hands numerous times after Lambert Hitchcock's death in 1852, and it eventually was forced to close down as mass furniture production shifted to Grand Rapids, Michigan. Forgotten in history, even the town of Hitchcocksville was renamed Riverton to avoid confusion with the similar-sounding Hotchkissville. Happily, two twentieth-century entrepreneurs have revived and modernized the old plant, created a small museum, and put the Hitchcock chair back in production. The stenciling is applied by airbrush but all other features are exactly the same.

DECORATIVE TOUCHES

All Hitchcock chairs have one or more wide back rails, which provide a flat surface for decorative painting and bronze powder stenciling. Early patterns included grapes, melons, peaches, and pears with surrounding foliage. In the 1830s, "liberty" patterns featuring eagles, flags, stars, and motifs from antiquity became popular. Female artisans applied the bronze powders by fingertip, rubbing them into the still-tacky varnish on the furniture surface. Originally, several different stencils were overlayed for one motif, creating a subtle layering of color and form. Ultimately, the need to speed up production led to just one stencil and hastily applied powders, producing a flatter appearance with little shading or detail.

Other parts of the chair also offered opportunity for decoration. The chair stiles and legs had multiple ring turnings, with heavy clusters just above and below the seat join. These turnings were highlighted with bronze or gold paint. The stiles were planed above the seat, offering a flat surface for fine-line striping, often in bright yellow. Seat fronts, "pillow" rails, and other curved surfaces were painted freehand with small motifs, and striping often framed the stenciled designs. Many early furniture gilders had spent their apprenticeships with carriage makers, learning how to paint a fine, steady line on the outside of a coach.

POPULAR HITCHCOCK STYLES

All of the Hitchcock styles were rooted in the Sheraton fancy chair. The rail-back chair was popular in the 1820s. It is also called the two-slat chair, since it has one wide, slightly curved rail mounted on top of the side posts and a second rail underneath. Both rails offered broad areas for stenciling. Another style, the crest-back chair, has a deep curved top rail with a rectangular crest rising up at the center top. It is similar to the crest used on early Boston rockers.

The most widely recognized Hitchcock chair is the pillow-back. The crest rail is narrow and bowed, and the center is turned so that it bulges out slightly in a cylindrical or oval shape. This convenient handgrip is called a "bolster" or a "pillow." One wide or two narrow rails join the side posts below.

See also Sheraton-Style Fancy Chair. See also under Rocking Chairs—Boston Rockers.

LEFT: A newly made Hitchcock side chair has a built-up pillow handgrip in the crest rail. Stenciling decorates the handgrip, crossrail, stiles, and front seat rail. The multiple ring turnings in the legs, front stretcher, and stiles are highlighted with bronze paint.

HORN FURNITURE

Furniture made of animal horns captivated the Victorian imagination. It was odd, outdoorsy, and accentuated an imaginative, romantic view of life in the wild. As the nineteenth century drew to a close, it was quite clear that industrialization and the many changes it brought—new products, growth of cities, faster transportation—were the wave of the future. In America, the upper classes in particular were stricken with a sense of duty to preserve the remaining wilderness, and a nostalgia for the early hunting and cattle days on the frontier set in.

This Victorian sensibility paid tribute to the "Old West" and the hardships and dangers of frontier life with parlor furniture made from animal horns, hides, and sinews. Horns from the Texas longhorn steer were most prevalent. Other materials were buffalo and antelope horns, prairie dog hide, and sheepskin. All types of furniture were assembled: chairs, hatracks, hall trees, tables, stools, plant stands, settees, armchairs, even rocking chairs. Most were made in Texas to be sold on the eastern seaboard and at exhibitions and state fairs. Needless to say, such fanciful pieces were quite unlike anything the original settlers would have used.

Horn furniture was found in private homes as well as libraries, hunting lodges, and gentlemen's clubs and billiard rooms. Related furnishings included wall-mounted buffalo, bear, and antelope heads, and wildcat and bearskin rugs. Furniture for rustic mountain camps featured the antlers of moose, stag, and elk. Some of the horn pieces used in gentlemen's clubs were made in Austria and Germany, where they had been popular earlier in the 1800s.

ABOVE LEFT: Table fashioned from elk horns. *ABOVE RIGHT:* An elk horn chair offers in novelty what it lacks in comfort.

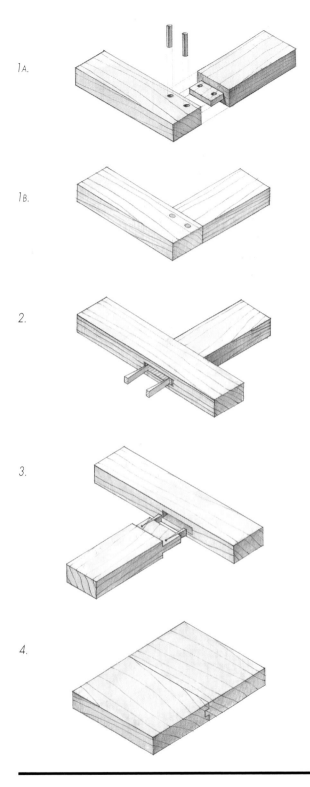

1A.

1B.

2.

3.

4.

1A and 1B. Pegged. The mortise and tenon are chiseled and checked for fit, and corresponding holes are drilled through both pieces. Tapered wooden pegs are driven through the holes, drawing the join together. 2. Wedged. Two small splits are started in the end of the tenon. The tenon is inserted into the mortise and small, tapered, straight-grained wedges are driven into the splits. 3. Foxed. Wedges are partially inserted into the tenon, which is then fitted into the mortise and driven in. 4. Tongue and groove. This method is used to join long edges. A rectangular groove is cut down the center of a board, and a second board is cut with a protruding tongue to fit into it.

JOINING AND TURNING

JOINING AND TURNING ARE THE TWO BASIC WOOD-WORKING SKILLS BY WHICH FURNITURE IS CONSTRUCTED. JOINERY REFERS TO THE WAY DIFFERENT PIECES OF WOOD ARE CONNECTED TOGETHER, AND TURNING IS THE TECHNIQUE OF CREATING CYLINDER-SHAPED PIECES OF WOOD, SUCH AS CHAIR LEGS. THE MOST SIMPLE JOINS ARE CHAIR LEGS WEDGED INTO HOLES BORED IN THE UNDER-SIDE OF THE SEAT. THE MOST COMPLEX ARE DOVETAIL JOINS, IN WHICH NARROW PIECES OF WOOD ARE SPECIALLY CUT AND THEN INTERLOCKED AT RIGHT ANGLES WITHOUT NAILS OR GLUE. THE CRAFTSMEN WHO PRACTICED THESE TRADES WERE CALLED JOINERS AND TURNERS, AND IN COUNTRY AREAS A SINGLE CRAFTSMAN OFTEN PRACTICED BOTH, PRODUCING CHESTS, CHAIRS, TABLES, PLATE RACKS, AND OTHER HOUSEHOLD FURNITURE.

The refinement of dovetailing in the eighteenth century led to more sophisticated furniture, lightweight for its size, with broad flat surfaces that could be veneered. The special skills needed for fine dovetailing and veneering gave rise to a new type of craftsman, called a cabinetmaker. Since the trades of turning, joining, and cabinetry were learned by apprenticeship and took years to master, they were not immediately abandoned when new styles took hold, especially in country areas. Rather, older styles of construction persevered, with craftsmen incorporating city-inspired techniques, tools, and design motifs into their work as they could. Two examples are country Chippendale chairs and provincial French armoires. Country chair makers worked in the new Chippendale motifs above the seat but retained the old-style turned legs with stretchers below the seat. Armoires were built from solid wood and used asymmetrical framing and carving to mimic *bombé* shaping and ormolu. Country cabinetmakers were not

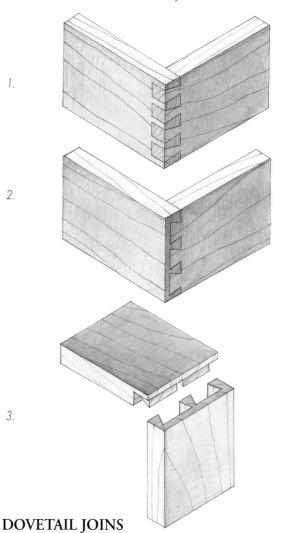

necessarily less able than their city counterparts, only less specialized, with diverse customer orders and perhaps even a farm and livestock clamoring for their attention.

MORTISE-AND-TENON JOINS

A mortise is an opening chiseled in a piece of wood, and a tenon is a projecting arm from another piece of wood that fits into it. The mortise can be a long channel, as in tongue-and-groove construction, or a small rectangular hole. A mortise can be cut partway through a piece of wood so that the tenon is concealed within it, or it can be cut straight through so that the tenon is visible or even projecting on the other side. The tenon can be pegged, wedged, nailed, or glued for a tight fit.

Paneled chests provide a good study of mortise-and-tenon construction. The posts and crosspieces are cut with mortises and tenons so that they fit together at right angles for the corners. A narrow groove is cut along each inside edge. Then these framing pieces are assembled together around wood panels with bevelled edges that slot into the grooves. Each panel is cut slightly smaller than the overall mortised opening. The panels are securely held, yet the wood has room to expand and contract with changes in temperature and moisture. This helps prevent cracking and splitting.

Mortise-and-tenon joins are durable, sturdy, and long-lasting. Historically they preceded the dovetail join and are found on joint stools, framed chests, trestle tables, settles, four-poster beds, gateleg tables, armoires, and many other types of furniture. In New Mexico, furniture with through tenons continued to be made into the nineteenth century. Factory-made furniture adapted mortise-and-tenon construction for mass production. Instead of a rectangular mortise join, two posts are drilled with corresponding holes and held together with dowels and glue. These modern joins are inferior because the glue eventually dries out and the joins loosen.

DOVETAIL JOINS

Dovetailing is used to join boards into L-shaped corners to make drawers, chests, and boxes. The dovetail is a specialized mortise that is shaped to flare out just like a dove's tail. To create dovetails, cuts are made into the edge of the wood, and the excess wood is chipped out with a chisel. Opposing cuts are made on the second piece of wood so that the two fit together like a jigsaw puzzle. Dovetail cuts vary in size according to the type of wood and period of construction. Before 1800, dovetails were narrow, with perhaps two to a drawer join. On Empire furniture of the early 1800s, three dovetails were used. Later during the 1800s, the dovetails evened out in

1. Through dovetail. This basic dovetail joins two boards of even thickness in an L-shape. It was used for chests and small boxes. *2.* Lapped or stopped dovetail, first developed around 1700, was used for drawers. The mortises on the drawer front were not cut all the way through, leaving a plane surface for staining or veneering. The drawer base was slotted into long channels cut along the inside. *3.* Mitered or secret dovetail. This dovetail is used to create a strong but concealed join. The side pieces are cut as for a drawer front, and the top is cut with an overhanging rebate.

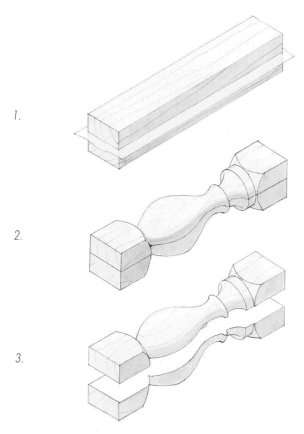

size and increased in number to fill up the entire join. Machine-cut dovetails began appearing in the mid to late 1800s. They match one another perfectly, whereas hand-cut dovetails often show extra cut marks beyond the chiseled-out area. Ponderosa pine chests made in the American Southwest use very large hand-cut dovetails, 2 to 3 inches (5 to 7.5cm) wide.

TURNING

Turning is the woodworking technique for creating dowels from squared wood blanks. The finished dowels can be smooth, as in simple stretchers for a kitchen chair, or decorative, such as the legs in a gateleg table. Very thin dowels, such as those used in Windsor chair backs, were generally not turned but were straight green sticks that were shaved and smoothed with a knife. Later, in the nineteenth century, machine-powered lathes allowed very thin spindles to be turned with elaborate rings, balls, spools, and coves. Examples of these can be seen in pressed-wood spindle-back chairs and rockers. Factory-made spool furniture had abundant turnings, though the patterns tended to be repetitive spool and ball shapes, rather than the graceful, varied designs produced by hand-turning.

To turn a spindle, the turner first planed a length of wood on four sides so it was square when viewed on end. The blank had to be wide enough to contain the widest diameter of the finished turning. The excess wood at the corners was planed off to more closely approximate the finished round shape. One end of this octagon-shaped blank was secured to a lathe. The lathe turned the blank, exposing the surface in continuous rapid rotation so the entire circumference could be evenly shaped. The turner first applied a gouge to rough out the basic forms—curves, indents, balls, spools—then used various chisels to create sharp indents and smooth tapers. If several identical turnings had to be made, such as four legs for a table, the turner would follow a paper pattern and choose matching wood.

Turning patterns varied from region to region and also from workshop to workshop. They had intriguing names, like bread and ball, ball and reel, spool, and barley sugar twist. Variations on the large double ball turning were seen in the front stretchers of many Dutch and English chairs. To ensure strength and stability, turners did not shave away wood in spots where joins would be made. Windsor chair side stretchers, for example, bulge out in the center where the cross stretcher is joined. Wood blanks can also be partially turned, so that they remain squared where extra strength and support are desired. Such squared sections are seen on gateleg tables and kitchen work tables. Chamfering helps make a graceful transition between turned and squared sections.

Today, modern machine lathes support the wood blank at both ends, turn at very high revolutions, and use microchips to remember and duplicate measurements and patterns. While reproduction turnings can be made fast, they remain expensive because of the sophisticated machinery and also because the raw material, wood, is not in as abundant supply as it once was. When historic patterns are copied, the level of precision eliminates the odd quirks and variations that characterize turnings shaped by hand-held gouges and chisels.

ABOVE: 1. To turn a half-banister, the woodworker first glued two wood blanks together. *2.* The piece was turned as usual. *3.* The completed turning was soaked in water to dissolve the glue and separate the pieces.

KAS

KAS IS THE AMERICAN SHORTENING OF THE DUTCH WORD *KAST*. EITHER TERM REFERS TO THE COMMODIOUS DUTCH STORAGE CABINET USED FOR HOUSEHOLD LINENS. LARGE BAROQUE *KASTEN* WERE BUILT IN THE NETHERLANDS IN THE SEVENTEENTH CENTURY, BUT SIMPLIFIED COUNTRY VERSIONS CONTINUED TO BE BUILT IN AMERICAN DUTCH SETTLEMENTS UP AND DOWN THE HUDSON VALLEY AND IN NEW JERSEY THROUGHOUT THE EIGHTEENTH CENTURY.

The base was a broad, low two-drawer chest resting on thick ball or bun feet. A massive two-door cupboard fit on top of the chest and was held in position by a thick surrounding molding. A broad overhanging cornice recalled the early baroque influence and provided visual balance against the heavy bottom. Inside were two or three widely spaced shelves. Collectors should be sure to distinguish the *kas* from the German *Schrank*, which had pegs inside and was used to hold clothing. Another form of the *kas* had just two doors, in the English wardrobe style. The doors were decorated with black and white paintings of fruit in a style called grisaille.

By the beginning of the nineteenth century, machine-made textiles became more widely available and preserving a family's linens became less important. Houses also were larger, with separate bedrooms upstairs. Many Dutch families moved their old *kasten* to upstairs rooms and decorated their downstairs rooms with more up-to-date furniture.

KITCHEN FURNITURE

Country kitchens in all cultures had to be well-run, well-stocked, and orderly in order to maintain the health and economy of the family home. The kitchen was a hub of activity, for the chores of daily life were ongoing—baking, cleaning, preserving, dairying. In many areas by the middle of the nineteenth century, the kitchen had become a separate room, but in some peasant cultures, cooking and food preparation continued to be done in the main living area. Yesteryear's kitchen furniture received hard daily use, and ways to improve and streamline its function, durability, and ease of care continued into the twentieth century.

ABOVE: A heavy cornice, applied molding trim, and bulbous bun feet characterize a Dutch-American *kas* of the late colonial period.

The Recycled Pie Safe

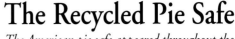

The American pie safe appeared throughout the midwest, Texas, California, Utah, the Oregon territory, and other areas. One of the easiest ways to make a pie safe on the treeless frontier was to recycle wooden packing crates and food tins. By the 1830s, iron sheets were being coated with tin to prevent rust. This allowed large cans of pickled foods, such as oysters, to be shipped west. The empty cans could be snipped open, unrolled into large sheets, then punched with a nail into decorative patterns. The tiny holes let in air but discouraged insects. It was not unusual for settler homes to have some fancy furniture from the east in the parlor and a pie safe made out of the packing crates in the kitchen.

FOOD PREPARATION

BUTCHER BLOCKS

A deep wood chopping block on strong, broad legs was a familiar sight in German and French kitchens. In the days before built-in kitchen counters, it provided a work surface for all kinds of kitchen chores: plucking poultry, trimming meat, scaling fish, and slicing vegetables. It had to be scrubbed scrupulously clean after each use. The first butcher blocks in America appeared in Pennsylvania German kitchens. Today, old butcher blocks from commercial meat shops sometimes end up on the market. They are less expensive than farmhouse antiques but received enough dents and scratches from heavy use to suggest a long history. Contemporary tables with thick wood tops show the continuing popularity of the butcher block look today.

DOUGH BOXES

Dough boxes were part of the once-a-week ritual of home breadmaking. They were made in various sizes and heights but can be recognized by their troughlike shape and flat lift-off lid. The dough was kneaded on the lid surface, then set inside the box to rise. A separate partitioned section inside the trough was used to store flour.

Dough boxes could have attached legs or separate stands. The French *pétrin* was the most decorative type. It stood on four turned legs or rested on a cupboard with Louis XV–style door panels. In America, dough boxes were portable, allowing them to be moved to a warmer spot in the room, perhaps near the chimney or stove, for the dough to rise. During the rest of the week, the box came in handy as a side table or ironing board.

One region where the dough box did not appear was Scandinavia. Here, bread was baked only once or twice a year. The loaves were round and flat, with a hole in the middle, and they were strung up on a line that hung across the room. The bread was eaten hard and dry, like a cracker.

CLEANING AND WASHING UP

In the days before indoor plumbing, the water used by the household had to be brought in by the bucketful from a clear-running stream or spring, a deep well, or the village fountain. This included water for drinking, cooking, washing dishes, and bathing. Elegant city homes were first fitted with pipes for indoor plumbing around 1865. This know-how led to the luxury of hot and cold running water, indoor bathrooms, and built-in drainage systems. More modest town and country households relied on a dry sink in the kitchen and a privy out back, a system that continued in rural areas into the early twentieth century. In continental Europe, long shallow stone sinks were used in kitchens with stone floors. Stone sinks had drains that ran outdoors into alleyways or yards, but they still had to be filled with fresh water by hand.

BUCKET BENCH

The bucket bench was placed convenient to the kitchen or scullery, either just inside the door or in a passageway. It held buckets and basins of fresh water on the lower, heavier shelves and empty buckets ready for refilling on the upper shelves. Fetching fresh water daily was often a chore for the children. In addition to empty buckets, the upper shelves also held dippers, soap, pitchers, clothes forks, and scrubbing boards. German-American carpenters added many upper shelves and nailed on a diagonal strut, instead of a backboard, for stability. Continental Europeans dressed up their bucket benches with scalloped edges and painted designs. Today, people use old bucket benches to hold plants, books, magazines, crockery, overshoes, and garden supplies.

DRY SINK

The dry sink teamed up with the bucket bench as the farmhouse kitchen's water supply and cleanup center. The term "dry" refers to the fact that water was poured into the sink by hand. This changed in the late 1800s, when hand pumps that could draw water directly from a well were mounted on the sink.

Early dry sinks were home-built, but by 1860, most were factory-made. The smarter-looking sinks were enclosed and given cabinet doors. The "sink" part of the dry sink was a wooden trough, usually pine. The Penn-

sylvania Germans designed the trough to overhang the base, creating a comfortable kickspace. They also built a small counter to one side. These practical features caught on and became popular in factory-made dry sinks.

The wooden trough could be bare but was more often lined with zinc, tin, or enamel; the enamel was the easiest by far to keep clean. The dirty dishwater drained out through a hole in the bottom into a bucket below, which was emptied outdoors. To wash dishes, the housewife plugged the hole with a piece of cork or corncob. Fastidious housewives heated the water on the stove first, for better sudsing. Dry sinks were used for cleaning more than dishes—fresh vegetables, fruit, flowerpots, clothing, even children were popped into the water for a healthy scrub.

FOOD SAFES AND CUPBOARDS

The idea of using ventilated cabinets to prolong food's shelf life goes back to the sixteenth century. At that time, churches were equipped with small cupboards called hutches. Instead of solid wood panels, some of the frames were filled in with turned spindles in order to let in air. Middle-class parishioners placed donations of bread loaves into the hutches, and almswomen came to collect them the next day.

In the seventeenth century, ventilated food cupboards came to be used in the home. The English and Welsh

OPPOSITE PAGE, TOP: Two large punched metal panels depict bowls of grapes—an appropriate theme for a food safe. The legs are handsomely turned, and a tiny turnbuckle at the top keeps the doors latched. *OPPOSITE PAGE, BOTTOM:* A pine dough box from Tasmania, Australia. *ABOVE RIGHT:* A Pennsylvania German dry sink.

livery cupboard had wooden spindles, a pierced metal panel, or a wicker grill to let in air. This small cupboard was set at the bedside to keep liveries—food and drink—on hand for refreshments during the night. In the late eighteenth century, this bedside cupboard was enlarged and moved to the kitchen to hold bread and other perishables. The paneled oak construction featured upper and lower cupboards, often with a drawer in between. The turned wooden spindles forming the grille were about 8 inches (20cm) long. Later versions had drawers in the bottom half.

A similar piece of furniture, called a *garde manger*, was used in French kitchens. It, too, had an upper cabinet ventilated with pierced metal panels. At the bottom was an open display shelf surrounded by a spindled gallery. The German *Milchschrank* was used for dairy products such as milk and cheese. The opening was filled in with parallel or gridwork wooden bars spaced close together to keep out the cat. Gauze or screening was added behind the bars to keep out insects. A smaller French cabinet, the *panetière*, was mounted on the wall. It is thought to have originated in Provence in the late eighteenth century. The entire framework is made of turned spindles, which allowed the housewife to see how much bread was left inside. Like the much larger armoire, the *panetière* door was attached with a long buttress hinge, and a decorative escutcheon was mounted over the lock.

Pioneers and settlers in Australia and America also used ventilated cabinets. They were known by various names—food safes, pie safes, meat safes, tin closets—but the concept and construction were basically the same. They were simply framed and stood off the floor on tall legs. The legs were set in tin cups filled with water to prevent ant infestation. When placed in a cool corner of the kitchen or in a cellar, the safe could keep meats, dairy items, and baked goods fresher for longer periods. Australians also used wire mesh to ventilate the lower cabinets of dressers.

The coolgardie meat safe is a unique air-cooled safe that originated during Australia's 1892 gold rush. This safe could be freestanding or hanging but was always situated in a cool spot, such as in a breezeway or under a tree. A water trough rested on top. The water trickled down strips of flannel hung on each side and into the drip tray below. Breezes blowing past the wet flannel helped cool the meat inside.

TOWARD THE TWENTIETH CENTURY

HOOSIER

The hoosier brought the American housewife into the twentieth century. Here was the modern factory version

ABOVE LEFT: An Australian hanging meat safe was constructed by wrapping a perforated metal sheet around circles of wood, which could be salvaged from shipping barrels. OPPOSITE PAGE, TOP: A hoosier with pull-out enameled work surface. OPPOSITE PAGE, BOTTOM: With its wood and hardware restored, a hoosier can serve as an informal buffet.

of the kitchen dresser. It provided storage for food, dishes, and cooking utensils and was a work center besides. Like the dresser, the hoosier was constructed in two parts. The lower section had a cabinet, storage drawers, and a tin-lined "bread box." The upper section had glass-fronted cabinets for dishes and swing-out doors that put measuring cups, graters, and staples like sugar, coffee, and tea at one's fingertips. Not an inch of space was wasted. The inside cabinet doors were fitted with plate holders, spice racks, and hooks for

utensils. The hoosier even had its own bake center: an upper moisture-proof bin stored flour, which could be measured directly through the built-in sifter to a bowl waiting below. Kneading was done on the pull-out work surface. Some hoosier models even had built-in rotary mixers for extra convenience.

Hoosiers were made in Indiana by various companies from 1900 to about 1930. The most well-known was Hoosier Manufacturing, which gave this work center its popular name. The cabinets themselves were made of maple, pine, oak, or walnut. They were given a natural finish or painted with shiny enamels. The pull-out work surface was wood or metal; on later models, the metal was porcelain-enameled. A major selling point was the hoosier's easy-to-clean surfaces.

Today, hoosiers add a quaint, cottage touch to the kitchen, but it's easy to see how all the gadgetry and compact efficiency was once considered the height of modernity. The kitchen isn't the only place to display vintage hoosiers: they can be converted to sewing cabinets, computer work stations, audio and video storage, and novelty buffets.

ICEBOX

The iceman was a familiar sight on early twentieth-century streets. He delivered fresh blocks of ice all year long, dispatching them with a big pick directly into the home and the waiting upper cabinet of the kitchen icebox. This wooden food box worked something like the Australian coolgardie safe. As the ice melted, the cold water trickled down the interior walls, cooling the meat, milk, eggs, and vegetables kept inside. The entire family knew not to open the icebox any more than necessary, and the housewife had to remember to empty the drain tray at the bottom to avoid flooding the kitchen floor. Old iceboxes with their simple lines and utilitarian hardware offer interesting storage possibilities today. They are especially nice as a wardrobe for children's clothes and accessories.

See also Dressers, Kitchen Work Table. See also under New Mexico Late Colonial Furniture—*Armario* and *Trastero*, Framed Chests.

QUALITY CHECKLIST

- The true age of old dough boxes is sometimes camouflaged. If you find a dough box with the top nailed down and a door cut in the slanted front, don't dismiss it too quickly. Old dough boxes were sometimes "improved" in this way when no longer needed for weekly breadmaking. The price generally will be lower than for one that is not altered, and you can always remove the nails and turn the added door toward the wall to keep the authentic look.

- If you plan to use a hoosier in a working kitchen, make sure all the parts are functional. You won't enjoy your hoosier if you have to struggle with stuck drawers or rusty sifters. Check that the hardware is present and in good working order. The pull-out shelf should slide in and out easily. If it is stuck fast, the framework may have gotten wet at some point and expanded; it may be possible to file down the frame to restore easy motion. Small knicks in the enamel can be repaired with epoxy paint.

- American and Australian pioneer pie safes often were made from recycled packing crates. Examine old safes carefully for any telltale markings or company names. These may give clues to the safe's history. Don't neglect painted areas—paint can be thin and markings can show through.

- Replacement tin panels on old pie safes are an unavoidable and acceptable repair. Do, however, try to verify that the designs are original.

- Pie safe legs were prone to rot since they stood in cups of water. It is not unusual to find old pie safes with the legs cut down or replaced. A pie safe with its original tall legs is a rare find.

KITCHEN WORK TABLE

Next to the dresser, no piece of furniture says "country kitchen" more readily than the massive refectory-inspired work table. In England and her colonies, these two pieces formed the hub of the well-run eighteenth- and nineteenth-century kitchen. The table was rectangular and solid, not a knock-down like the trestle table. The thick wood top was used for all kinds of tasks—rolling out pastry, cleaning fish and game, and polishing brass and copper. It was scrubbed vigorously after every use.

OPPOSITE PAGE: An oak icebox with heavy brass hardware. The drain tray is behind the bottom panel, which pulls out. *ABOVE:* Richly turned legs featuring balls, teardrops, and large rings support an overhanging tongue-and-groove tabletop.

At night, a chenille or wool cloth would be draped over the top and the family would gather around with their books and needlework for a little socializing before bedtime. The table doubled as a bed for the visitor, and the dead were laid out on it before burial.

REFECTORY TABLE ORIGINS

The refectory table originated in the communal dining halls of medieval monasteries. It is long and substantially built, with heavy turned or chamfered legs, low stretchers, and a solid top without leaves or extensions. A frieze runs around the entire table and the top can overhang it slightly. In the twentieth century, the refectory table continued to be in use in boarding schools, college and university residence halls, and clubs. Examples sometimes come on the market.

DESIGN AND CONSTRUCTION

The earliest English kitchen work tables were built like the refectory table, with straight or chamfered legs and low stretchers. The stretchers were omitted in the late eighteenth century following the Hepplewhite influence. The Empire style, which followed soon afterward, led to turned legs with massive ball and cylinder shapes. These large legs were so stable, no additional support was required. A solid block was left unturned at the top of each leg to support the corners of the tabletop. Drawers were built into the frieze, either at the ends or in the sides, to hold utensils. Racks were sometimes added underneath to hold pots and pans. Huge kitchen work tables continued to be made for English homes through the nineteenth century up until 1930. They were standard in the basement kitchens of townhouses.

The Perfect Kitchen Work Table

Whether you are shopping for an antique table or a reproduction, here are the features to look for.

- *Four or six heavy legs made of oak, ash, elm, or maple. The legs may be turned, straight, or chamfered but must be massive.*

- *A plain or shallow-carved frieze. Drawers in the frieze are a real plus.*

- *A table height of 33 to 36 inches (84 to 91cm). This is slightly higher than the average dining table and is ideal for chopping, mixing, and other chores best accomplished while standing or sitting on a high stool.*

- *A thick natural wood top. The base of the table may be painted or show natural wood tones, but the wood top is scrubbed clean. Old pine-topped tables may show the scouring marks left by the scrub brush. Modern tables are likely to have a hardwood maple or sycamore top with a natural-colored protective finish. Ask the retailer about a protective oil finish if you plan to use the tabletop as a butcher block for chopping. A rounded bullnose edge eliminates sharp corners and is a safety feature worth considering in active households with young children.*

ABOVE: Massive legs with ball and ring turnings support a draw-leaf tabletop that has seen years of service. With the leaves extended, the surface area nearly doubles. The end drawer becomes inaccessible when the table is fully opened, but unfortunately, the draw-leaf mechanism prohibits placing a drawer in the side frieze. Wheels were added to make the piece easier to move. *RIGHT:* In a large kitchen, a work table can also be used for dining.

German Kitchen Table

German cooks adapted the central work table idea. They used a small refectory-style table, made especially for cottage kitchens. It had low stretchers and a solid wood platform underneath. Often, the entire table was painted.

Irish Kitchen Table

Irish work tables can be recognized by two end stretchers that are joined by parallel double stretchers running underneath the center of the table. These two stretchers were close enough to serve as a slatlike shelf for holding pots and pans. It would have been easy to pull in a chair, given the recessed stretchers, though the Irish preferred to gather around the hearth to eat.

Swedish Kitchen Table

The Swedish used a knock-down central work table in their kitchens. The massive tabletop rested on high stools. When the table was no longer needed, the top was lifted off and hung on heavy iron rings mounted on the wall.

ABOVE: Baroque legs and a pedestal base support an early twentieth-century kitchen table. The draw-leaf top is enameled metal. Plank seat chairs are included, and the entire set is painted with quick brushstroke flowers for a Germanic look.

Quality checklist

- Sometimes an English-style table appears with drawers and turned legs on one side of the table but straight legs and a plain frieze on the other. These features indicate that the table was specifically built to be placed up against the wall. It may be of Irish or Scottish origin, where the custom of a large central kitchen table was not as widely practiced.

- A refectory-style table with shallow, even carving on the frieze indicates a Victorian or early twentieth-century reproduction.

- Be sure to consider the height of the stretchers and depth of the overhang if you plan to use the table for dining. Low stretchers and a shallow overhang make it difficult to pull a chair up to the table.

L

LADDERBACK CHAIRS

LADDERBACK CHAIRS ARE ONE OF THE MOST POPULAR COUNTRY CHAIRS EVER MADE. THE TURNINGS, STILES, AND LADDER RAILS CAN BE PLAIN OR FANCY, BUT THE RUSH SEAT ALWAYS SUGGESTS A COUNTRY ORIGIN. THE SAME CONSTRUCTION WAS USED FOR SETTEES.

ABOVE: Slat-back chairs line up on a weathered porch.

A BRIEF HISTORY

One of the earliest records of the rush-seated ladderback chair is found in seventeenth-century paintings of ordinary middle-class Dutch interiors. Rushes were abundant in the watery lowlands, and the Dutch may have devised the method of wrapping them around a turned seat frame. The tall ladderback chair appeared in England, Spain, and France at about the same time, and the style was transported to America in the mid to late 1600s by Dutch and English colonists.

Many rich provincial styles developed over the next two centuries that made this chair attractive and fairly

the front legs can end at the seat or extend up to support arms. Normally, this straight, erect construction would be very uncomfortable, but ladderback makers strove to overcome this problem. By cutting the crossrails from thin pieces of wood and steam-bending them, they were able to introduce a slight arc that conformed to the natural shape of the human back. These curved slats were inserted between the stiles at the same time the lower stretchers were joined. Everything was held together by pegs or clamps, which prevented the slats from unbending as they dried. In some regions, the slats were thicker. These were cut, rather than bent, into their curved shape.

The slats took on many interesting shapes. In England and New England, four or more slats were used on each chair. Typically, they were straight on the bottom, gently arched on top, and graduated in size so that they became deeper near the top of the chair. Dutch, Pennsylvania German, and northwestern English slats were highly ornamental with crisp decorative cuts, indents, and points. French Canadian rails were called salamander slats because they were cut into two round curls at the center.

The seat of the ladderback chair was woven directly on the finished frame. Rush seats were typical, though other natural materials also were used. American pioneers used corn husks and hickory splints. French Canadians and settlers in the American West used rawhide strips. The Shakers created a special wool cloth tape called listing for weaving seats. In France, the seat rails were slightly bowed, giving the seat a rounded contour.

comfortable. In the nineteenth century, as factory-made furniture entered the market, the plain slat-back chair common in rural America and Australia was all that remained of the ladderback legacy. Then, in mid-century, a surprise popped up as the Shakers began turning out beautiful New England-style ladderbacks, including a new invention—the ladderback rocker.

THE BASIC FRAME CONSTRUCTION

Ladderback chairs of all types can be identified by two characteristics: horizontal rails—the ladder "rungs"—that form the backrest of the chair and a seat that is woven on to the chair frame. Most ladderbacks have turned legs, stiles, stretchers, and seat frames, but there are exceptions. Some French ladderback styles, for example, have gently curved stiles and legs.

Construction of the ladderback is straightforward. The back legs extend straight up to become stiles, and

FAVORITE ENGLISH LADDERBACKS
LACEMAKER'S CHAIR

This special ladderback chair was used by bobbin lacemakers in the late eighteenth century. Bobbin lace was worked by hand using a small, dark-colored pillow as a work surface. Many threads were used to create a single pattern, and each strand was wrapped around its own small wooden spindle to keep the threads from getting tangled together. The lacemaker inserted pins into the pillow to hold the completed lace as she worked.

The lacemaker's chair was specially designed to help her hold the pillow in her lap. The chair had no arms or rockers and sat lower than other chairs. When the lacemaker sat down, her knees came up slightly and her lap was very deep. Lacemaking was intense work and to economize on the cost of candles, up to four lacemakers would gather around a special adjustable candlestand.

MACCLESFIELD LADDERBACK

This regional eighteenth-century armchair was a bit "dressier" than most English ladderbacks. The four ladder rails were curved on top but had a downward-pointing tip. A round stay rail with barrel-shaped tips is believed to have been inspired by the "picking stick" used in the Macclesfield silk factories to knock the shuttle along the warp. Chair maker Charles Leicester also showed extra concern for comfort by crafting gracefully curved arms and stiles that bent back slightly just above the seat. Other features in this detail-rich chair included pear-shaped finials, pad feet, decoratively turned underarm supports, and protective wooden edge strips to prevent the rush seat from wearing out.

NURSING CHAIR

The English nursing chair is deliberately constructed 4 to 5 inches (10–13cm) lower than usual, with low arms. These modifications were for the benefit of mothers who were nursing their babies. They could rest their arms more comfortably as they held the baby, and the lower center of gravity provided stability and a deeper lap. Some chairs had rockers attached to the legs. Tie-on cushions made the seat softer.

CONTINENTAL EUROPEAN LADDERBACKS

Ladderbacks from the European continent are more decorative than those originating or influenced by the British Isles. The rails may be thicker and cut rather than bent into their curved shape. The back stiles also show more sophistication, angling back slightly above the seat. In France, the slats are always decoratively

shaped. A common version shows a cupid's-bow on top and a point on the bottom. Stiles may show gentle side-to-side curves. In Spain, pronounced turnings run all the way up the stiles, leading the eye toward a high, rounded, ornamentally carved crest. The rails are scalloped or wavy. A broad, decoratively cut apron is detached from the seat rail to allow for the rushes to be woven on. Some chairs show double stretchers with matching ball turnings connecting the front legs.

AMERICAN SLAT-BACK CHAIRS

The American slat-back chair is a nineteenth-century rusticated version of the English ladderback. Straight "broomstick" legs, stiles, and stretchers have few, if any, turnings, and the horizontal slats are straight-cut, without any decorative shaping. Maple, hickory, and chestnut were among the woods used. Stretchers were shaped from dry wood, and as the green wood shrank around them, strong joins were created without nails or glue. Seats were woven of wet rushes, cornhusks, or wood splints, which shrunk tight on the chair as they dried. Extremely short legs may indicate a chair used for butter churning. Two chairs built together provided "Sunday" seating in farm wagons. Slat-backs continued to be made in outlying rural areas into the twentieth century.

See also Rush Seats. See also under France—*Chaise à Capucine;* Mexico—*Toluca;* Shaker Furniture—The Shaker Ladderback.

Quality checklist

- To determine if a shorter English-style ladderback is a nursing chair, examine the foot. If the foot is tapered and evenly turned, the chair is probably a nursing chair. If it is cut straight across, the chair was probably a full-size ladderback cut down to eliminate rotted wood or to make it more comfortable for sitting by the fire.

- Be suspicious of an "old" chair that has perfectly round stiles or legs. Wood shrinks unevenly as it ages, and chair parts that were round when new should appear oval when aged.

- A slat-back chair with steeple-shaped finials and heavy slats may have been made in the American South before 1830 or in the Southwest at any time throughout the 1800s.

- Slat-back chairs made in the American midwest are recognized by their flattened posts, called "rabbit ears" or "donkey ears." Midwest legs taper to form a foot and slats show gentle arcs along the top edges.

MEXICO

MEXICAN FURNITURE HAS A RUGGED, PRIMITIVE ELEGANCE THAT CAPTURES BOTH THE GRANDEUR OF THE EUROPEAN RENAISSANCE AND BAROQUE PERIODS AND THE FOLKLORIC MOTIFS OF A NATIVE CULTURE. THE BASE OF THE STYLE IS THE BOLD, MASSIVE FURNITURE OF FIFTEENTH-, SIXTEENTH-, AND SEVENTEENTH-CENTURY SPAIN. DECORATIVE PAINTING AND NATIVE FURNITURE CONSTRUCTION METHODS LIGHTEN THE LOOK AND LEND AN AIR OF INFORMALITY.

Mexico was one of Spain's most sophisticated colonial centers. Unlike New Mexico, located in the remote area to the north, Mexico was the center of Spanish trade between the homeland and China. Mexico was also somewhat more open to Anglo influence than was New Mexico, despite Spain's strict rule that trade with other areas had to be conducted through home ports. When new information did get through, it was often fractured or incomplete, resulting in curious interpretations such as gateleg-style tables that had no movable parts.

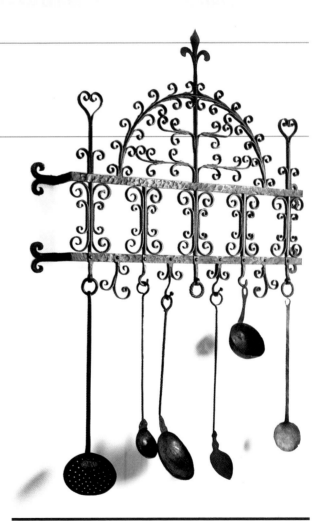

OPPOSITE PAGE: Wavy rails become larger as they ascend the stiles of a high New England ladderback chair. The stiles are topped with acorn finials, and ball turnings appear on the front legs and stretcher. *ABOVE:* Ornamental ironwork displays the delicacy achieved by Mexican artisans.

SPANISH-MOORISH INFLUENCES

The Moors occupied large parts of Spain during most of the Middle Ages, and they left an imprint on Spain's arts and culture that was unique in Europe. The European Baroque style encouraged exaggerated curves and heavy, pronounced ornament. Elaborately scrolled chair aprons and tall crownlike cornices on beds and cabinets are examples of the Baroque style. The Moorish presence, in contrast, emphasized geometrics. Both of these influences made their way to Mexico.

One distinctively Moorish feature is geometric motifs carved in heavy, deep relief. Rectangles, squares, diamonds, triangles, and other geometric shapes appeared throughout Mexico on chests and cabinet doors as well as on interior and exterior doors. The arrangements were typically asymmetrical and therefore very lively. Furniture made in the nineteenth century carried through on this style using miter-cut moldings that were nailed in place.

Repeated geometric shapes are seen also in decorative latticework. The artisan cut the edges of each lath with small notches at regular intervals. When the lattice was assembled from these cut laths, a strong overall pattern resulted. Latticework was often used as window coverings and room dividers as it allowed air to circulate yet afforded a sense of privacy. It provided the perfect screening in the warm climate of Spain, and it transferred beautifully to Mexico. Lattice was used in food cupboards, such as the *armario*, to provide ventilation, and it was also laid over solid panels as decoration.

Another form of ornament combines shallow grooving and chip carving. These two folk arts developed hand in hand in provincial seventeenth-century Spain. The narrow grooves were incised with gouges, and the rhythmic repeat chips were impressed with a chisel. The artisan used both methods together to create flowers, vines, and geometric designs, generally on chair rails and seat aprons.

A final carryover from Spain is the decorative ironwork used on chests and other wood furniture. These highly decorative escutcheons, hasps, hinges, and strapwork were forged of black iron with pierced openwork designs. The delicacy of the work creates a striking contrast to the strength and solidity inherent in the iron. Native artisans became particularly adept at the art of iron forging.

ABOVE AND LEFT: Side and front panels of a nineteenth-century Michoacan chest exhibit the tradition of native Mexican lacquerwork.

NATIVE DECORATIVE PAINTING

The Indian culture indigenous to Mexico also contributed to the colonial style. Guilds were opened to native Indians, who participated in the bicultural society. One art form that entered Mexico by way of trade with both China and Spain was lacquerwork. Native Indians' fascination with this art encouraged them to pursue it using pigments and resins extracted from local plants. The result was a brilliant new folk art that incorporated native flowers, vines, birds, geometrics, and storytelling scenes. The colors were particularly striking as they combined brilliant and soft shades in the same piece. Chests, chairs, and cabinets were painted, and the industry has continued into the twentieth century, serving a lively tourist trade today.

MEXICAN FOLK CHAIRS

BUTACA

The *butaca* is a low-slung chair with origins in the Renaissance. The side supports are X-shaped, and the gently sloping seat and back are covered with wood slats. The slats are covered most often with a sheet of leather attached with brass nailheads. The *butaca* is related to the nineteenth-century Louisiana campeche chair, named after the Campeche area of Mexico's Yucatan peninsula. Collectors should be alerted to the resem-

blance between the today's popular *butaca* and the Creole antique.

EQUIPAL

The *equipal* is a native chair that has become synonymous with Mexican folk style. It is lightweight, affordable, and can be seen with matching tables in cafes and on patios throughout Mexico and the American Southwest. The name *equipal* is the Spanish translation of the native word *icpalli*. The chair is rounded and tublike, with a circular seat and curved backrest. The base is formed of split cedars that cross one another diagonally, and the backrest is framed by tree branch uprights and bent reeds. All of the structural pieces are lashed together. Traditionally, the seat and back were woven with rushes or covered with animal skins or tanned hide. The tanned hide version is the most common today.

TOLUCA

The *toluca* is a low rush-seated chair in the ladder-back tradition. The stiles are decoratively turned and often end in small ball finials. The chair frame is painted in a solid color and the crossrails are decoratively painted with pictures of flowers, birds, or other motifs. Sometimes a hide seat is used instead of woven rushes.

See also New Mexico.

TOP LEFT AND RIGHT: An equipal. ABOVE: A Michoacan painted toluca with woven rush back and seat.

MISSION OAK

Mission Oak furniture, made from 1900 to about 1920, is often viewed as the first popular modern furniture. It grew out the nineteenth-century Arts and Crafts "mission" led by John Ruskin, William Morris, and others. These writers, designers, and philosophers reacted against the excess and eclecticism of the Victorian-industrial era and called for a return to hand craftsmanship.

In America, the Arts and Crafts movement was furthered by architect Gustav Stickley. The furniture he designed was rectilinear, with pronounced horizontal and vertical lines. Chairs and settees featured straight vertical slat backs and broad flat armrests. Tables had perfectly straight legs with a wide central stretcher. Cabinet glass was framed with windowlike muntins. This strict monotony was interrupted by graceful, shallow arches on armrests, chair aprons, and toeboards. The famous bow-arm Morris chair is an example. Although the furniture was factory-made, it was given a handcrafted look with pegs and through tenons. The oak was stained or fumed to a very rich, dark color.

Arts and Crafts furniture was produced by Stickley's Craftsman Shop, Elbert Hubbard's Roycroft Shops, California's Greene and Greene, and others, and the new style soon reached the mainstream. By 1910, many other manufacturers joined in, producing plain desks, chairs, dining suites, and cabinets, all simply designed and assembled with exposed recessed screws. The furniture was well received by the public, especially in California and the Midwest. It appealed equally to urban and country markets, and farm families could order it by mail from Sears, Roebuck & Co.

Today, Mission Oak is enjoying widespread popularity, and prices on Stickley originals have soared. The more affordable mass-marketed pieces are a favorite among beginning furniture restorers because the flat, plane surfaces are so easy to strip.

See also under New Mexico—Mission-Style Reproductions, 1900–1940.

NEW MEXICO

THE CHUNKY, MASSIVE, GEOMETRIC QUALITY OF
EIGHTEENTH- AND NINETEENTH-CENTURY SPANISH NEW
MEXICAN FURNITURE IS UNMISTAKABLE. THOUGH IT MAY
SEEM PRIMITIVE AND INDELICATE COMPARED TO
AMERICAN, ENGLISH, AND FRENCH CABINETRY OF THE
SAME PERIOD, IT WAS ACTUALLY CRAFTED FOLLOWING A
STRINGENT, DISCIPLINED GUILD SYSTEM OF MEASURE-
MENTS, DESIGN PLACEMENT, AND WORKSHOP ROUTINES.
EARLY NEW MEXICO FURNISHINGS WERE SPARE, WITH
ALACENA CABINETS BUILT INTO THICK ADOBE WALLS AND
TARIMAS, OR LOW BENCHES, HUGGING THE PERIMETER OF
THE ROOM. AS A HOUSEHOLD PROSPERED, ITS FURNITURE
INVENTORY GREW TO INCLUDE ANGULAR ARMCHAIRS, AN
ARMARIO FOR DISHES AND PRESERVED FOOD, AND SIDE
TABLES. FOR MEALS, FAMILIES SAT ON LOW STOOLS OR ON
THE FLOOR, AND THE FOOD WAS BROUGHT IN FROM THE
KITCHEN AND LAID OUT ON A LOW TABLE. DEVELOPING
TRADE ROUTES BROUGHT NEW INFLUENCES, FIRST FROM
MEXICO TO THE SOUTH, THEN IN A SUDDEN BURST FROM
THE WESTWARD-EXPANDING UNITED STATES.

A BRIEF HISTORY

UNDER SPANISH AND MEXICAN RULE, 1540–1846

Spain's New World colonies were politically and
geographically isolated, but they were not internally
static. Though the society was formal and hierarchical,
with laborers placed at the bottom of the social scale, the
skills needed to survive in the harsh desert climate, the
opportunities for land ownership, and the presence of an
indigenous population somewhat blurred the picture. A
flourishing multi-tiered guild system allowed Native

OPPOSITE PAGE: This Mission Oak suite includes a small cushioned bench, two armchairs, and a table. *ABOVE RIGHT:* Zigzag strips that imitate streaks of lightning provide ventilation on these *alacena* doors from the late 1800s.

Americans to train as apprentices and prepare for the
guild examinations. Workshops were strictly run,
production was monitored, and construction secrets
were closely guarded. This approach contrasts sharply
with the practice of eighteenth-century English and
French cabinetmakers, who printed and distributed
pattern books of their designs. Rather than cultivating
innovation and interpretation, New Mexicans prized
their furniture for its conformity.

ANGLO-AMERICAN INFLUX BEGINS, 1821

Following a period of slow but perceptible maturing in
the late 1700s, bicultural New Mexico had its world
turned upside down in the 1800s. Mexico's independence from Spain, the opening of the Sante Fe Trail,

ABOVE: This room in Mesilla in southern New Mexico reflects the New Mexico style.

United States military occupation, the California gold rush, and the laying of railroad tracks brought drastic, irreversible changes to the region. Americans from the eastern seaboard brought new tools, soft goods like calico and carpeting, and factory-made furniture like rocking chairs, sofas, daybeds, and washstands. The old New Mexican desert economy, based on finding and conserving precious resources, was overturned by an Anglo-American economy that produced and distributed material goods through a network of wholesaling, banking, shipping, and credit. Goods shipped west for newly arrived Americans were also purchased by the wealthy Hispanic class. The *carpinteros* saw for the first time the work of newly arrived cabinetmakers from the eastern seaboard, France, Germany, and Ireland. They adapted the new tools to their own tradition, creating unique and charming interpretations of both Anglo and New Mexican styles.

LATE COLONIAL FURNITURE

New Mexico furniture can be identified by three distinctive characteristics: ponderosa pine, distinctly "boxy" proportions, and through mortise-and-tenon joins.

Ponderosa pine is a soft, light-colored, easily worked wood. Because of its relatively light density, it had to be cut in thick pieces in order to make strong furniture. Chair legs and chest posts, for instance, are obviously chunkier than those of furniture from other regions. Even though they were using a new wood, New Mexico *carpinteros* continued to build furniture according to Spanish guild guidelines. The base unit of measure was the *vara*, which is equal to about 33 inches (84cm). Each piece of furniture conformed to a specific set of relationships based on the *vara*, and the resulting proportions were more cubelike than those of English and French furniture. Another guild guideline is through mortise-and-tenon joins, in which mortises were cut clear through the wood, so that the tenon showed (though it did not protrude) on the opposite side. The joins were pegged, not nailed, and the dry, arid climate

caused them to shrink tight. These visible mortise-and-tenon joins are a hallmark of the New Mexico style.

Only the most basic tools were available during the colonial period: straight saws (like serrated knives), adzes, planes, chisels, augers, grooving planes, simple hand-cranked lathes for turning, and knives for cutting pegs. The marks left by these simple tools have led many collectors to erroneously conclude that the pieces were made by inexperienced part-time woodworkers.

Many of the following examples from the colonial period continued to be made into the Anglo period.

ALACENA

The *alacena* is a niche built into the deep adobe wall, where foods could stay cool on the shelves inside. The two *alacena* doors swing open and closed on pintle hinges. The framed doors can be solid or built with spindles or decoratively cut slats to let in air. All that remains of most old *alacenas* are the doors, rescued from

ABOVE: Turned spindles form the grillwork on a reproduction trastero.

homes destroyed long ago. Present-day owners frequently mount them on the wall as art.

ARMARIO AND TRASTERO

The *armario* is a tall, freestanding, upright framed cabinet. It was used to store household items, including clothing, food, dishes, and crockery. The cabinet framework can be fitted with solid panels or with spindles or openwork slats to allow ventilation. *Trastero* is the nineteenth-century name for the spindled version, which was used solely for food and kitchen items. Either style is easily recognized by the decorative cornice that protrudes prominently at the top of the cabinet and fits into the four thick corner posts. The cornice can be horizontal, with decorative scalloping, but the most distinctive ones arch up high in a baroque Spanish and Mexican style.

Inside the *armario* or *trastero* are shelves; larger pieces have interior drawers, sometimes with secret access that involves removing an entire interior cupboard and opening the drawers on the backboard side. An overwhelming number of *trasteros* have round scooped-out depressions in the bottom shelf. The function of these hollows has so far stumped historians, but it is suspected they had something to do with food preparation or storage.

ARMCHAIR

Early twentieth-century collectors often referred to New Mexican armchairs as "priest's chairs" in the mistaken assumption that they were made for use only in mission churches. Historians now know from surviving household inventories and wills that New Mexican armchairs were indeed used in homes. They were important and valued pieces of furniture. Despite their low height—the seat is typically only 16 inches (41cm) off the floor—they afforded great respect to those who sat in them.

Collectors will recognize features from the European folk chair: the legs are straight, with stretchers at different heights to add strength. The New Mexican seat apron and top rail often were decoratively cut, chip-

carved, or incised in matching designs, and these delicate patterns helped offset the chair's cumbersome quality. Stepped designs represented the Pueblo dwellings, horizontal parallel lines represented the heavens and rain, and a Y-shaped symbol with curled ends represented cornstalks. Triangles were cut into the edges to create M-shaped patterns.

BENCHES

Tarimas, the simplest New Mexican benches, were low, backless, and set right up against the wall around the perimeter of the room. A fabric "dado" was tacked to the wall to prevent the powdery white residue from rubbing off onto clothing. The *banco* was a far more imposing piece, really a long settee, with a back support and arms. Like the armchair, it was constructed in *vara* units and exhibits the same boxy proportions.

The backrest of the *banco* was ingeniously patterned with a series of decoratively cut vertical splats. These board splats were slotted into the upper and lower rails; they could either touch or be positioned with spaces between them. The traditional Spanish saw made it

difficult to cut patterns in the center of a board, but it was easy to cut out geometric shapes, such as triangles, from the board edges. When similarly cut boards were arranged side by side, powerful repetitive patterns of mass and void resulted. Two opposing triangle cuts, for instance, formed a diamond.

ABOVE LEFT AND RIGHT: A New Mexico chair and a twentieth-century reproduction.

BOARD CHEST

Dovetailed board chests were less common than framed chests in New Mexico, but they were often prettier. The ponderosa pine tree yielded boards up to 3 feet (0.9m) wide, a real find for the collector. Chest tops and sides were smoothed with a plane, then carved in relief for decoration. Popular motifs were rosettes, pomegranates, vines, lions *regardant* (backward-looking), the sun, and Indian-inspired geometric motifs. Board chests could also be left plain or decorated with applied molding. The practice of applying molding to board chests so that they resembled framed chests is a good indication of the higher prestige of the latter.

The other striking feature of the New Mexico board chest is the incredibly large dovetails, up to 3 inches (8cm) wide. European and American cabinetmakers, by way of comparison, were creating dovetails ¼ to ½ inch (6–12mm) wide during this period. It is because ponderosa pine had to be cut in such chunky boards, 1 inch (2.5cm) thick or more, that the dovetails were so broad. The cruder tools lent the dovetails a rectangular rather than angled shape, which made for a weaker join.

To better secure the chest, *carpinteros* wrapped a strip of rawhide clear around the top of the chest to help hold it together. This was especially important on plain board chests that would be used mostly for shipping. L-shaped iron straps were another type of reinforcement.

FRAMED CHESTS

Joined frame-and-panel chests were the most common type of chest built in late-eighteenth-century New Mexico. Unlike the board chest, which was set into a separate stand, the framed chest was constructed with its own legs, which were extensions of the four corner posts. A distinguishing feature is the pair of braces that ran diagonally from the front legs up into the bottom rail. Rather than miter-cut the braces, the *carpinteros* cut openings in the legs and rail and fit the rectangular braces into them so that their full rectilinear shape was visible. This complex construction was apparently part of the *carpintero* guild specifications. It helped the legs to remain straight even after the wood had shrunk and the joints had loosened.

The top of the chest could be flat or coffered. It opened on eyelet or iron strap hinges and locked with an iron clasp. A close look at a New Mexican paneled chest will show that the outside surfaces were planed smooth, but that the inside surfaces were adze-finished only.

The *harinero* is a framed chest designed to hold milled flour. It was the largest piece of furniture in the New Mexican house and a prominent sign of prosperity. Its function demanded that it be strong, in order to hold a lot of weight and be resistant to rodents. To make it gnaw-proof, the *carpintero* worked multiple panels—four in each end and twelve or sixteen on the front and back. Extra-strong floor slats were mortised into the lower rails, and a transverse board was attached underneath for additional support. The top of the *harinero* was so heavy that only part of it was cut and hinged for a lid.

LEFT: A reproduction bench displays New Mexico motifs and cutout techniques.

Sante Fe-Style Decorating

Today's Sante Fe Southwest style starts with New Mexico's carpintero-built furniture, then goes south of the border to Mexico for colorful accessories. These include handwoven jerga *strips for the floor and* saltillo *blankets in rich colors like red, orange, yellow, and black. On the walls are tinned "silver" wall sconces and mirrors with delicately incised designs. Other possibilities from Mexico include a painted chest or* trastero *and the* equipal *chair with leather seat and back.*

One of the most important features of the Southwest style is adobe. These thick mud-brick walls kept interiors cool in the hot desert sun. In modern interiors, fresh white paint can give walls the same cool look and provide the proper backdrop for tinware and textiles. A panel of bright cotton fabric tacked to the wall around the edge of the room is especially authentic. With the availability of pine reproduction furniture and a few accessories, the Sante Fe Southwest look is one of the easiest and least expensive styles to put together.

TABLE

The New Mexican side table can be recognized by its open-frame construction and large single drawer that is visible not only from the front but from the sides and back of the table as well. The framework consists of four legs joined by rails and stretchers all around. Cleats join the leg stiles at the top sides and support the boards that form the tabletop. The dovetailed drawer fits in under the tabletop and slides in and out on an openwork H-shaped support. These drawers were very cumbersome since they were very heavy and there were no slides or grooves to guide them. Even though the entire drawer is visible through the framework, a hasp and staple lock keeps the contents secure. Below the drawer, vertical turned banisters or splats may connect the rails and stretchers, contributing further to the unusual open-yet-enclosed look. Surviving tables often are missing the drawer, but the open-frame construction has such a modern silhouette, a person not knowing about the drawer might not even miss it.

THE ANGLO-AMERICAN INFLUENCE

The new tools introduced to New Mexico by the Americans included the frame saw, which allowed close, curved cuts, molding planes for shaping convex and concave curves, and steam-powered mortising machines and lathes. Milled lumber became available through Sante Fe's first sawmill in 1847. A number of distinctive innovations appeared on New Mexican furniture made between 1860 and 1880 because of these changes.

The *carpinteros* used molding planes and miter boxes to cut deep ogee cornices for the tops of *trasteros*. They also cut triangular moldings and nailed these on in groups of four to create raised squares and diamonds. Dovetails became finer, with more pronounced angles, and drawer bottoms were slotted into grooves instead of pegged on. More finely turned spindles and curved splats began to appear on *trasteros, bancos*, daybeds, and

ABOVE: A Mission-style rocker.

cribs. New Mexicans also began using brightly colored contrasting paint and wood graining to accentuate their geometric designs.

New forms of furniture also appeared. The *carpinteros* learned about the chair-table from the army, where it was used as a laundry table and ironing board. They borrowed the drop-leaf desk form to create a new kitchen storage piece. The lower section was a chest with slanted lift-up lid, replacing the *harinero*. The top section was a blind cupboard for canned goods and dry staples. Other new furniture included Empire-style

daybeds and chairs. The Empire curves combined with the thick ponderosa pine made for an unusual pairing of grace and mass.

MISSION-STYLE REPRODUCTIONS, 1900–1940

New Mexican furniture was associated with poverty during the late 1800s, and it was not until the early twentieth century that interest in it was renewed. The colonial revival period grew out of the need to reassess

QUALITY CHECKLIST

Eighteenth- and nineteenth-century *carpintero*-made pieces and twentieth-century revival pieces all have their place in history and are worth owning. Buyers should make sure they can recognize the differences between them.

- Original New Mexico chairs are blocky and chunky, with the seat dividing the overall chair height in half. Revival chairs tend to be taller, with vertical lines, to appeal to the Anglo-American taste.

- Diagonal braces on original chests are "let in" to the frame and the legs. On revival pieces, they are mitered and the angled cuts butt the frame.

- Original pieces were made only of ponderosa pine. Revival pieces were made of pine, spruce, juniper, and cedar and often were given a dark stain.

- Original pieces have "gentle" dimensions because of wear on the frame edges. Revival pieces have much sharper, crisper edges.

- Only through mortise-and-tenon joins appear on originals, but on revival pieces the tenon either protrudes or sometimes is concealed.

- Any "modern" furniture form—a sideboard, dining table, coatrack—is a revival.

Additional notes:

- Sometimes a piece that seems original still doesn't look quite right. It may have been assembled from parts rescued from damaged originals. The *vara* system of construction made these sorts of marriages possible.

- Old board chests were sometimes "improved" with rosette carvings to attract early twentieth-century buyers. To determine authenticity, examine carvings carefully, checking for symmetry, position, similarity of tool marks, and color of wood.

- An original *trastero* may have repairs to lengthen the back legs. In adobe homes, the dirt floor was packed higher near the walls and to balance the furniture, the back legs were cut shorter.

the effects of industrialization, recapture the romance of the past, and restore craftsmanship to production. In Sante Fe, this Anglo yearning resulted in the restoration of the three-hundred-year-old adobe governor's palace as the site of the Museum of New Mexico. Furniture constructed in 1917 for the Woman's Boardroom is the earliest known example of Spanish Colonial revival. The look was not historically true, only interpretive, and included furniture forms, woods, and construction techniques not used by the *carpinteros*. Tenons, for example, protruded through the mortises in the Arts and Crafts style, which was popular from 1900 to 1920.

The revival continued through the Great Depression, as a network of Works Progress Administration (WPA) vocational schools trained Hispanic-Americans to make furniture suggesting a romantic colonial past. Today, this sturdy furniture can be seen in public agencies, institutions, and national parks; domestic pieces, such as china cabinets, were offered for sale in consumer shops, including Sante Fe's "The Native Market." The movement finally waned as inexpensive, factory-made furniture overtook the market.

See also Mexico, Reproductions.

CARE TIPS

To care for a *carpintero*-made piece:

• Before you clean a piece, carefully check the concealed areas (undersides of chair seats, interiors of cabinets) for penciled inscriptions, dates, and even lengthy correspondences. Such records are common and part of the piece's history. You do not want to remove or damage them inadvertently.

• Make all repairs by hand using tools of the *carpintero*. Do not use power tools.

• Clean with turpentine (use a light touch), then wax with a clear carnauba paste wax. Polish with a soft brush.

• For an authentic look, allow the piece to mellow to a soft, dull finish. Originals were not repeatedly waxed and shined.

OFFICE AND STORE FURNITURE

YESTERYEAR'S OFFICES, SHOPS, SCHOOLS, AND INSTITU-
TIONS LEFT BEHIND AN ARRAY OF UTILITARIAN
FURNITURE—DESKS, SHELVING, CABINETS, AND CHAIRS.
MADE OF OAK, MAPLE, PINE, CEDAR, AND ALSO IRON, SUCH
PIECES ARE STURDY AND FUNCTIONAL, YET STILL OLD-
FASHIONED IN THEIR APPEAL. EVEN THOUGH THEY
WEREN'T DESIGNED FOR RESIDENTIAL USE, THEIR BASIC,
UNCLUTTERED LINES COMPLEMENT COUNTRY ANTIQUES AS
WELL AS MODERN FURNISHINGS. THE SMOOTH WOOD
SURFACES ARE EASY TO REFINISH.

Specialized commercial furniture such as apothecary
cabinets and store fittings can solve all kinds of modern
storage needs. Apothecary cabinets extended up to the
ceiling, and the doors and drawers were often glass-
fronted so the pharmacist could see the bottles inside.
General merchandise stores, shoemakers, tailors, and
other shops used multiple-drawer cabinets to sort and
hold the thread, buttons, laces, and other small items that
they sold directly to the public or used in their trades.
These cabinets lined the walls behind the counter.

ABOVE LEFT: Banks of drawers rescued from yesteryear's businesses, such
as a nineteenth-century apothecary, can provide ample storage in a
modern interior. *ABOVE RIGHT:* A custom-cut glass top and brass handles
help this oversized counter make the transition to a dining room buffet.

Glass-paneled display cases, once used for handkerchiefs, gloves, jewelry, and accessories, can make novel vitrines for collections and memorabilia. The locking lids are a bonus to keep the contents safe from children. Similar display furniture was quite popular during the late Victorian era for fossils and rock collections. Another store display piece is the iron baker's rack with marble slab shelf which helped to keep pastries cool. Today, baker's racks can hold plants, books, crockery, or even the kitchen microwave or a portable television.

Other opportunities for innovative storage are card catalogs, printers' type trays, and post office sorting cubbies. Card catalogs weren't used just in libraries. Index card files were important in business and government offices, schools, and other organizations to keep records, names, and addresses neatly alphabetized and handy. Large card catalogs can be removed from their stands and set directly on the floor as low tables.

Avid cooks can turn smaller units into extended recipe files. The shallow pull-out trays used for printer's type or architects drawings are perfect for organizing papers, art prints, photographs, postcards, clippings, and other documents and keeping them flat and protected. Files with the original small brass label holders are the most in demand.

Yesteryear's business offices were also filled with sturdy, practical, long-lasting furniture. Stacking barrister's bookcases had a separate glass-fronted door on each shelf. Each shelf could lift off, making a move to a new office easy. Other finds include huge locking rolltop desks (Cutler is a popular brand), partners' desks, and surprisingly comfortable oak desk chairs that swiveled, tilted back, rolled on castors, and adjusted to different seat heights. Huge wall files with sliding tambour doors can make unique dish dressers and are perfect for book lovers or those who save all their old magazines.

PAINTED FURNITURE

EVER SINCE THE EIGHTEENTH CENTURY, PAINT HAS BEEN A FAVORITE FINISH MEDIUM FOR COUNTRY FURNITURE MAKERS. IT CAN MIMIC EXPENSIVE WOOD GRAINS, SUBSTITUTE FOR EXPENSIVE OR TIME-CONSUMING CARVING, OR SIMPLY BRIGHTEN A PIECE OF FURNITURE SET IN A DARK LOG-WALLED ROOM. WHEN SEVERAL DIFFERENT WOODS ARE COMBINED, AS IN A WINDSOR CHAIR, PAINT CAN CONCEAL THEIR MISMATCHED GRAINS.

OPPOSITE PAGE: Different-sized drawers are neatly laid out in this American colonial shop fixture. *ABOVE:* Spontaneous brushstroke flowers and freehand striping decorate the crest and crossrail of this kitchen chair from Pennsylvania.

EUROPE

In Europe, most painted furniture emerged east of the Rhine and north into Scandinavia. Furniture from the British Isles was generally plain in design, and the damp climate helped prolong the life of the wood. In France, country furniture makers relied on asymmetrical framework, scalloping, and cabriole legs for design interest. It is only in the peasant cultures of Central Europe and Scandinavia that painting developed into rich symbolic decoration.

The exact style of the painting varies from region to region, but the common motifs of flowers, vines, birds, and animals reflect a way of life that is close to nature. Decorative painting was often done on dower chests and furniture given as wedding gifts. In Sweden, solid white and pale shades of gray were popular as well.

NORTH AMERICA

North American painted furniture reflects the many rich backgrounds of its immigrant settlers. Eighteenth-century pine furniture typically was grain-painted in black over a red undercoat to resemble mahogany. In the nineteenth century, settlers from the midwest north to Ontario coated their furniture with solid primary colors of milk paint, a mix of buttermilk, turpentine, and cow's blood. The Pennsylvania Germans were masters of color and employed graining, brushstroke painting, striping, and other techniques to decorate dower chests, chairs, cupboards, and other household furniture. The American democratic spirit seemed to inspire free expression in pioneer settlers, and unique examples of their stained, sponged, and stenciled folk art creations are highly collectible. In Mexico, folk painting in vivid and surprising color combinations brought life to beds, chairs, and tables. Spindles were painted in contrasting colors to highlight the decorative turnings.

During the early nineteenth century, the United States produced vast numbers of decoratively painted furniture in factories. An experienced factory painter took less than five minutes to add sweeping brushstroke graining to a painted chair. At first, all painting was done by hand, but the need to step up production and reduce costs eventually led to stenciling, fewer colors, and less elaborate designs. By mid-century, most factory furniture was painted in solid colors with some simple stenciling or striping as the only decoration.

See also Hitchcock Chair, *Kas*, Sheraton-Style Fancy Chair. See also under Central Europe—Hungary; Mexico—Native Decorative Painting, *Toluca*; Scandinavia— Rosemaling, Dalarna Painting.

BELOW: Grain painting simulates the look of natural wood and creates the illusion of framed paneling on a plain board blanket chest. *OPPOSITE PAGE:* Plates, crockery, and a disk of flat, dry bread lean forward against the thin wood guard strips of a Scandinavian wall-hung rack. The wood wall boards are visible through the open-backed rack, and gracefully curved side supports allow for shelves of varying depth. Flatbread was baked with a hole so it could be hung on a string.

Care tips

- Place painted furniture out of direct sunlight. White window curtains are helpful for diffusing harsh light.

- Painted furniture fares best in an unheated or air-conditioned room with controlled humidity. With repeated changes in humidity, the wood pores open and close, allowing the paint to scale off.

- Removing recent layers of paint without disturbing the original finish requires great skill and is best left to a professional restorer.

PLATE RACKS

Wall-mounted plate racks have long been a country fixture throughout Europe, North America, and Australia. In the early 1700s, large plate racks became incorporated into the sideboard, giving birth to the dresser. Smaller wall racks continued to be mounted above tables, dry sinks, and doorways into the twentieth century.

BASIC CONSTRUCTION

Plate racks are simply contrived, with one or more boards joined into side mounts. They rarely had backs as the extra weight, combined with that of the plates, would have placed too great a strain on the wall.

English Plate Racks

English plate racks typically became deeper toward the top. As on the dresser, the uppermost shelf held large platters that were used only occasionally, and the middle and lower shelves kept dinner plates, saucers, and bowls within easy reach. Cups and mugs were hung from small hooks screwed into the underside of the shelf. Another English feature was the narrow groove or channel cut into the back of each shelf. The plates

rested in the groove and leaned back against the wall. This style was carried to America and appeared on early American plate racks.

Continental European Plate Racks

While the English tilted their plates back against the wall, the Dutch, French, Germans, Scandinavians, and other continental Europeans preferred to tilt their plates forward. To do this, they installed a narrow wooden strip several inches above the shelf for the plates to lean against. The strip could be plain, decoratively carved, or scalloped. This design allowed the rack to be mounted high on the wall, out of the reach of children, and the plates could be tilted forward and down so family and guests could admire them. Some peasant cultures mounted decorative plates high on the wall all around the perimeter of the room. In Sweden, the safest place was considered above the door frame. Peasant plate racks were often painted in dark solid colors, to better show off white plates, then decorated with striping, brush-stroke flowers, and other designs. Today, this continental-style plate rack can make a handy cookbook rack in the kitchen. The books are slipped in face forward so their covers show.

STANDING PLATE RACKS

The standing plate rack, used in large estate houses, held earthenware and pewter platters that were too large for the dresser or wall rack. It could stand several feet off the floor. The framework was constructed from horizontal pine boards joined by many pairs of vertical dowels. The plates slipped in between the dowels, which held them upright and kept them separate. This type of rack was quite heavy when full. The head cook could set up the platters in the right order for serving a multicourse meal, and the less-experienced help could pull them out as they were needed.

Smaller versions of this rack could be moved in front of the fire to dry or warm dinner plates. Similarly styled plate racks were built above kitchen sinks all over Europe. The freshly washed dishes were placed above the sink to drip-dry and remained there until needed for the next meal.

PRESSES

The press is a double-height stacking cabinet used for linens or clothes. Presses first appeared in the William and Mary period and continued to be used into the middle of the nineteenth century in England, North America, and Australia. Ultimately, they were replaced by full-length wardrobes and built-in closets, where clothes could be hung, instead of folded, for storage.

The bottom unit of the press was a chest with three or four levels of long drawers. The upper, taller section was a cupboard with blind paneled doors. Inside were three or more slide-out drawers with tapered or shaped sides. The drawers had shallow fronts, allowing the contents to be easily viewed and removed. If the housewife were especially meticulous, she might take the time to place freshly laundered linens at the bottom and let the weight of each stack press out the residual wrinkles. Some presses, such as the late-eighteenth-century "gentleman's wardrobe," were built in one piece but still retained the upper and lower divisions. In Sweden, the lower section was built in the *bombé* style. Achieving this level of workmanship would have admitted the country cabinetmaker to the city guild.

The meaning of the word "press" can be confusing. The seventeenth-century linen press was an actual mechanical device used to crease table linens. Napkins and folded table linens were placed between two boards. The boards were laid into a frame, which was then tightened upon them by means of a large wooden screw. These presses were kept on top of chests, and when the linens were creased, they were removed and transferred to the drawers below. In the eighteenth and nineteenth centuries, "press" came to mean simply a cabinet or cupboard.

ABOVE LEFT: An antique press provides extra bedroom storage without taking up any more floor space. *ABOVE:* This Shaker press rests on top of a single-drawer table.

QUALITY CHECKLIST

- Presses with the upper sliding shelves still intact are a good find. As wardrobes became more popular, owners often removed the press shelves and installed wooden pegs to hang clothes. Wooden battens along the interior side walls, or a change in wood tone where they were removed, indicate an old press. Unfortunately, missing trays devalue the piece and are difficult to replace.

- Because presses are composed of two stacking units, there is always the possibility of "marriages." Examine antique presses carefully and make sure the upper and lower sections truly belong together. Signs to look for are matching wood grains, moldings, and hardware.

- If you're unsure of the origin of a piece, check between the drawers in the lower cabinet for dustboards. English cabinetmakers installed thin dustboards between drawers, but American cabinetmakers did not.

REPRODUCTIONS

REPRODUCTION FURNITURE IS NEWLY MADE FURNITURE THAT COPIES OR REPRESENTS FURNITURE OF PAST HISTORICAL PERIODS. THE CONCEPT OF REPRODUCTIONS FIRST APPEARED IN THE NINETEENTH CENTURY. DURING THIS TIME, FACTORIES, STEAM POWER, AND ADVANCED TOOLS TURNED FURNITURE MANUFACTURE FROM A HANDCRAFT INTO A MASS-MARKET BUSINESS. THE VICTORIANS TURNED OUT VAST AMOUNTS OF FURNITURE IN A HODGEPODGE OF HISTORICALLY INSPIRED STYLES. IN AMERICA, THE SHEER EXCESS OF FACTORY-MADE GOODS AWAKENED A CONCERNED MINORITY TO THE IMPORTANCE OF THEIR COLONIAL PAST AND THE NEED TO PRESERVE IT BEFORE IT SLIPPED AWAY ENTIRELY. THE 1876 CENTENNIAL EXHIBITION WAS A FIRST CATALYST TOWARD SERIOUS PRESERVATION.

Generally, antiques collecting and reproduction manufacturing go hand in hand. A small group will begin collecting antiques from a particular time or place, generating interest and historical awareness. As the demand grows, the antiques become more expensive, and reproductions step in as affordable examples of the newly popular style. This occurred in Edwardian England, when the shortage of eighteenth-century oak and elm farmhouse dressers led to pine reproductions. In America, reproductions of colonial styles abounded in the 1920s and 1930s.

It is important to remember that a reproduction is not a forgery. It is an honest copy of something that came before and always should be presented that way to the buyer. Most reproductions can be identified by the way they are constructed—they may look authentic on the outside, but inside are modern screws, saw marks, and plane marks. An exception is handcrafted reproductions, which are often made using antique tools. Many different types of reproductions are available, and there is no right answer when it comes to selecting between a reproduction and an antique. The buyer must consider cost, care, whether the primary goal is decoration or investment, and what type of use the piece will receive.

DO-IT-YOURSELF KITS

The most affordable source for reproduction furniture is the kit the customer assembles at home. All the major woodworking is completed at the factory—sawing, planing, turning, and drilling. The kit comes complete with hardware, special finishes, and instructions, but the customer supplies basic tools such as a screwdriver, hammer, and paintbrush. Assembly is usually with screws, glue, or both.

ABOVE AND RGHT: Reproduction Shaker table and chair made from ready-to-assemble kits.

For a little sweat equity, it is possible to own a Shaker-style chair or a punched tin pie safe and save money on the cost of a floor-ready reproduction. Building kit furniture is also a good hands-on way to learn about construction and finishing. It may help you decide whether you want to try restoring an antique piece for your next project.

MANUFACTURED FURNITURE

Commercially manufactured reproductions are generally a good buy for the consumer. The reproduction may be a direct copy of an antique, but is more likely an adaptation or interpretation. Modern tools, machinery, hardware, and production methods help keep the furniture affordable, though sometimes prices can exceed those of lesser quality antiques. Antiqued finishes, such as milk paint or distressing, can give the wood an aged look without the disadvantages of flaking or peeling. Another plus, especially on primitive or settler look-alikes, is that all the drawers open and close smoothly, doors catch closed with magnets, and the interiors can be ready-fitted to hold high-tech audio and video equipment. Manufacturer's reproductions are a good choice around children and pets, who are sure to give furniture some hard knocks.

MUSEUM-LICENSED REPRODUCTIONS

A relatively new and exciting category of reproductions is the museum-commissioned piece that is built by a furniture manufacturer. Licensing programs offer the public direct copies of antiques in the museum's collection, down to wood, finishes, and exterior hardware. The museum curators work with the furniture maker to choose pieces suitable for factory reproduction and to oversee their design and manufacture for the contemporary market. The furniture maker can be a large-scale manufacturer, a small workshop, or sometimes an individual craftsman. Large manufacturers tend to offer their furniture through their usual retail markets, but licensed furniture from smaller manufacturers is often sold directly through the museum's own store or catalog.

As more people visit museums and become accustomed to seeing quality antique furniture, the demand for museum-authorized reproductions will continue to grow. They offer the more sophisticated buyer an authentically designed piece. Interestingly, since museums try to acquire the best historical examples they can find for their collections, authorized reproductions can show more outstanding details than an actual antique that is mediocre in quality or design.

QUALITY CHECKLIST

- One reason antiques are so exciting is their size—they are either larger or smaller than contemporary furniture and thus create visual tension and drama in a room. Quality reproductions will capture this nuance.

- Check reproductions carefully for integrity in construction. Hardware should be authentic for the period represented. Hinges should be set into the wood, not simply screwed on to the surface.

- If you're trying to choose between a comparably priced reproduction and an antique, consider the wear and tear the furniture will receive. A set of reproduction chairs might be a better choice around a busy kitchen table. You can save the antique Windsor for a quieter spot in the house, such as a bedroom.

CUSTOM CABINETMAKERS

The ultimate source of reproduction furniture is the individual artisan or small workshop. These craftspeople have developed their skills over a period of years and take pride in the hand tools and traditional methods they employ. They select and age their own woods and are totally involved, from designing a piece to rubbing in the final finish.

The increasing desire for high-quality, handcrafted, one-of-a-kind furniture has enabled the most talented artisans to build thriving businesses, with back orders of up to several years. Their work is expensive but worth waiting for. Many collectors see today's fine handcrafted furniture as more likely than some antiques to appreciate in value.

See also under New Mexico—Mission-Style Reproductions, 1900–1940.

RESTORING OLD FURNITURE

Hands-on furniture restoration is not for everyone, but properly pursued, it can turn bargains found at country auctions, estate sales, and flea markets into real treasures. Buyers should be careful not to buy rickety furniture beyond their abilities to repair. Beginners should start with a simple piece, perhaps a small chest or wall shelf with flat surfaces. Repairing, rather than replacing, damaged parts helps restore value as well as good looks to the piece. Once repairs are made, the surface finish can be restored or stripped and finishes added.

OPPOSITE PAGE: A reproduction trundle bed slides under its low four-poster companion. The birdcage Windsor rocker is also a new piece.
ABOVE: A furniture restorer must step back in time and use only hand tools to create replacement parts for damaged antiques.

MAKING REPAIRS

Many things can go wrong with old furniture, particularly country pieces that received heavy use over the years, then were stored in damp sheds and basements when they went out of fashion. Chairs are especially prone to loose or broken legs, stretchers, and backs. The tops of tables and chests can warp, or the boards can lift up. Other problems include worn drawer slides, missing drawer stops, sagging cabinet doors, swollen doors that won't close properly, broken or missing dovetails, rotted bracket feet or table legs, missing sections of molding, loose joins, and cracked or split panels. All of these problems can be corrected by woodworkers with the proper skills and equipment and are acceptable repairs providing they are done properly. Repairs should be as inconspicuous as possible, and any replacement woods—such as a filler in a damaged molding—should match the original finish and grainline. The buyer should avoid pieces that have been repaired with nails or metal braces screwed into the wood; instead of addressing the original problem, they weaken the structure further.

To make repairs, the woodworker first disassembles the furniture parts that are damaged. This might mean removing all four legs of a wobbly chair or unscrewing the hinges of a sagging door with a cracked panel. Numbering the parts and drawing a diagram will ensure the correct reassembly. Wooden mallets, rags, and wood scraps are used to prevent damage to the pieces as they are pried apart.

Repairs are made either with water-soluble polyvinyl acetate glue, commonly known as white glue, or with traditional animal glue, called Scotch glue. The animal glue is set in a container of hot water and applied warm. The old dried-out glue must be completely removed from the join if the new glue is to adhere. The glue is applied sparingly and the wood parts are held together with clamps until dry; excess glue oozing out of the join is wiped immediately. Furniture with many loose joins is glued and assembled in sections to make certain no stress is placed on the joins as they dry. Sometimes disassembly will reveal damaged tenons, dowels, or dovetails; replacements must be cut before the repair can be undertaken.

STRIPPING

Stripping furniture of old paint and varnish has advantages and disadvantages. Restoring the original finish is always preferable to stripping the wood and starting from scratch. If the current finish is an old milk paint or grained finish, removing it will devalue the piece. It is better to clean the surface carefully with oil soap and as little water as possible. Dirty shellac and lacquer finishes can be dissolved with denatured alcohol or lacquer thinner, revealing clean wood underneath that can be touched up and resealed.

If the surface is loaded with a grimy wax buildup on top of varnish, or if it is alligatored or blistered, a total stripping may be the only way to restore life to the piece. Ideal candidates are pieces that were sealed when new, then subsequently painted. Stripping down to just the sealer coat will help preserve the wood. Scraping at an inconspicuous spot with a piece of broken glass will reveal what's underneath.

There are two basic ways to apply wood-stripping chemicals: by immersion and by brushing them on. Immersion in caustic soda is best left to the professionals. It works well with pine but tends to darken other woods. Even when the soda is neutralized with oxalic acid, it continues to leach out of the wood for months afterward. Too much time in the solution will draw off the wood's natural oils, raise the grain, and dissolve glues.

The weekend furniture restorer is better off using a commercial stripping agent that brushes on as a liquid or gel. The chemicals work their way into the finish in 10 to 20 minutes, causing it to bubble up so it can be scraped away with a putty knife. A chisel is helpful for removing the gummy stripper from corners, and wire brushes and fine-grade steel wool work well on carved areas, moldings, beadings, and turnings. It is best to work small areas at a time and to finish stripping the entire piece in one day. If there are many coats of paint, a heat gun can be used instead of a stripping agent to soften the topmost layers. When it is completely stripped, the piece is given a final coat of stripping agent, scrubbed down with warm, soapy water, and rinsed with a garden hose. The piece should be set in the shade or brought indoors to dry. Some commercial strippers rinse off with methylated spirits, which is not as convenient to use as water from the hose but dries more quickly and does not raise the grain.

REFINISHING

The ideal refinishing job restores furniture to the way it looked when it was made. Wood may be stained or left a natural color, but it should be sealed to protect against dirt and excess moisture. The color of the natural finish can be tested by wiping a small amount of turpentine or paint thinner on the bare wood; touching a wet fingertip to the wood gives much the same result. If the color and

Furniture Stripping Tips

- *If possible, work outside on a warm day out of direct sunlight. Ventilation is very important, and the warm air will help the stripping agent act.*

- *Read and follow all the directions on the product can, especially the safety notes. Wear protective eye goggles, long sleeves, jeans, and industrial rubber gloves. If stripper accidentally splashes on the skin, rinse the area of contact in cold water immediately.*

- *Remove doors and drawers so you can strip them separately. Remove all hinges, metal handles, and other hardware and set them aside. Use peelable white artist's tape to mask off any areas you don't want to strip, such as a cane seat.*

- *Set the furniture up on an old table so you can walk around it and work on it without bending over. Place old newspapers underneath to catch the drippings and lay down more paper on top when the area gets messy.*

- *Figure out an order for stripping, and finish stripping one area before moving on to the next. Generally, it's best to work from the top down, so drippings don't fall on the clean areas. Work plane surfaces first to get the feel of working with the stripper. Pull the scraper toward you along the grain. Wipe the scraper with a rag after each drag so that you don't transfer the sticky residue back to the piece.*

- *On the final rinse, scrub all sections of the piece, inside and out, to prevent water stains and warping.*

- *To remove a stubborn layer of varnish beneath paint, soften it with stripper and rub it off with fine steel wool.*

OPPOSITE PAGE: Bare wood before staining and sealing. *LEFT:* Using steel wool to remove an old finish.

grain are handsome, as in ash or cherry, sealing with shellac or varnish and rubbing in a good wax polish are the only steps remaining.

STAINS

If the natural color is not attractive or the grain is uninteresting, the wood may be stained or bleached. Stain always darkens the wood, and bleach lightens it. Stain can be used also to alter the color, adding red, gray, black, brown, or green tones. Stains can be water-based, oil-based, spirit-based, or reactive. Successfully preparing and applying stains to repaired areas so that the new and original woods match is a true test of the restorer's art.

Water-based stains are easy for the beginner to use. They can be applied by brush, cloth, or sponge, and if the aniline color becomes too dark, the wet stain can be lightened by wiping with a damp cloth. The water does, however, raise the grain, making sanding necessary both before and after application.

Oil-based stains provide good color, can be mixed (within the same brand) to create new colors, and do not raise the grain. Pigment oil stains work best on close-grained and soft woods, such as maple and pine. Penetrating oil stains are best on open-grained woods such as oak and walnut. They should be sealed with shellac before varnish or wax is applied, though sometimes letting the stain harden for up to three days will seal it adequately.

Spirit-based aniline stains offer many colors, including blue and green. Because the spirit base dries very rapidly, the stain is best applied with an airbrush.

Reactive stains are actually chemicals that bond with the wood to change its color. Potassium dichromate reacts with tannic acid, present in oak and mahogany, to produce a rich, brown color. Light woods such as birch or pine can be brushed with tannic acid and then treated with potassium dichromate to darken them. Ferrous sulphate will gray walnut or oak and tone down mahogany. Sycamore grayed with ferrous sulphate is called harewood. Potassium permanganate gives pine a warm, brown hue. All of these reactive stains are water-soluble but should be handled and stored with care.

Rubber gloves should be worn when mixing and applying them.

Fuming with ammonia gas is another way of creating a reaction with tannic acid. The furniture is sealed in plastic bags along with an open container of ammonia and left for several hours or overnight. The color change is dramatic, yet the wood grain stays clear and visible. Note that care must be taken to avoid inhaling the fumes and to let the furniture air thoroughly once the fuming is complete.

SEALERS, POLISHES, AND WAXES

A sealing coat is necessary both to keep wood from drying out and to prevent excess outside moisture from seeping in. Polishes and waxes applied over the years build the patina that gives old wood its luster and depth. If furniture is stripped to the bare wood, it will be impossible to restore the lost patina, but a rich finish still can be developed.

Shellac provides a thin, hard finish that dries fast and protects wood well. It was a favorite of furniture makers in the nineteenth century. Unfortunately, heat and water can damage the surface, leaving behind white marks.

French polishing is the process of rubbing shellac and oil into the wood surface in many repeated layers. The applicator, called a rubber, is a wad of cotton or wool inside a linen cloth. The process is time-consuming, but the reward of the labor is a glasslike surface with brilliant shine. Unfortunately, it is vulnerable to heat, water, and alcohol, and the surface shows up every scratch. French polishing was very popular in the nineteenth century. Orange shellac was used for mahogany and cream polish for light woods. Most country-made furniture was not French-polished.

Natural varnish is used as both a sealer and a finish coat and dries slowly to a hard, protective surface. It is applied by brush, and special care must be taken not to create bubbles. The work surface and room must be absolutely dust-free and at an even, warm temperature.

Polyurethane is a synthetic varnish that protects even better than natural varnish but lacks its warmth and softness. Even though it is more durable, it is sometimes shunned for restorations in favor of natural varnish. Like natural varnish, it can take a paste-wax finish.

Penetrating sealers provide a durable finish that sinks down into the wood rather than resting on top. There is no surface polish to be marred by scratches, yet the wood is resistant to water, heat, and spirits. These sealers work best on wood that has previously been chemically stained or fumed. Professional restorers have their own favorite recipes for a sealer made of varnish, linseed oil, and turpentine. The mixture is applied hot, and care must be taken as it is flammable. After it penetrates the wood, the excess is wiped off. In a few days, the surface of the piece is rubbed vigorously. Repeat coats with increasing percentages of varnish are added over a period of weeks. Commercial penetrating finishes, known as Danish, tung-oil, or resin-oil finishes, have a sealer built into them and require fewer applications than varnish-oil-turpentine mixtures.

Lacquer is a popular contemporary finish that is used commercially and is available in spray cans for home use. Lacquer finishes dry hard and clear and are resistant to water and heat, but they are difficult to apply evenly, tend to become "stiff," and are prone to cracking.

Beeswax polish is a soft mixture of beeswax, pure gum turpentine, and oxide powders, which add brown or yellow coloring. It can be purchased ready-mixed. The wax is rubbed into sealed or sanded bare wood surfaces with the finest grade steel wool. It is important to push the wax into the wood fibers; an old toothbrush can help it to penetrate corners, carvings, and the crevices in turnings. The wax is allowed to dry for several hours, then the wood is rubbed hard with a lint-free cloth, such as silk or linen. The process is repeated in two days, again in one week, again in one month, and finally once every year. The rich, mellow finish is perfect on country pine.

Oil finishes bring out the grain and give stripped pine an especially mellow tone. Teak oil is preferred to boiled linseed oil because it is quick-drying and doesn't pick up dust. It is rubbed into the wood with a soft cloth, and the excess is wiped off. Oil finishes are easily renewed with repeat applications. A light touch is recommended to prevent the surface from getting gummy.

CARE TIPS

- Do not oil surfaces that have been previously waxed—the oil will not penetrate properly. Oiled pieces, however, can be waxed.

- Always work in a dust-free environment when applying sealers, polishes, and waxes. Keep the floor and work surfaces spotlessly clean so that dust is not raised when people move about. Some restorers wipe a tack cloth over surfaces about to be coated to prevent dust particles from being trapped in the finish.

- Protect all furniture, but especially newly sealed pieces, from sunlight, radiators, and sudden changes in temperature and humidity.

- To remove white spots or rings from shellac, wipe with a soft cloth dipped in denatured alcohol, ammonia (squeeze out excess), or turpentine. For dark spots, use laundry bleach or ammonia, let stand for 15 minutes, and wipe off.

ROCKING CHAIRS

The rocking chair is quintessentially American—pragmatic, innovative, and rooted in the past but not wedded to it. While nineteenth-century British commentators lamented the sloth and casual lifestyle the rocker purportedly promoted, Americans bustled about their business manufacturing, selling, and buying them to furnish their parlors. No one knows for sure when someone first got the idea to combine rocker blades, like those used on cradles, with a chair, but there is no disputing that American know-how capitalized on the invention.

A BRIEF HISTORY

The earliest known rockers, which date from the mid-1700s, were converted from existing chairs. They were not considered appropriate for formal rooms or occasions, but rather provided comfort in bedrooms, nurseries, and kitchens—the private spots in a home. They were associated with the elderly and infirm, and the rocking motion was considered a good way to take exercise, soothe jattered nerves, or lull oneself to sleep.

Chairs designed from the start as rockers first appeared between 1790 and 1800. They tended to be

awkward and imbalanced, with high backs, no arms, and a jerky "ride." Over the next few decades, refinements would come one after the other, resulting in the now classic Boston rocker of the mid-1830s. Many diverse styles followed. By mid-century, the rocker was upholstered and had become an acceptable parlor furnishing. It was used enthusiastically by men and women, young and old, and typically was viewed as the most comfortable seat in the house. Many Victorian homes boasted several rocking chairs.

American-made rocking chairs were sold in Europe and Australia and sparked a modest industry abroad. The Boston rocker was eagerly copied in Finland. In the late nineteenth and early twentieth centuries, rockers made of wood, wicker, bentwood, willow, and cane were popular as both indoor and porch furniture. Reproduction Boston rockers were first available in the 1920s and are still being made today. All have contributed to a rich and varied legacy for today's rocking chair aficionado.

ABOVE: A mid-nineteenth-century Boston rocker lacks the flamboyant seat curves and elaborate crest of earlier versions. The low-slung seat and high backrest were important refinements to rocking chair design.

EVOLUTION OF THE ROCKER BLADE

The first commercially made rocking chairs were turned out by the same workshops that made Windsor and Sheraton-style fancy chairs. Rocker blades could be narrow and high, with chair legs mortised and bolted onto them, or broad and low, with legs socketed into them. Early rocker blades typically were short and extended the same distance front and back. The chair legs were generally straight or slightly splayed, and the blades were parallel.

Gradually, between 1800 and 1815, the blades were cut longer in the back; by 1825, the rear blades were extending by as much as 10 inches (25cm). Other modifications included shorter back legs, a more pronounced splay to the legs, and blades canted toward the center back. The idea was to safely tilt the chair back, alter the center of gravity, and provide a wider, smoother, more stable swing. The one drawback was that the long rocker blades stuck out behind the chair and people inadvertently tripped over them. Placing the chair in a corner helped somewhat, but since rockers tended to "migrate" during use, the legs sometimes damaged walls and furniture.

BOSTON ROCKERS—
THE "GOLDEN AGE"

The extremely popular Boston rocker was made in many parts of the northeastern United States, not just Boston, and may have originated in Lambert Hitchcock's Connecticut chair factory sometime between 1826 and 1829. The chair silhouette underwent change over time, reaching the peak of comfort and good looks in the 1830s—the "golden age" of American rockers. During this period, the crests were decoratively cut, the pine seat had a pronounced roll, and the gently sloping arms ended in scrolled handgrips. Since the rocking motion created stress on the chair, maple frequently was chosen for its durability.

Early Boston rocker crests are especially striking. They can be recognized by a rectangular section that juts out above and below, giving the effect of a built-in headrest. This shaping was highlighted with striping,

and the wide, flat surface was painted or stenciled with fruit, cornucopias, scenic vignettes, or patriotic motifs such as the eagle and flag. The earliest examples featured simple rosettes. Later, curled leaves and finally scrolled designs were added. For head comfort, the crest was steam-bent into a sweeping curve, and the long Windsor-style spindles were similarly shaped to cradle the seated person's back and support the lumbar region.

The seat of the Boston rocker was saddled in the Windsor tradition. By the mid-1820s, it had assumed a distinct S-curve, rolling forward in the front, for more comfort behind the knees, and curving up in the back. At first, the rolled seat was shaped from a single piece of pine or whitewood, but the more pronounced curves introduced around 1840 had to be shaped separately and joined together. Maple, oak, hickory, and ash were used for the legs, spindles, stretchers, and arms. Arms were also shaped from cherry and apple and were given a natural finish even though the rest of the chair might be painted. Graining colors included the popular black over red to imitate mahogany; later offerings included yellow, gray, and dark green backgrounds as well.

ABOVE: A handcrafted rocking chair by an Australian woodworker who strived hard to copy the Boston rocker design. He achieved the rolled seat, but neglected the shorter, splayed legs and characteristic backward tilt that made rocking chairs so relaxing.

Variations on the Boston rocker were made through the 1860s. The original was so enormously popular that people used the name loosely to refer to all kinds of rockers. One Hitchcock version featured a rush seat with three horizontal slats across the back. A midwestern version, the fiddleback Boston rocker, was factory-made in Ohio and Indiana beginning in the late 1840s. It exchanged some of the vertical spindles for a vase-shaped splat—yet another flat plane to decorate.

OTHER FAVORITE ROCKERS

AMISH BENTWOOD ROCKER

The Amish first devised this ingenious rocker, but commercial firms, such as the Old Hickory Chair Company, manufactured and marketed it at the turn of the century. Like the Shakers, the Amish were highly interested in comfort. They steam-bent long, narrow hickory slats, shaping them to conform to the human spine and support the lumbar region. The slats were spaced slightly apart near the seat, then drew together toward the top of the chair. The chair frame is constructed of bent hickory saplings.

GOOSENECK ROCKER

The upholstered gooseneck rocker, or Grecian rocker, was popular from 1835 to 1860. The wooden arms scroll downward and the entire chair is characterized by the soft Empire curves and an S-shaped back. In the early twentieth century, journalists began referring to it as the "Lincoln" rocker because it was the style rocker President Lincoln was using when he was assassinated.

THE LITTLE BOSTON

"Nursing chair" was another name given to the armless rocker called the Little Boston. Manufactured around 1850, it was smaller than the Boston rocker, with only five spindles. It was a popular bedroom chair and comfortable for mothers who were nursing infants.

MAMMY BENCH

This Windsor-style rocking settee came into fashion on the heels of the Boston rocker. It had curved arms, often with comfortable handrests. A short removable gate could be fitted into holes at the edge of the seat, creating a cradlelike bed along one half of the bench. The mother could sit in the free half and rock herself and her baby, as she did handwork, shelled peas, or chatted with a visitor. The gate was easily removed, returning the bench to a two-seater. The mammy bench appeared throughout America. It was also known as a bench rocker, rocking settee, or cradle settee.

MOTTVILLE ROCKERS

The Mottville rocker is a plain, sturdy, slat-back rocker that was sold in great quantity from 1880 through 1930, especially to hotels and resorts. It was durable, light in weight, and had an honest elegance reminiscent of Shaker furniture. Woven seats provided extra resilience and also were cooler in summer. Original Mottville rockers can be identified by narrow grooves in the stiles and legs, which were highlighted with black paint. Similarly styled porch rockers were very popular and widely available during the same period.

PATENT PLATFORM ROCKER

American ingenuity came up with the platform rocker as a solution to the rocking chair problem. Rocker blades weren't called carpet cutters for nothing—daily rocking did indeed wear out carpets. Another inconvenience was tie-on pads that slipped and long rockers that stuck out behind the chair and were easy to trip over.

The new patented rocker was comfortably uphol-stered, with semicircular wood rockers that rolled back and forth on their own platform. The seat was kept on

track by strong springs mounted underneath. The platform remained stationary and took up no more floor space than an armchair. The rocking motion did have a different feel than traditional rockers—it was shorter and quicker, but pleasant. Silencing fabric strips glued to the arcs cut down on noise. For those with limited floor space or too many memories of bumped shins, the platform rocker hummed of progress. It was first sold in the 1850s and was especially popular from the 1870s through the 1890s as part of parlor suites.

See also Bentwood Furniture, Hitchcock Chair, Shaker Furniture, Sheraton-Style Fancy Chairs. See also under Scandinavia—Finnish Furniture.

OPPOSITE PAGE: An Amish bentwood rocker with steam-bent slats. *ABOVE RIGHT:* A Texas-German rocking chair features turned armrests, a leather-bound seat, and an unusual bent crest. The back slats are similar to those found on Mottville rockers. *RIGHT:* A mammy bench.

RUSH SEATS

The rush seat is the hallmark of the country chair. It appeared on ladderback chairs, the American-Dutch fiddleback chair, country-made Queen Anne– and Chippendale-style chairs, provincial European chairs, and others. To wrap the rush, the seat frame had to be open. A back splat couldn't touch down on the seat but had to end in a low crossrail instead. Rush seats were especially favored by the English and the Dutch but appeared in many other regions as well. They remained popular into the nineteenth century and are still used today.

A BRIEF HISTORY

Since antiquity, rushes have played an important role in everyday culture, serving as bedding and weaving material. In medieval times, rushes were spread on dirt or stone floors to insulate them. As the rushes became matted down with dirt, fresh rushes were laid on top of them. The entire floor was swept out and renewed only once a year. This annual summer harvesting of fresh rushes led to a chairmaking cycle. Early rush weavers were itinerants, traveling from town to town and hiring out to weave seats on the chair frames built over the winter by joiners and turners. In northwest England, a ceremonial gathering of the rushes lingered until the end of the nineteenth century.

ABOVE: A corner of a rushed seat. The most common chair-rushing pattern creates a single, large X on the chair seat.

RUSHING A SEAT

Rush weaving requires a strong hand, for the rush must be twisted as it is worked into a tight, cordlike strand. The twisting is done only on the top side of the seat, however, not on the underside. The rush is wrapped around the seat rungs, covering them completely, so that only the corners are left showing. The rushes must be kept moist and supple during the process. Freshwater rushes stay damp with just a simple sprinkling, but saltwater rushes are soaked for two hours, then wrapped in a wet blanket and drawn from as needed.

Rushing begins near an outer corner and proceeds around the chair frame in a continuous circle. The seat area is filled in from the outside in. New lengths of rush are added as needed, usually underneath so their cut ends don't show. At the first corner, the rush is wrapped over and under one rail, then over and under the second rail. The rush is pulled tight to "lock" the corner in place. Next, the rush is carried straight across *under* the seat frame (no twisting required here) to the next corner. Here it is passed under and over each rail in turn and again drawn tight.

The work continues from corner to corner. Each successive cycle conceals some of the rush already laid and creates an X pattern in the chair seat. As the seat nears completion, the rushes have to be packed tight to make room for the last few rows.

There are other aspects to rushing, including different patterns and compensating for chair arms and angled or bowed seat frames. Materials, tools, and instruction manuals are readily available and give the full details to those interested in this aspect of chair restoration.

CARE TIPS

- Vacuum a rush seat with a brush or wand attachment to draw out bits of grit, sand, and dust. If the seat is not old or fragile, you can turn it upside down and press the underside with your hand to loosen bits of dirt before you vacuum.

- To wash a rush seat, use a soft rag that has been dipped in warm soapy water and wrung out. Rinse-wipe several times with clean water and a new rag. It is especially important to remove any trace of soapy residue, which may cause mold or mildew. Work on a sunny, dry day and place the freshly washed rush outside to dry.

RUSTIC FURNITURE

Rustic furniture encompasses a surprising range of styles and functions. It includes utilitarian chairs and benches fashioned on the frontier, romantic "woodland" garden pavilions and shelters, and the grand-scale furniture of the back-to-nature camps and mountain hotels of the late nineteenth century.

FRONTIER CONSTRUCTION

Frontier stick furniture is strictly utilitarian. Prospectors, trappers, and pioneers put together simple furniture without paying too much attention to symmetry or permanence—the goal was simply a seat to sit down on. On the Australian outback, bushmen used available branches and primitive tools to assemble Windsor-style chairs. Seats were rough-shaped with an adze, and limbs were wedged in for chair legs and backs. Joins were secured with nails, not glue. Even though the furniture was assembled spontaneously, without much planning, sometimes the natural fork or curve in a branch made its way into the design. Chairs, benches, even bedframes were made in a similar way in American frontier areas. In the west, settlers lashed together pieces of bent willow, cottonwood, or green ash with rawhide thongs.

THE ENGLISH GARDENS

While stick furniture was a make-do necessity on the frontier, it was valued in populated areas for its rustic simplicity. In late-eighteenth-century England, furniture made of roots, branches, and bark beckoned to strollers in romantic gardens. Rustic branch-built summer-houses, gazebos, arbors, pergolas, fences, and gates suggested a romantic, pastoral innocence. The fashion reached American shores by the 1840s and accentuated the Victorian love of fresh air and the outdoors. Furniture incorporating tree stumps, forked branches, gnarled roots, and white birch bark "veneer" began appearing indoors as well as on porches and in gardens.

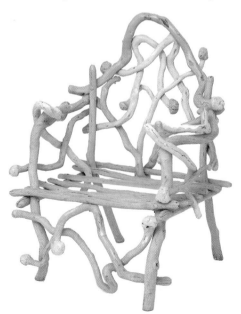

TOP: A well-planned Gothic design and tree limbs of uniform diameter give this rustic chair an air of formality. *ABOVE:* The weight of the sitter causes the legs of an Australian settler's stick chair to wedge more tightly with every use, eliminating the need for stretchers. *LEFT:* A chair fashioned from vines and stick timber.

THE MOUNTAIN CAMPS

As cities became more crowded and industrialized in the mid-1800s, annual summer migrations to mountain resorts and religious campgrounds became popular. It was the middle class who initiated these pilgrimages, though the trend is most frequently associated with the great mountain camps of the wealthy. Areas attracting vacationers included the White and Green Mountains of New Hampshire and Vermont, Michigan's Upper Peninsula, the Minnesota lake country, the Rocky Mountains, the Pacific Northwest, and, most notably, New York State's Adirondack Mountains. All of these regions developed independently, though the rustic furniture created for them is often referred to today as Adirondack furniture.

The effort to recapture raw survival on the frontier was more romantic than actual, as the huge lodges and outlying "cabins" were lavishly furnished with rustic handcrafted beds, dressers, sideboards, desks, dining tables, clocks, lamps, and chairs for sitting and reclining. The most interesting pieces were constructed on-site by the summer guides, trappers, and handymen, who stayed on at the camps over the winter. Cedar was used frequently, as it was light in weight, fairly strong, resistant to insects and rot, and pleasant-smelling.

A number of novel construction techniques were used. These included birch bark veneers, half-round stick moldings, and stick moldings for surface decoration. Peeled cedar poles were used to make four-poster beds and chairs. Hickory saplings were bent in amazingly graceful forms for chairs, table bases, sofa frames, standing lamps, and other pieces. Burls were true treasures. A burl is a growth that protrudes from the tree as a result of an infection or irritation—the process is akin to how an oyster creates a pearl around a grain of sand. The swirling, knotted patterns found in burls were highly prized for tabletops.

In addition to custom-built pieces, a number of furniture factories also produced rustic pieces. The Old Hickory Chair Company, located in Martinsville, Indiana, was among those turning out chairs, settees, and swings for hotels and camps between 1890 and 1940. Such factory-made pieces lacked the idiosyncratic touches of the hand-built pieces, but they were sturdy

ABOVE: A rustic settee was obviously made for genteel enjoyment of the outdoors. The legs show sensitive Empire curves, the sides cleverly suggest rolled arms, and the backrest rises in a classical pediment.

and intriguing enough to capture the imagination of those who were city-bound most of the year. During the Depression, bentwood chairs were made and sold by Gypsies roaming America's South and Midwest. In Australia, artisans used the coastal tea-tree. This tree grew in extraordinary bends and grotesque shapes that could be converted to table bases and chair backs.

Today, interest in rustic furniture is on the rise again, with new firms offering bent willow chairs and settees,

Windsor-style twig chairs, birch bark lamps, and similar items. Individual artisans are the best source for unique pieces.

See also under Australia—Stick and Slab Furniture; Rocking Chairs—Amish Bentwood Rocker.

ABOVE: Vinelike willow branches twist and swirl to form the back and armrests of a rustic rocker.

S

SCANDINAVIA

THE NORTHERN COUNTRIES OF SCANDINAVIA—FINLAND,
NORWAY, AND SWEDEN—ARE BOTH SIMILAR AND
DISSIMILAR IN THEIR FURNITURE STYLES. ALL HAVE GIVEN
THE WORLD A RICH WOODWORKING TRADITION, AND
SWEDEN ADDED THE PARED-DOWN, LIGHTENED LOOK
THAT HAS COME TO CHARACTERIZE THE MODERN
COUNTRY INTERIOR. MANY OF THESE INFLUENCES CAME
ABOUT LARGELY THROUGH ACCIDENTS OF GEOGRAPHY.

The countries of Scandinavia are located in the
extreme northern latitudes. They have up to eighteen
hours of daylight in summer and long, dark nights in
winter. To keep occupied and productive during the
many winter hours spent indoors, farmers and peasants
turned to woodworking, furniture building, and other
handcrafts. In Norway, medieval woodworking
traditions continued into the nineteenth century.
Remote villages on the dramatic seabound fjords
remained largely isolated from the influences of France,
Germany, and England. Sweden, with its more
accessible ports, enjoyed more trade and cultural

exchange, and its provincial furniture reflects these
influences. By the end of the eighteenth century, light,
delicate classical designs from England, France, and
Italy had entered Sweden and were being copied. In the
nineteenth century, Empire furniture was emulated.
Pine settees were built with scrolling arms and backs
that rose in high central pediments.

Certain furniture forms appeared throughout
Scandinavia. Cupboard beds lined up end to end against
the wall are evidence of the cold winters. The bases were
often fitted with drawers or cabinets to store bedding
during the day. If the wallspace was long enough, a
cabinet could be built in between the beds. A bed built
into a corner might have a cabinet built onto the open
end to accentuate the room-within-a-room aspect of the
bed compartment.

ABOVE: Wood predominates as a building material in a Norwegian
interior. The built-in cupboards feature baroque carvings and painted
panels. The chair backs are carved in relief. *OPPOSITE PAGE:* The Finnish
tupa, center for many varied family activities, is heated in winter by a
large fireplace. Among the furnishings are locally made rocking chairs.

The pine settee also was used throughout Scandinavia. It featured a spindled or vertical slat back and open arms. The flat plank seat could rest on straight or turned legs or on a box base that pulled forward to form a bed platform. A plump feather bed, clean white sheets, and fresh pillows made it ready for sleeping. The pull-out bed was used more often in the summer, to take advantage of breezes.

Scandinavians also used trestle tables with broad tops and angled legs, simple plank stools and benches, and plank chairs. A three-legged Swedish chair, called a *bordstol*, had a hinged seat that could unfold and convert to a small table. Folding tables with enormous drop leaves were also common, as were smaller drop-leaf styles. Blind cupboards built in two stages had the three-sided pediment and canted corners typical in northern and central Europe. Contrasting paint was used to pick out the door panels and moldings. A closer look at the traditions of each country follows.

FINLAND

Finland remained largely rural until well into the twentieth century. In the 1940s, about sixty percent of the population was still living in the countryside. Life revolved around hunting, fishing, and farming, and country people traditionally made all their own tools. The simplest homes were made of logs and had a central chimney. (It was seventeenth-century Finns who built the first log cabins in America.) The summerhouse or country cottage is a long-standing tradition in Finland, as it is in Sweden. Even farmers have a weekend place where they go for relaxation.

THE FINNISH *TUPA*

The rural Finnish home had one central room called a *tupa*. The *tupa* was used for many activities, including cooking, eating, sewing, woodworking, and sleeping. A single oven was used for baking as well as heating.

Open space for doing handcraft work was an important part of the design of the *tupa*. The area had to be large enough for several centers of activity. A weaving loom might occupy one corner, and another corner was kept available for building furniture. This arrangement allowed the family to take advantage of the central heat source and enjoy one another's company as they worked on their projects.

FINNISH FURNITURE

Finnish country furniture is a sturdy peasant style. Bare wood was preferred, with woven textiles and rya rugs providing color. Built-in benches around the perimeter of the *tupa* provided extra seating and could fill in as spare beds when needed. Plank seat chairs and other furniture often were presented from groom to bride as a wedding gift. Most of the bare wood furniture received little decoration, except for wedding furniture, which had decorative geometric cutouts or repeat carved motifs. The western Swedish-speaking part of the country introduced Gustavian pieces. These included white-painted Queen Anne–style chairs and colorful cupboards with rococo cornices.

Unexpected pieces also turn up in Finland. The Finns were fond of using natural wood forms, such as tree roots and branches, for stool and table legs. Another surprise is the rocking chair. News of America's Boston rocker reached the shores of Finland sometime in the nineteenth century. The Finns fell in love with it and enthusiastically went about making their own versions, complete with rolled seats and amazingly long rocker blades. Some Finnish rockers show two extra rear legs extending out to support the rockers.

NORWAY

Norway's tall pine forests give a hint of this country's rich woodworking tradition. Practically everything—furniture, tools, the house itself—was made of wood and decorated with rich carving. In the eighteenth century, paint came to replace carving and helped to relieve the monotony of wood tones inside the house. Because so many parts of Norway were geographically isolated, many areas managed to remain out of the mainstream of the industrial revolution until the nineteenth century. The concept of a wardrobe, for instance, never appeared as a native furnishing in Norway. During the eighteenth century, when the rest of Europe was using armoires, *Schränke*, and wardrobes, Norwegians continued to fold and store their clothes in trunks.

"NATURAL CURVE" FURNITURE

The dome-lidded trunk is a good example of a trait peculiar to Norwegian furniture. Norwegian woodworkers were fascinated by the natural curved form of the tree trunk. Rather than steam-bending wood into a curved shape, they hewed it from the log and allowed the natural form of the tree to suggest the contours. Other examples of furniture that display this technique include the *bandestol*, the bow-front cabinet, the cylinder-lid desk, and the *kubbestol*.

The *bandestol* is a three-legged chair with a U-shaped seat and surprisingly clean, modern lines. There are two legs in front and one in the back center. The chair is a bit tippy, and people sitting in it have to be careful not to shift their weight off-center. The legs extend up above the seat and support a naturally curved wood rail that functions as both chair arms and back support. In all, only seven pieces of wood are needed. The braces could be decoratively carved or plain.

The bow-front corner cabinet was first made in the eighteenth century. Sophisticated British and continental European cabinetmakers began using steam to bend pine

LEFT: A Norwegian bandestol. OPPOSITE PAGE, BOTTOM: A bow-fronted corner cabinet incorporates a tree trunk's natural curves into its design. OPPOSITE PAGE, TOP: A cylinder-top desk.

panels into quarter-cylinder doors and cabinet facings. The cabinets they built were richly veneered and very elegant, with a price tag to match. The cabinets were first introduced into Scandinavian cities around 1800, and knowledge of the style filtered into outlying areas from there.

When traditional Norwegian woodworkers saw the bowed doors, they were reminded, of course, of the dome-lidded trunk. They seized on the design and began making their own version of the bow-front cabinet using techniques familiar to them. The cabinet doors and front, instead of being bent to shape, were hewn from a tree trunk and smoothed with narrow planes. In a peculiar quirk of history, Norwegian immigrants carried this construction idea with them, resulting in elegant bow-front corner cabinets being made in the heart of the American prairie.

The cylinder-top desk is another sophisticated piece of cabinetry that required knowledge of wood-bending and veneering to construct. Instead of a drop lid, the desk contents were protected by a quarter-cylinder door that lay on its side. To use the desk, the writer unlocked the door and rolled it up and back on the inside curved channels. The Norwegian version featured the same type of quarter-cylinder door used for the bow-front cabinet. Norwegian woodworkers also included a pull-out writing surface, pigeonholes, and small drawers.

The *kubbestol* is a unique chair crafted from a hollowed-out section of tree trunk. It was first created during the Middle Ages. The base of the *kubbestol* is a cylinder that arches in at the center. The curved backrest continues up from this base in one continuous piece. It is rounded at the top and may slope back slightly. More primitive *kubbestoler* show less sensitive shaping and have a more up-and-down appearance. Rich carvings often decorate the base and chair back—they were no doubt completed during the dark Scandinavian winters. A round plank seat is set in loosely, which allows the wood to expand and contract without stress. Considering that no joining is involved, the seat is surprisingly functional. Artisans have kept the *kubbestol* craft alive into the twentieth century.

OTHER NORWEGIAN FURNITURE

The furniture in the Norwegian home emphasized practicality and function. Huge tables with leaves that hung down to the floor were common. Small fold-up tables that rested on single legs were hinged to the wall. Freestanding tables were placed in corners, and it was traditional to hang a corner cupboard above them. A standing corner cupboard, called a *skop*, has a closed cupboard below and open tiered shelves above. Gay scalloping danced up the two backboards of the *skop* until they crested in the center. The Norwegian love of woodcrafting led to elaborate cupboard interiors as well. A surprising multiplicity and complexity of drawers and shelves could be lurking behind closed cupboard doors. Holes for hanging spoons were often added to shelf edges as a way of showing off possessions.

One tall cupboard was traditionally positioned just inside the door to the home. This cupboard, used for crockery, stood on bracket-type feet that are extensions of the board sides. For some reason, perhaps to add a kickspace, the feet are recessed. This made the entire cupboard top-heavy, so that it had to be bolted to the wall for stability. The shelves are protected by large double doors.

Jumbo diamond motifs, made of molding, are often seen on Norwegian cupboards and can help identify them. Norwegian-Americans cut diamonds and circles in door panels and filled them with screening for their food safes. Scalloping is another common motif that requires wood-working skill. In one design, the scalloping alternates with small curved horns that end in a point. Each alternate horn points in a different direction, creating a lively cut edge full of activity and a sense of motion.

The Norwegian woodworker did so much carving, utensil making, and furniture building that he devised a special work-bench, called a box bench. The box bench takes its inspiration from the box tables used in Scandinavia in medieval times. These tables were low, and the family would gather around them on the floor to eat. The legs of the table were recessed on the sides, so that the tabletop was almost twice as long as the base.

The box bench is much smaller but similarly proportioned, so that when the woodworker sat down the bench seat extended a foot or so on either side. Perhaps woodworkers foresaw the need for extra space to set down their tools. A special tool storage compartment was built into the base of the bench, directly under the seat. All the craftsman had to do was slide open the small door and reach in for the tool he needed. He didn't even have to stand up.

ROSEMALING

Rosemaling is the Norwegian style of decorative brushstroke folk painting. It first appeared in the early eighteenth century and reached its fullest artistic flowering over a one-hundred-year period beginning around 1750. Up until the early eighteenth century, most Norwegian peasant homes were dark and sooty with central fires and no chimney. All construction was in wood, and carving and textiles provided the only design and color.

ABOVE: A kubbestol, or log chair, features symmetrical relief carving on the back.

the house, such as beams and lintels, were decorated. Different districts developed their own preferences for motifs and colors, though in all areas, colors were generally deep and muted.

Rosemaled furniture and objects were brought into the United States during the mass Norwegian migration in the second half of the nineteenth century. Very little new rosemaling actually was done by the new immigrants, though, because they were busy establishing their homesteads. In the twentieth century, popular revival of the craft eventually led to a study of rosemaling as originally practiced in Norway.

SWEDEN

The Swedish love of the countryside is most evident in the numerous country houses that dot the land. Most of these houses are small family hideaways located by the shore, on a lakefront, or in the hills. The custom of escaping to the country for rest and relaxation is enjoyed by all levels of society. Even families with modest incomes own country retreats.

As in other Scandinavian countries, early Swedish peasant homes made of wood were dark. Today, the style is quite different, and Sweden is known for its spare, open, airy look. Woods are blonde or painted in light colors, rather than dark and somber. There is also a sense of whimsy, playfulness, and informality. This look developed over time and was influenced by the Gustavian period in the late 1700s and later by the painter Carl Larsson, whose watercolors of his own family's home were published around 1900.

SWEDISH PEASANT FURNITURE

The country life of Swedish peasants emphasized hard work and thrift, but also beauty and creativity. Furniture and possessions were well cared for and decorative, and handcrafts were a normal part of the Swedish way of life.

Several new developments changed the Norwegian interior, making it more receptive to painted design. Better windows brought in more light, a corner stove was cleaner and more efficient, and milled lumber allowed for wood-paneled walls. At the same time, baroque and rococo scrollwork and acanthus leaf designs filtered into Norway from the continent. Traveling craftsman mingled these new designs with old Viking motifs used in wood carving, and the rosemaling style evolved. It featured flowers, geometric designs, scrolling, and sometimes human figures or animals. Furniture, utensils, and even architectural features of

TOP AND BOTTOM: An antique cupboard made in Norway and a mid-twentieth-century Norwegian-American *bandestol* show how migration influenced rosemaling style and technique. In the late twentieth century, the older rosemaling techniques began enjoying a revival.

Swedish Country Style

Swedish country decorating is light, cool, and refreshing, never heavy or overdone. Walls are painted white with a tinge of gray, and the mellow pine floorboards are covered with handwoven linen runners. Window treatments are always simple. Full-length sheer curtains or simple swags of muslin, striped cotton, or linen let in the maximum amount of the soft northern light. White and a soft blue are the preferred colors for upholstery fabrics, as they suggest summer days by the water during the long, dark winters.

Furnishings are kept simple, reflecting the Gustavian influence. To maintain the feeling of open airiness, rooms are sparsely rather than overly furnished. Handcrafted or informal accents, such as hand-crocheted doilies or bunches of wildflowers, are preferred to expensive porcelains.

A must in any Swedish country house is the floor-to-ceiling tiled stove, used instead of a fireplace. These elegant stoves, with their blue-on-white painted tiles and sculpted mantels, provided heat as well as decoration. If the fire was well-stoked during the day, the tiles would continue to radiate heat through the night and into the early morning.

A wife's embroidered towels, for instance, were hung for display on a special wooden towel rack made by her husband. This rack was mounted just inside the "best room" door, where visitors would be sure to see it. Another small display unit, called a *tavelett*, featured rectangular shelves supported by turned columns. It was used to display the household's decorative objects and to hold books. The *tavelett* could be hung on the wall by a leather thong or it could stand directly on a cupboard or tabletop.

One special display area in southern Swedish homes is the trunk room. The typical peasant dwelling consisted of just two rooms off a central hall—a living room and a trunk room. Each family member owned at least one dome-lidded trunk to hold church clothes, embroidered textiles, household items, dowry gifts, and other treasures. All the trunks were boldly painted and signed with initials and dates. Together, they created a rich, colorful assembly. On holidays, murals painted on linen were unrolled and hung around the room. The more trunks and paintings a family had, the richer it was considered to be.

DALARNA PAINTING

Swedish Dalarna painting first appeared around 1780 and lasted about one hundred years. In Dalarna and provinces to the north, the second large room in the peasant house was not used for trunks but was reserved as a large festival room. Removable benches lined the walls and a huge tile stove in the corner provided heat. The room was used only for weddings, holidays, and other special occasions. Painted linens were hung around the room, and in Dalarna, the walls themselves were painted with murals depicting biblical scenes. Every inch of wall was covered. These Dalarna-style paintings, particularly the flowered borders, sometimes made their way onto cupboards, as well.

THE GUSTAVIAN STYLE

The formal furniture styles that developed in England and France during the seventeenth century were received with great interest in Sweden, but it was simply not important to the Swedes to copy them slavishly or to mimic the lifestyles that went with them. Even the Swedish court developed its own version of rococo that reflected Swedish traditions.

The lighter colors associated with Swedish country decorating today were introduced during the Gustavian period. The formal Gustavian period extended from 1770 to 1810, but the style continued to thrive, particularly in northern Sweden, through 1825. Two kings reigned during this period, Gustav III, from 1771–1792, and Gustav IV, from 1792–1809. King Gustav III was very interested in the cultural and artistic trends in Europe, particularly the emerging neoclassical revival of ancient Greek and Roman designs. In his court, the heavy rococo colors were replaced by pale gray tints and shades of off-white.

By the reign of Gustav IV, the new classical style was firmly established. It emphasized symmetry and straight

OPPOSITE PAGE: A drop-leaf table with heavy baroque legs, a Gustavian chair, a practical stepladder chair, and a painted hanging cupboard furnish a corner of this Swedish kitchen. *ABOVE:* This Swedish cabinet front, painted in the Darlarna style, depicts the biblical story of Jacob's dream.

rather than curving lines. An overall delicacy and restraint replaced the flamboyance of the earlier baroque and rococo influences. In addition, Sweden enacted many antiluxury laws during this period that limited the ornamental use of woods and metals. All of these influences contributed to the leaner, pared-down, lighter look that has remained a part of the Swedish consciousness into the twentieth century.

Gustavian-style furniture combines both formal and informal elements. The Gustavian bed, for instance, featured a high rococo-style headboard but was painted in a light solid color with floral decoration. The bed itself was a practical pull-out style that, when closed, resembled a settee minus the seat. A typical Gustavian chair features a rounded back with wheat sheaf splat, a formal design associated with English Adams-style architecture. The legs could vary from round and tapered (the expected style) to William and Mary–style turned legs to Queen Anne–style cabriole legs, all with stretchers. Once the chairs were made, they were painted white or light tints of blue, gray, or green. This innocent mix of different formal styles in a single chair and the

light, unpretentious paint colors are keys to understanding Sweden's relaxed attitude toward its furniture.

Swedish cabinetmakers also copied Europe's formal table styles, including desks, bedside tables, and side tables. They especially loved half-round and rectangular side tables with delicate tapering legs. When two half-round tables were made in a set, they could be hooked together to form a circular table or placed as extensions on the ends of a square or rectangular table. The versatility of such furniture fit in with the impromptu Swedish spirit. In the early nineteenth century, France's Empire-style furniture continued the neoclassical look. Swedish woodworkers copied this also, working deeply scrolled arms onto their daybeds (a form of the original Scandinavian sleigh bed). The new furniture fit in well with traditional peasant cupboards, bed-settees, and drop-leaf tables, and the Swedes seemed unconcerned about mixing different styles together in a single room.

OTHER EUROPEAN INFLUENCES

Other European styles also influenced Swedish woodworkers. One of these was the French *fauteuil*, a

roomy ladderback armchair with loose seat and back cushions. The Swedish country version featured turned legs with stretchers instead of French cabriole legs. The arms could be turned, or they could be shaped and padded in the French manner. Two matching chairs and a cushioned footstool often were made together as a three-piece ensemble. The stool was the same height and width as the chairs and could be placed between them to form an extended lounger.

Another Swedish ladderback style was made in Uppland during the eighteenth and nineteenth centuries. The decorative back rungs could be thin and steam-bent or thick and cut to shape with a saw and knife. It differs from the traditional rush seat ladderback in that the seat is wooden and dropped into the seat frame, rather than being woven on the chair itself. Some seats were padded with horsehair and covered with fabric. A faster, less costly alternative was to tie on a loose seat cushion.

The Swedish wooden chandelier is another country accessory that owes its inspiration to continental Europe. It was made in imitation of costly brass and bronze chandeliers, which were introduced to Sweden during the 1700s. In the Swedish version, the center column

was turned from wood and painted. The arms were wood or wrought iron. Woodworkers first made them for use in churches and prominent homes.

CARL LARSSON

The world got its first taste of Swedish interiors through the charming watercolors that artist Carl Larsson made of his home and family. Carl Larsson was an acclaimed painter whose work was in demand. He had studied in both Stockholm and France, and he received many commissions, including the large fresco in the hall of Stockholm's National Museum. In the late 1800s, he and his wife Karin were given a house by her aunts in the Dalarna country town of Sundborn. The house was called Little Hyttnäs, meaning "the hut on the point." The Larssons made Little Hyttnäs their home and raised eight children there. They added on to the house as needed, and the villagers got used to their artist neighbor and his funny house with its extra rooms and odd passageways.

When the Larssons first moved in, the rooms were dark and dreary, as they were in most simple Swedish homes throughout the 1800s. When he wasn't busy with his many paintings and commissions, Carl Larsson took to painting the interior of his house to cheer it up. Over a period of years, woodwork, walls, moldings, and ceilings were painted in both light and bright colors and decorated with murals and written messages, such as the greeting above the studio threshold: "Carl Larsson and his spouse welcome you to their house."

OPPOSITE PAGE: Fabric loops are informally slipped over the finials to keep the cushion on a Swedish armchair form shifting. The Gustavian side chair features turned stretchers. The tile stove is a replica of the room's original stove, which stands across the room. *ABOVE LEFT:* A pull-out section converts a Swedish daybed for nighttime sleeping. *ABOVE RIGHT:* A boxlike sleigh bed in the home of Carl and Karin Larsson.

Carl Larsson so loved to paint that in his spare time he made charming, realistic watercolors of his family in their home. The scenes were typical household vignettes, not formal interiors, though the details of furniture and decorating are clearly shown. He captured his son Pontus brooding in the "punishment corner," his daughter Suzanne watering plants, butter churning in the kitchen, and the children getting dressed on a Sunday morning. His pictures were published in the book *Ett Hem (A Home)* in Sweden in 1899, and they captivated the country. The book was republished abroad, and the rest of the world welcomed the Carl Larsson style as a refreshing change from the over-abundance and clutter of Victorian interiors. Many of

his pictures depict the furniture and accessories associated with Swedish country decorating today: Gustavian-style chairs, blue and white striped upholstery, and linen floor runners.

See also Sleigh Bed. See also under Beds—Swedish Trestle Bed; Drop-Leaf Tables—Scandinavian Gateleg Tables.

ABOVE: The living room of Little Hyttnäs, home of Carl and Karin Larsson and their family. The white Gustavian chairs are plumped up with blue and white seat cushions. The sleigh bed settee was used for sitting or daytime napping. The round table in the foreground is composed of two half-round units that are joined with simple hook-and-eye hardware.

SETTLES

The high-backed, hard-seated settle was the most comfortable bench furniture in the seventeenth- and early eighteenth-century farmhouse or cottage. Settles were used for seating, storage, and sleeping, and as partitions. Ultimately, the high solid back and arms were replaced with open spindles or slats, and the couch or settee was born.

A BRIEF HISTORY

The settle first appeared in the 1600s and likely grew from the medieval practice of placing low benches for seating right up against the wall, which served as a backrest. The settle is best thought of as a bench with the wall built into it. The high back, constructed of tongue-and-groove wainscot paneling, went right down to the floor. The full-length sides ended in shaped or angled wings. The resulting furniture offered protection against drafts to the feet, shoulders, neck, and head. When drawn up to the hearth at a right angle and plumped with a soft squab, the settle became a warm, cozy seat for two or more to eat, talk, or do handwork. Some settles were built in an arched shape so that those seated could see each other without craning their necks. Others had a small boxlike table on the seat for resting refreshments or needlework.

The earliest English settles were made of oak, followed by ash and pine. American settles of painted pine continued to be made into the early 1800s. Planks were either joined or nailed together. The seat was thick and hinged to reveal a storage compartment underneath. Some owners treated settle backs as room dividers, fitting them with towel holders or shelving or pinning them with maps or pictures. In bars of inns, settles fit in close to the wall or were built in; some were L-shaped to fit into corners. The shine on British pub settles is said to be due to a polish that included home-brewed ale.

For multipurpose seating, Swedish peasants retained the old medieval turnover settle. This settle was positioned at long trestle tables across from the bench that was built in along the wall. This arrangement gave everyone at the table a comfortable backrest. When the meal was over, rather than turning the heavy settle around to face back into the room, its backrest simply pulled out of a groove and slotted into parallel grooves on the opposite side.

Around 1740, the back of the English settle became lower and the solid sides were replaced with open arms. The seat frame was laced with rope, like a bed, to support loose cushions for seating. In coaching inns, these low settle-couches could be used as emergency beds.

THE SETTLE-BED

Some settles were designed to convert into low box beds. They were space-saving in small, crowded rooms and

Using Old Settles Today

Today, high-backed farmhouse settles are not generally considered comfortable enough for living room seating, but they can be practical in an entrance hall or mudroom as a place to set packages or to sit while taking off boots. The under-the-seat compartment is perfect for stowing bulky outdoor gear, and some are even partitioned. Old frame-and-panel pub settles, stripped to bare pine, can be especially inviting around a table. Simple nineteenth-century farmhouse settles are a common component of country decorating in America and Canada.

ABOVE: A *banc-lit*, or fold-down settle-bed, from Canada.

offered a warm sleeping spot close to the last glowing embers of the evening's fire.

The fold-down settle-bed appeared in Ireland and northern Scotland, though not in England. The seat portion of the bench flipped forward and down, so that the front rested on the floor. The straw bedding and linens stowed inside were then arranged in this boxlike frame. This settle-bed style was carried to Canada, where it was adopted by the French-Canadians as the *banc-lit*. From there, it spread south into northern Vermont, New Hampshire, and Maine, but did not appear elsewhere in the United States.

The pull-out settle-bed was more common in continental Europe. The seat lid lifted off, and the lower portion pulled forward, extending the size of the bed. Sleeping close to the floor invariably meant sharing the bedding with mice and insects. The Scandinavians solved this problem by introducing a fold-out sleeping platform that raised the bed up off the floor. Nineteenth-century Norwegian settlers introduced a slat-back settle-bed with curved armrests to the American prairie.

SHAKER FURNITURE

Of the various Utopian communities that arose in eighteenth- and nineteenth-century America, the Shakers were the only ones to leave behind a legacy of elegant, expertly constructed furniture. Their pieces were wholly functional, reflecting the purity, simplicity, and integrity they pursued in their communal life. Conspicuously absent are ornamental embellishments, such as carving, decorative painting, veneering, and inlay, which were considered worldly and capable of diverting the believer's attention from God. Today, Shaker pieces attract admirers because they seem so crisp and modern, and it is hard to believe they were designed over a century ago.

ABOVE LEFT: A sense of protection and enclosure is offered by a high-backed American settle with narrow board "ceiling." *ABOVE:* This bank of floor-to-ceiling drawers and cabinets in an upstairs hallway imitates the Shaker penchant for orderly storage. The buttonlike knobs are also Shaker-inspired. *OPPOSITE PAGE, TOP:* A Shaker ladderback rocker has mushroom-topped handgrips and a rod across the top rail for securing a shawl or lap robe. *OPPOSITE PAGE, BOTTOM:* A neat, trim, unadorned bedstead was nonetheless crafted to last a lifetime. Since the Shakers were celibate, single beds in dormitory-style rooms were the norm.

A BRIEF HISTORY

The Shaker movement began in England in 1747, when James and Jane Wardley formed a small faction that broke from the Quakers. Their worship emphasized physical exuberance, and they became known as the "shaking" Quakers, which was abbreviated to Shakers. Twenty-two-year-old Ann Lee joined the group in 1758 and became its leader twelve years later. In 1774, she and eight followers boarded the *Mariah* and set sail for America.

By the spring of 1776, the small band was settled near Albany, New York. The group aspired to social and spiritual order, a goal to be achieved through communal sharing of property, rejection of the world, and celibacy. New members were won through proselytizing in surrounding towns, and hard feelings resulted as new converts left behind their spouses and children to join the Shaker community. Towns and villages forewarned of the Shaker intentions did not give them a warm welcome. Nevertheless, by the middle of the nineteenth century, some 6,000 followers were living in nineteen villages throughout New York and New England. A second wave of conversions led to new settlements in Ohio, Kentucky, and Indiana.

The Shakers were self-sufficient, and the idealistic people who joined the communities possessed many diverse talents and skills—among them cabinetry. They built all their own furniture, and to help support themselves financially, turned to designing and building furniture for sale to the public after 1850. The New Lebanon community in New York State was the main center of chair production. Advance sales were made by illustrated catalogs, complete with religious messages, using a mail-order system. Among the most popular offerings were ladderback rockers in eight different sizes, which were seen by the masses of people who visited the 1876 Centennial Exhibition in Philadelphia. The rocker won awards for its "strength, sprightliness, and modest beauty" and continued to be made through 1930.

THE FURNITURE

The Shakers based their communal and spiritual life on four principles: celibacy, true peace, sharing the fruits of life, and the religious and secular equality of men and women. Their goal in all endeavors was perfection, and they followed leader Ann Lee's admonishment to "do all your work as though you had a thousand years to live, and as if you knew you would die tomorrow." The furniture produced by such a philosophy was thoughtfully conceived and painstakingly crafted. The Shakers didn't simply build furniture; they focused on the relationship between function and design and distilled earlier furniture, such as the ladderback chair, to its most basic forms. Their pursuit of comfort, utility, and ease of maintenance resulted in clean lines, rich, smooth surfaces, and striking clarity.

The Shakers' communal furniture was often oversized, as members lived and worked in groups. Dining tables were up to 20 feet (6m) long, with bench seats on either side. Massive built-in floor-to-ceiling cupboards had drawers and cabinets of varying sizes to keep workshop and household supplies clean, tidy, and organized. The Shakers pursued ways of streamlining maintenance and improving traffic patterns, important considerations when large groups of people shared living quarters. Chairs were built with low backs, to slip under a table when not in use. They could also be lifted up and hung on a peg rail, clearing the floor for easier sweeping.

The most beautiful Shaker furniture was made from 1825 to 1850—the "classic" period—for use within the community. Most surviving examples from this period are found in museums. The pieces reaching auction are generally from the later 1800s and represent Shaker furniture offered for sale to the public. Quality reproductions of Shaker furniture abound, though there are those who contend that even the most faithful reproductions do not transmit the spiritual essence of pieces made within the community.

THE SHAKER LADDERBACK

The signature Shaker chair is the ladderback. It has mushroom-shaped knobs for handrests and understated acorn finials. Communities in Kentucky and Ohio used deeper turnings and higher finials than the New York and New England groups, reflecting a more relaxed Southern influence. The chair frame is usually maple, though birch, cherry, hickory, and butternut also were used. Seats were woven of cane, rush, wood splints, and a woven wool tape known as listing. The listing tapes were woven onto the seat frame in two contrasting colors; tan with maroon and red with black were popular combinations. Early tapes were handwoven and hand-dyed, but by the middle of the nineteenth century they were machine-made to streamline production for the "sale" chairs. Both straight-leg and rocking chairs were built in varying sizes. The Shakers took special care to measure the human body and study its proportions to calculate the most comfortable chair dimensions.

OTHER SHAKER INNOVATIONS

The Shaker's thoughtful approach to furniture making yielded other practical innovations that were ahead of their time. Trestle tables had diagonal iron struts instead of a leg-hampering crossbar. Beds rolled on castors to make cleaning easier. Chairs were designed with footrests, swiveling seats, and rodlike top rails for tying on a cushion or draping a shawl. To lean back in a chair without tipping over, the Shakers devised special "tilters" that attached to the back legs. This ball bearing–like device became the prototype of the metal ball-and-socket foot found on contemporary chairs.

LEFT: The Shaker philosophy led to elegantly simple, pared-down designs, such as this circa 1850 candlestand with Queen Anne features.

SHERATON-STYLE FANCY CHAIRS

The English Sheraton fancy chair was first advertised for sale in New York in 1797. Affordable only to the wealthy, this chair nevertheless captured the imagination of American entrepreneurs who were beginning to see possibilities in factory construction and decoration. Over the next fifty years, prices dropped dramatically, and the factory-made painted or stenciled chair replaced the Windsor as the hands-down favorite of ordinary Americans. Fancy chairs were used in the parlors, dining rooms, and bedrooms of private homes, and also in public bars, hotels, and on riverboats, where they were called steamboat fancies.

DESIGN AND DECORATION

The first fancy chairs were light and delicate in color, overall design, and decoration. Legs were straight and slender, turnings were understated, and gold striping was applied sparingly. Over the next half century, the chairs would become bolder and darker, with more hasty brushwork and the expected loss of refined detail. Hand-painted decoration gave way to multiple-color stencils

and finally single-stenciled designs, tinted with a quick brush of transparent oil colors. With the stenciling so simplified, chairs that once took many days to paint could now be decorated in a short while by a handful of trained factory workers. Motifs for decoration included fruit, leaves, vines, urns, swags, and musical instruments such as horns, lyres, and harps.

FAVORITE CHAIR STYLES

The fancy chair style is named according to the shape of the chair back, not the design that was painted or stenciled on it. This practice arose in the factory, when the workers needed a way to identify the chairs being made before they got to the decoration stage.

Early fancy chairs had rectangular rail backs, but by 1815 the shapes became more interesting and included saw-cut eagles, shields, and cornucopias. These fancy shapes remained in fashion for about fifteen years. They were time-consuming to cut and decorate, and eventually manufacturers replaced them with symmetrical patterns that could be turned out more efficiently in the factory.

ABOVE: Early fancy chairs featured elaborately cut crossrails and scenic paintings.

ABOVE: Decorative painting and stenciling adorn every surface of this early nineteenth-century fancy chair. The crest shows stenciled fruit and striping, the cutout crossrail and front stretcher are painted with freehand brushstrokes, and the legs and stiles are grain-painted to resemble wood. The edges of the rush seat are protected with a split ring turning on the front and wood strips on the back and sides. *BELOW:* A Swedish daybed with sloped sides.

One of these simplified shapes was the turtleback. It was basically a large oval joined to the side rails by four short wavy bars representing the turtle's legs. Another style was the buttonback. This broad rectangle was joined to the crossrails by tiny round balls, called buttons. Both the buttonback and turtleback rails were gently curved for comfort and offered ample space for stenciled decoration. The vase-shaped Queen Anne–style fiddleback splat, reintroduced around 1840, was yet another move to streamline production and keep factory costs down.

By 1850, even the most basic stenciling was being phased out, and chairs were simply painted in solid colors and striped, or grained in black over a yellow or red background.

See also Hitchcock Chair.

SLEIGH BED

The sleigh bed is an old Scandinavian form dating back to the sixteenth century. The bed is deep and boxlike. Like a sleigh, the open side dips lower in the center, making it easier to climb up into bed. The side curves up at the ends to protect against drafts. Sleigh beds were often built against the wall, left open on just one side, and draped

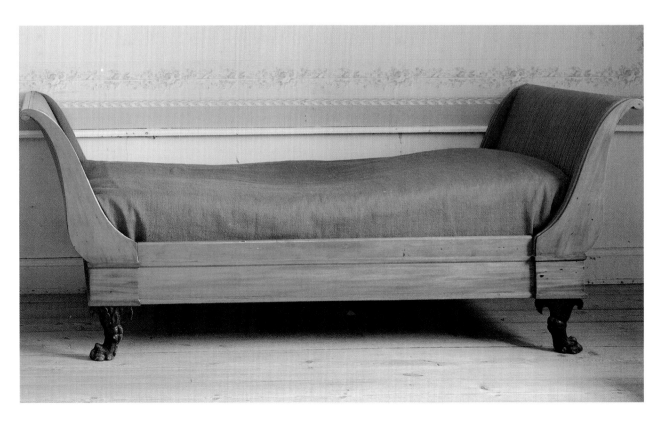

with privacy curtains. To save space and conserve heat, a home's beds were frequently banked along a single wall. Blankets and bed coverings were tucked down inside the bed rather than allowed to hang outside.

During the nineteenth-century Empire period, it became fashionable to place daybeds with the long side against the wall. A projecting arm or peg was anchored to the wall above the center of the bed. A soft curtain was draped over it and allowed to fall to each side, creating a tentlike canopy. This new style was called a French bed, but the gentle Empire scrolling reminded people of sleighs and eventually the name sleigh bed took hold. The head- and footboards were of equal height and curved up and out, each ending in a graceful rolled edge. Country versions often were constructed of straight endboards, with decorative cutting giving the illusion of sinuous curves.

SPICE CABINET

The spice cabinet has long intrigued collectors because of the multiple drawers, cubbyholes, and secret hiding places that are found behind its single locking door. On European estates, spice cabinets were large and stood on the floor, but in middle-class and country homes of the seventeenth and eighteenth century, they were small enough to stand on top of a chest or table.

A BRIEF HISTORY

Ever since the Middle Ages, Europeans had valued spices not solely for their flavors but also for their ability to disguise the first traces of rancidity. By the late seventeenth century, imported Asian spices were affordable to the middle class but still expensive enough to warrant storage under lock and key. The cabinets made for this purpose were kept in the living room, not the kitchen, and the spices were dispensed to the cook as needed.

By 1720, increasing trade brought spice prices down, and it was no longer necessary to lock the cabinet. Eventually, the doors were eliminated altogether, and the design was expanded to include small alcoves for jars. It was during this period that dresser racks came to be built with a row of easily accessible spice drawers. Locking

spice cabinets became less important in Europe but they remained popular in America, particularly around Philadelphia.

DESIGN AND CONSTRUCTION

Spice cabinets are charming miniature pieces of furniture. Made of oak, walnut, or fruitwood, they stand on bun or bracket feet and often feature compass-drawn inlaid designs and veneering. The interiors were arranged in two basic ways. An older style had a central cupboard with smaller drawers arranged symmetrically all around. A later style featured horizontal drawers, graduated in size to resemble a chest of drawers.

The little drawers were supported by thin wood dividers. The drawers held individual packets of ginger, nutmeg, cinnamon, mace, cloves, and pepper, but old records indicate they were also used for other small valuables such as documents and jewelry. The cabinets' small size, customer requests for secret drawers, and the possibility of including exotic, expensive woods gave the cabinetmaker a chance to play at his craft.

It is easy to see how the compact, orderly arrangement of drawers translated over time to today's "colonial" spice rack and the narrow built-in spice cupboards that have become standard in modern kitchen cabinetry. Old spice cabinets are especially appealing as a way to sort and organize small treasures. The Dutch led the way in the late eighteenth century by using their old locking cabinets to store valuable tulip bulbs.

SPOOL FURNITURE

Spool furniture was one of the most popular mass-produced styles available in the mid-1800s. Decoratively turned legs, rails, and bedposts were created by the same technology used to turn wooden spools for sewing thread. Manufacturers realized that instead of cutting the spool turnings apart and drilling holes through them for the textile industry, they could skip a step or two, leave the turnings intact, and sell them to furniture makers for chair and table parts. Using a machine-turned lathe to produce elaborate decorative ornament appealed to the Victorians' love of excess as well as their desire for efficiency. They were thrilled to create a material object in a fraction of the time—and cost—it would have taken by hand.

A BRIEF HISTORY

The first factory-turned spooling was done around 1815, but spool furniture didn't come into wide distribution until around 1850. It reached a peak over the next thirty years and continued in production into the twentieth century. Turned patterns included spools, bobbins, spirals, knots, buttons, sausages, and vase-and-ring shapes. Because of the way the machine lathes functioned, patterns tended to be repetitive and exacting, with sharp edges and pronounced rings. The style was called Elizabethan revival, and it enjoyed incredibly wide appeal in all classes. President Abraham Lincoln, in the moments following his assassination, was carried to the nearest available lodging, where reporters dutifully noted that he died in a walnut spool bed "too short for his frame."

STYLE AND CONSTRUCTION

Spool-turned furniture included beds, cribs, tables, washstands, and towel racks. Spool turnings were used in sofas, chairs, and ottomans, to support the shelves of whatnots, and as spindles in open-style canterburies. Spool-turned spindles were also split in the old half-banister style and applied as decoration to the fronts of chests of drawers.

Top-of-the-line spool furniture was made from mahogany and rosewood for drawing rooms, parlors, and libraries. It included marble-topped tables and small tables built in graduated sizes to form nesting sets. Other woods, including black walnut, maple, birch, and most notably pine, were stained to resemble the more expensive and desirable mahogany.

THE JENNY LIND BED

The spool-turned bed was one of the most popular styles of country bed ever made. When an adoring public found out that internationally famed songstress Jenny Lind slept in a spool-turned bed, it was christened with her name.

Three basic styles of spool bed were made. The first, appearing around 1830, had straight lines, spool-turned posts, and a high headboard that rose to form a

CARE TIPS

Stripping and refinishing spool-turned furniture can be extremely challenging. The many crevices and indentations are difficult to scrub out, even with a brush. A worse problem, though, is that the ball turnings expose the endgrain of the wood, which soaks up more stain than the outermost section of the ball. There are two solutions:

- Color-correct the differences when you restain, making the outer surfaces darker.

- Disassemble the furniture and put the spool-turned sections on a simple lathe. As the lathe turns, carefully sand or chisel away the ⅛ inch (3mm) of stained endgrain that's causing the trouble.

pediment. The crossrails, spindles, and pediment trim were all spool-turned, making for a rich display of form, shadow, and ornament. Around 1850, the structure became less angular, and manufacturers began offering a curved top rail that joined the post in a style resembling simple cast iron beds. A final style was fully linear, with horizontal rails and multiple vertical spindles. Because of the machine construction, spindle beds were quite affordable for working people yet still carried an aura of luxury and style. They frequently were purchased for servants and children.

STOOLS

The stool has been around since antiquity. It can stand on three or four stick legs or have two plank legs. Small stools can be made from odd pieces of wood, tree branches, or board ends left over in the workshop. Tops can be round, square, oblong, or shaped by nature, and the legs can be rounded, squared, or chamfered and they don't have to match perfectly.

The primitive slab stool, smoothed with an adze, was among the first pieces of seat furniture early settlers made for themselves. The three-legged stool, which remains stable on uneven ground or stone flooring, was commonly used for milking or open-fire cooking. More sophisticated stools, such as the four-legged joint stool, required joining and turning skills and a flair for decorative carving.

COUNTRY STOOLS

The simple country stool with three or four flared legs is constructed easily: the leg holes are bored through the seat on an angle; the legs are then inserted through the holes from the underside, wedges are driven in from the top to hold them tight, and the ends are shaved off even with the seat surface. An alternate construction is to bore partial holes and secure the legs on the underside with fox wedges. Either method makes the inevitable leg replacement easy.

Wood from apple, pear, and other smaller-growing trees frequently was "used up" on small projects such as stools, though a strong wood, like ash, was reserved for the legs. Simple country stools could have been painted but most often were left natural since they were considered expendable utilitarian furniture. An exception is Wales, where legs were painted red, and western England, where they were painted green. If the piece was to be left outdoors, the top would be painted as well.

JOINT STOOL

The seventeenth-century joint stool was a stout, sturdy oak seat with a decorative frieze that enjoyed a revival during the Victorian era. The rectangular seat was cut 1 inch (2.5cm) thick with the grain running lengthwise. It was edged with a simple molding. The four legs were decoratively turned and slightly splayed. Dowel pegs joining the seat to the frame normally showed on the surface of the seat. The bench version, called a form, was constructed the same way for use at trestle tables. Similar stools were built slightly taller in pairs to support coffins, and people in subsequent generations were loath to have them in the house as furniture. During the

OPPOSITE PAGE: A spool-turned Jenny Lind bed has a pedimented headboard. *LEFT:* A three-legged slab stool is topped with a smooth plank seat. *ABOVE:* An American colonial joint stool made around 1640 has a plain frieze.

Victorian Jacobean revival, joint stools were factory-made by the thousand. Assembly was the same, but all the cutting, drilling, and even the frieze carving was done by machine.

PLANK STOOL

The plank stool was typical of the eighteenth- and nineteenth-century folk furniture of northern and central Europe. The basic stool construction was boxlike, slightly canted, and quite simple. The sides extended down and were cut out in a triangle shape at the bottom to form legs. The overhanging plank seat was trimmed front and back with a wood apron, and often a cutout in the seat center served as a handhold. In many folk versions, the leg and apron edges were cut into scallops or curves that mimicked high society rococo styles.

TALL STOOL

Tall stools were used throughout the eighteenth and nineteenth centuries in factories, accounting and legal offices, schools, and other places of business to offer relief from standing. Workers in England's eighteenth-century workshops and factories used crudely made potter's stools with thick seats and chamfered legs. In America, clerks working at tall desks used three- or four-legged Windsor-type stools; some had built-in footrests, but on others, a stretcher had to suffice. Schoolteachers at tall desks also used stools. By the nineteenth century, tall stools were factory-made. They remain very popular today for use around kitchen breakfast bars.

ABOVE: A three-legged stool with uneven stretchers, a ball foot, and a well-worn saddle seat.

QUALITY CHECKLIST

An antique stool is a special find because, commonplace as such stools once were, they received hard use, were easily replaced, and therefore were not especially treasured.

- An old low stool should not be rejected simply because the legs look newer than the seat. Leg replacement was common on stools.

- If you plan to use a four-legged stool, always check to make sure it doesn't wobble.

- If a tall stool is presented as an antique, check the rungs for signs of wear. They probably were used as footrests and there should be some sign of gentle depression or indentation.

- Assume that joint stools offered for sale are revival pieces. Original seventeenth-century stools are distinguishable by their deep, irregular carving and warpage.

STRIPPED PINE

The honeyed warmth of stripped pine furniture is one of the most popular looks in country decorating today. Pine has never been a formal wood, and for centuries it was used solely for utilitarian pieces, painted furniture, and carcases that would be covered with veneering and overlay. Once shunned as inferior because of its grain imperfections and knots, pine is now appreciated for its natural beauty. Pine is easy to live with, especially in homes with children, pets, visitors, and lots of activity. It requires no extraordinary care or polishing, and its appearance mellows rather than suffers from the inevitable knicks, dents, and scratches.

Most of the antique pine furniture sold today is from nineteenth-century English houses. Pine was used for breakfront bookcases, library shelves, corner cupboards, kitchen dressers, and cabinets of all kinds. Late Victorian homes contained huge, solidly built pine cupboards for linens, china, crockery, and food. They featured locking drawers, bun or bracket feet, and slide-out trays.

Elegant pine furniture has also become available. These are the carcases of commodes, small desks, and bow-fronted cabinets that were once elaborately veneered or gilded. Stripped down to the bare humble pine, such furniture instantly becomes countrified yet still retains its air of nobility and prestige.

Pine can be stripped at home, but most pieces are best done professionally. The furniture is dipped into a caustic soda solution, which unfortunately eats away at the glue in the joins as well as the old paint and sealers. A good restorer will check all the joins after the stripping process is complete and reinforce any loose sections before offering the piece for sale. Caustic soda also removes patina, leaving the wood a pinky white color. Some people like this fresh-scrubbed look, but it can be mellowed out by waxing and polishing with a soft cloth.

RIGHT: Stripped of its original paint, a solid pine kitchen dresser takes on a mellow, honeyed warmth. Glazed and blind cabinets give this piece exciting decorating and storage potential.

Pickled Pine

Pickling, or liming, is a special process used to lighten or darken wood. It was originally done in the seventeenth century to darken oak, though today pickling generally refers to a lightening process. White paint is brushed onto the pine, then wiped off with a cloth within 20 to 60 minutes, before the paint has had a chance to set. The lingering white residue highlights the grain and accentuates the folds and curves of carving. Candidates for pickling include raw, sanded, stripped, or even lightly sealed woods. Pickling can also come to the rescue of a once-painted piece by evening out the mismatched tones left after stripping.

TRESTLE TABLE

THE TRESTLE TABLE WITH BENCH SEATING HAS BEEN USED IN ALL PARTS OF THE WESTERN WORLD, FROM ARISTOCRATIC HOMES TO SMALL FARMS AND PEASANT DWELLINGS. IN RURAL AREAS, IT SURVIVED INTO THE NINETEENTH CENTURY, AND REPRODUCTION LOOK-ALIKES ARE BEING MANUFACTURED TODAY.

THE TRESTLE SUPPORTS

The trestle table is a knock-down design. It calls for boards that can be assembled or disassembled quickly and that can store flat in little space when the table is not in use. These features evolved during the Middle Ages and possibly earlier, when dwellings were small and rooms were used for more than one function. The trestle table could be readily set up for eating, then just as easily dismantled and cleared away when the meal was done.

The design is simple and uncluttered. Two thick side supports—called trestles—are supported in an upright position by a long, central stretcher that runs between them. The ends of the stretcher are inserted into mortises cut through the trestles, then locked in place with removable wooden wedges or pins. Once the trestle assembly is set up, a large flat board is laid on top as the table surface.

ENGLISH I-TRESTLE DESIGN

In England, the trestles were I-shaped. A thick plank rested directly on the floor to form the foot of the trestle, a straight upright formed the vertical support, and a second horizontal plank crossed it at the top to buttress the tabletop. These three pieces were connected by mortise-and-tenon joins, and the resulting support was solid and stable. English settlers carried this design with them to America and Australia.

CONTINENTAL EUROPEAN TRESTLE DESIGN

The peasants of continental Europe developed a different trestle support that was shaped something like an inverted V. This V support was cut from a single piece of wood. It was thick and solid at the top to support the table board but branched out into two distinct legs on the floor. Legs were thick, chunky, and strong, and they were often decoratively cut for a sort of peasant rococo flourish. The connecting stretcher joined these trestles at the upper, broader section.

SAWBUCK TRESTLES

The sawbuck trestle appeared in Germany and Scandinavia and was popular among the Pennsylvania Germans and German immigrants in Australia. Two boards were notched and fitted together to form an X-shaped trestle. The joining stretcher ran through the center of each X. This base could be made permanent by nailing long boards to the trestles to create an under-the-table trough, which was used to store flatware and bread. Narrower stretchers joined the supports closer to the floor and served as footrests.

ABOVE: This knock-down sawbuck table, probably used for large gatherings, was made by German settlers in Australia in the late 1800s.
OPPOSITE PAGE: The connecting boards of this sawbuck table form an under-table trough suitable for holding flatware and napkins.

THE BOARD

Early tabletops for trestle tables were huge solid planks, cut in one piece from large trees. As Europe's virgin forests—the source of these wide boards—were destroyed, woodworkers anchored two or more narrower boards together on the underside to form the tabletop. Wide boards continued to be available in newly colonized regions, such as Australia and North America, long after European supplies were depleted. In the seventeenth century, trestle tables were commonly 12 feet (3.65m) long, but by the nineteenth century, half that length was more usual. A wide variety of woods were used, and tables generally were unpainted.

TRUNKS

The first "trunks" really were trunks—they were sections of felled trees, split and hollowed out. The bottom outer surface was hewn to lie flat, but the top "lid" remained rounded, following the natural form of the tree. Log trunks were prone to rot when placed on cold stone or dirt floors, leading to the practical solution of wooden stands to raise them up and away from the moisture. As the flat-topped chest form developed in the seventeenth and eighteenth centuries, the stand evolved into permanently attached legs.

The round-top trunk continued to be used for travel and by sailors, because rain and seawater rolled off the top curved surface. The Spanish protected their round-topped trunks with sheets of leather affixed with decorative nails, a practice they carried to their colonial territories in America. Norwegian and Swedish tradition kept the round-top trunk for storage as well as travel.

See also Chests. See also under Scandinavia— Norway, Sweden.

UNITED STATES

MANY RICH TRADITIONS HAVE CONTRIBUTED TO THE
COUNTRY FURNITURE OF THE UNITED STATES. THE
AMERICAN STYLE IS ROOTED IN THE FURNITURE FORMS OF
THE EARLY ENGLISH COLONISTS. ENGLISH-MADE BOARD
CHESTS, I-BEAM TRESTLE TABLES, SETTLES, BENCHES, AND
CUPBOARDS HAVE BEEN INFLUENCING THE AMERICAN
TRADITION FOR OVER THREE HUNDRED YEARS. PIONEERS
AND SETTLERS FROM OTHER COUNTRIES FOUND THESE
STYLES EASY TO COPY AND ADDED THEIR OWN FLOURISHES,
SUCH AS DECORATIVE PAINTING AND SCALLOPED EDGES.
THE INFLUENCES OF DUTCH AND GERMAN SETTLERS
WERE ESPECIALLY STRONG.

OPPOSITE PAGE, TOP: Thick trestles, decoratively shaped in the continental
European tradition, support a long tabletop made of tongue-in-groove
planks. A protruding stretcher is visible in the foreground. *OPPOSITE
PAGE, BOTTOM:* Rosemaling and ornamental metal banding decorate this
Norwegian trunk with curved lid. *ABOVE:* A banister-back chair, slat-
back armchair, Windsor chairs, gateleg table, and fireplace settle are
among the American colonial pieces represented in this inviting living
room.

In the nineteenth century, America grew more
industrialized, and factories began producing furniture.
This furniture was purchased by people of all classes as
well as by newly arriving immigrants who wanted to
"feel" American right away. By mid-century, American
factories were shipping furniture all over the country
(and also to other countries, such as Australia). Such
widespread marketing helped to diminish regional
differences, and within one generation or less, many
immigrant groups were ordering all their new furniture
from the mail-order catalog.

In the early twentieth century, interest in America's
colonial past was reawakened. It led to historic preservation projects, such as Colonial Williamsburg in
Virginia, Dearborn Village in Michigan, and many other
smaller historic sites. This in turn promoted a lively
antiques market in colonial furniture, such as the
Windsor chair and the gateleg table. Reproduction
furniture made during this period also emphasized
colonial styles. Over time, historians, collectors, and
dealers began sorting out the rich legacy of other

American-made regional furniture. In the late twentieth century, these regional styles and their continental European origins are being rediscovered, researched, and appreciated once again.

Note: Many of the individual encyclopedic entries describe furniture made in the United States. See especially Adirondack Chair; Arrow-Back Chair; Cottage Furniture; Golden Oak; Hitchcock Chair; Mission Oak; New Mexico; Rocking Chairs; Sheraton-Style Fancy Chairs; Spool Furniture; Windsor Chairs. See also under Germany, Austria, and Switzerland—Pennsylvania Germans, Texas Germans.

VICTORIAN ERA FURNITURE

QUEEN VICTORIA'S RULE OVER GREAT BRITAIN LASTED FROM 1837 TO 1901, A TIME OF TREMENDOUS SOCIAL AND ECONOMIC CHANGE. FURNITURE MADE DURING THIS PERIOD IS EASY TO RECOGNIZE, YET HARD TO DEFINE SUCCINCTLY. IT COVERS A RANGE OF STYLES, FROM ORNATE AND CURVED TO PLAIN AND RECTILINEAR. THE UNIFYING ELEMENT BEHIND THE DIVERSITY IS MACHINE-POWERED TOOLS. WATER, STEAM, AND COAL POWER REVOLUTIONIZED THE WAY FURNITURE WAS CONSTRUCTED, MARKETED, AND ULTIMATELY DESIGNED. THE NEW CAPABILITIES UNLEASHED A TORRENT OF FURNITURE MANUFACTURING, PARTICULARLY IN AMERICA.

The first impulse to emerge from the new manufacturing methods was to re-create elite furniture from the past, substituting machine methods for expensive hand carving and joining techniques. The rising middle classes, giddy with the possibilities for improving their social status, were delighted to be able to purchase factory-made furniture in a variety of historical and romantic styles. Ordinary citizens found themselves sitting in upholstered chairs that just a few centuries earlier would have been reserved for a king.

In the United States, Canada, and Australia, where so many people were immigrants, furnishings that suggested an "instant" social lineage were enormously popular. The Victorians' fantasies about life in the past led them to Gothic cathedrals, classic Rome and Greece, opulent Renaissance estates, and the French court for design ideas. Finally, in a gasp of exhaustion, they turned to the straight rectilinear styles of Charles Eastlake and the Arts and Crafts movement. It was in these later styles that the crisp clarity and beauty of machine-planed surfaces came to be appreciated, and the modern sensibility was born.

Whether or not to consider Victorian furniture "country" is largely up to the taste and preferences of the beholder. In many country decorating schemes, the odd Victorian piece can provide just the touch of whimsy or eccentricity that is needed to keep the room relaxed and informal. Dark Gothic chairs and bookcases can be painted white and combined with chintz cushions or curtains for a country cottage look. Victorian furniture generally works well in an eclectic mix, and Victorian wicker will lighten the look.

"COUNTRY" VICTORIAN FAVORITES

In addition to numerous furniture styles, the Victorian era produced special furniture forms to suit the nineteenth-century lifestyle. Yesteryear's homes were

built differently than those of today, and the furniture needs were different. Wardrobes and washstands, for example, were essential in houses without closets or indoor plumbing. Today, these pieces can add a charming informal accent precisely because they reflect the mood of another era.

CLOSET SUBSTITUTES

Two serviceable pieces of furniture solved the bulk of the Victorian clothing storage problem. For outerwear, there was the enormous hall tree. Much more than a simple freestanding coatrack, it could include a mirror, small table, drawers, a built-in seat with lift-up lid, an umbrella stand, and even shelves for potted plants. Outer clothing was hung on wooden pegs, gloves went in the drawer, and galoshes went under the seat. Eventually, the wooden knobs were replaced by brass hooks, and by mid-century, cast iron ornamental grillwork was added.

In the upstairs bedrooms, wardrobes took the place of closets. The wardrobe is an enormous clothes cupboard that takes its name from an Old French word meaning "guard robe." The Victorian era wardrobe ranged from plain to fancy in design and woods. It might incorporate mirrored doors, interior drawers and shelves, hat and glove compartments, or a low bank of drawers beneath an upper cupboard. Some wardrobes opened to reveal a bank of drawers down the center, with hanging space on either side.

Mail-order catalogs offered wardrobes that could be knocked down and shipped flat. Wardrobes also came en suite with other bedroom furnishings, such as dressing tables, washstands, and beds. In all wardrobes, the clothes were hung facing forward—the space was simply not deep enough for the sideways hanging used in modern closets. Today, people often fit the interior of old wardrobes with shelving for audio and video equipment and recordings.

ABOVE LEFT: A huge wardrobe, bedstead, writing desk, washstand with mirror, and assorted chairs fill this Victorian bedroom to overflowing. Any one of these furnishings could be used to dramatic effect in a country-style interior.

THE CLUTTER PROBLEM

It makes sense that the Victorian era, which produced an increasing amount of material ornaments and souvenirs, would also come up with the furniture to display them. The great manufacturing binge of the Victorian age was targeted, ultimately, at the consumer. All kinds of manufactured products entered the Victorian middle-class home, from sentimental knickknacks, bibelots, and curiosities to greeting cards. Everyone faced the same problem: where to put them.

The quintessential Victorian display piece is the whatnot. The basic unit featured a series of open shelves supported by turned spindles or scroll-cut brackets. Many variations were made. The shelves could be the same size or tiered, and the unit could be rectangular, square, or triangular, to fit into a corner. People displayed anything they wanted on them—figurines, decorative pottery, vases of flowers, birthday cards, dishes of candy, books, and sewing supplies. In Australia, a popular turn-of-the-century craft was to build whatnots using empty wooden thread spools as the supports. Wicker and bamboo whatnots work well in contemporary bathrooms as towel racks.

For magazines, newspapers, and sheet music, the Victorians revived the eighteenth-century canterbury.

This low two-section rack sat on the floor and was typically found next to the piano or easy chair. Canterburies were made in many materials—wood, wicker, iron, bamboo—and were as common in Victorian era homes as televisions are today. As middle-class citizens began to join reading societies, subscribe to magazines, and register their children for music lessons, a practical stand to contain their cultural paraphernalia became most welcome.

The late-century Victorian parlor would not be considered complete without its potted palm plant. All kinds of stands were made specifically to hold palms. They ranged from plaster or marble columns to wood tables with three or four legs. The tropical ambiance is just as effective today, and many old palm stands are back in service.

THE VICTORIAN WASHSTAND

Before homes had bathroom sinks with built-in vanities, every bedroom had its own washstand. This piece of furniture was considered so essential, it was sold as part of a bedroom suite. The washstand was used for face and hand washing, shaving, tooth brushing, and moustache waxing. A basin placed on top of the stand was filled with fresh water from a pitcher. Some washstands have a circular hole cut in the top so that the basin is held snugly and doesn't slip. A marble or tile splash board, attached tilting mirror, and side towel bars all show thoughtful attentiveness to the washstand's function.

See also Wicker Furniture.

LEFT: A mail-order washstand provides Victorian era ambiance in an old house that has since been renovated to include plumbing.

An overview of Victorian furniture styles

Name	Dates Made	Identifying Characteristics
Early Victorian	1840-1866	Ostentatious, elaborate baroque elements with undulating curves; cabriole legs; realistic high-relief machine carving; marble tabletops.
Gothic	1840-1870	Pointed arches on chair backs, paneling, and glazed doors; tall, complex spires and finials; rectilinear forms; dark woods; some spool turnings; architectural built-ins.
Spool Furniture*	1850-1880	Machine-made spindles with turnings resembling sewing thread spools. Turnings were used for bedframes, shelf supports. Pine most common though fine-quality spool furniture was made of mahogany. Other woods include maple and birch.
Cottage Furniture*	1845-1890+	Simple utilitarian design and construction in pine, usually with painted finish. Matching bedroom suites very popular. Washstands with outward curving aprons to hold side towel bars show Empire influence.
Louis XV	1845-1875	Curvilinear shapes, cabriole legs, machine dowel-and-glue construction instead of mortise-and-tenon joins. Parlor suites with matching upholstered sofas and chairs very popular.
Renaissance	1855-1875	Tall arched pediments; machine-carved wood drawer pulls; circular marble-topped parlor tables; bedroom chests with handkerchief drawers and tilting mirrors; tall, massive headboards.
Louis XVI	1865-1875	Rectilinear design. Upholstered chairs have straight legs, open arms, H-stretchers. Burl panels popular instead of carving.
Eastlake	1870-1890	Uncluttered rectilinear design with pronounced absence of curves; shallow linear machine-incising; thin door panels; circular-cut dovetails.
Golden Oak*	1895-1910	Curvilinear with American colonial look. Typical pieces include large round tables, rolltop desks, pressed back chairs. Thin backboards; no dovetailing.
Mission Oak*	1900-1920	A "modern Gothic" style in dark wood. Geometric with vertical emphasis; little ornamentation; unconcealed round-head screws.

*See individual encyclopedia entry

WICKER FURNITURE

WICKER FURNITURE HAS BEEN FAVORED SINCE VICTORIAN TIMES FOR ITS GARDEN-FRESH LOOK AND ITS ABILITY TO BRING THE OUTDOORS IN. THE TERM "WICKER" CAN REFER TO RATTAN, WILLOW, REED, RUSH, GRASS, AND PAPER FIBER. THE TYPE OF FIBER DETERMINES THE DESIGN POSSIBILITIES, WHICH RANGE FROM ELABORATE, SCROLLED CURLICUES TO SMOOTH, EVENLY LOOMED SURFACES. VICTORIAN ERA WICKER COMBINES SEVERAL DIFFERENT FIBERS FOR LOTS OF DESIGN ACTIVITY AND CONTRAST. EARLY TWENTIETH-CENTURY WICKER IS MORE STRAIGHT-FORWARD AND MIMICS MISSION OAK FURNITURE. WICKER DIPPED IN POPULARITY BRIEFLY BETWEEN 1930 AND 1960, BUT IT HAS BEEN ON THE RISE EVER SINCE. IT IS A FAVORITE FOR COUNTRY DECORATING.

A BRIEF HISTORY

Victorian era wicker is a product of industrialized America. Cyrus Wakefield, a Boston grocer, developed the first large-scale wicker manufacturing operation. His odyssey began one day in 1844, when he joined in with a group of workers who were clearing the city wharves of rattan. This packing material had been discarded as waste by newly arrived cargo ships from the Far East. The rattan intrigued him, so he brought some home so that he could experiment with it. He tried wrapping it around an old wood chair frame and recognized its potential for furniture making. Soon he was jobbing in rattan and cane. Cane is the outer shell of the rattan reed and was used for caning chair seats. In 1855, he opened his own firm, the Wakefield Rattan Company, in South Reading, Massachusetts. In addition to furniture, his company produced woven floor coverings, window shades, and caned seats for railroad and trolley cars.

The Wakefield Company grew rapidly, with branch offices as far away as San Francisco. Its chief competitor was Heywood Brothers and Company, a long-standing chair manufacturer that had entered the wicker market. Heywood was making profitable sales from its machine-woven sheet cane that could be slotted into wood seats, eliminating hand caning. There were many other smaller manufacturers as well, and by the late 1880s, Sears, Roebuck and Co. and the Montgomery Ward Company were featuring their own wicker products in their mail-order catalogs. Finally, just before the turn of the century, the two giants, Wakefield and Heywood, merged into one company.

The early part of the twentieth century saw a major shift in all furniture design, including wicker. In reaction to the Victorian excess, wicker designed in Austria and Germany assumed a more angular, less flexible look. The exception was English wicker, called cane furniture, which featured graceful curves and had an art nouveau quality. To cut labor costs, American manufacturers introduced a more open weave that came to be known as the Bar Harbor style. A final innovation was Marshall B. Lloyd's 1917 invention of a power loom that wove sheets of wickerlike paper fiber. Workers then fitted the material over wooden furniture frames, which saved hours of hand-weaving time.

DESIGN AND CONSTRUCTION

Almost all Western-made wicker furniture, no matter how ornate the pattern, has three basic components: the frame, the spokes, and the fibers. The frame is built of sturdy hardwood, the spokes are added on to suggest the basic form, and finally the fibers are woven over and under the spokes to fill in the spaces and create solid surfaces. At first, only the shiny outer shell of the rattan was used for weaving, and the inner pith, called reed, was discarded. Once a machine was developed that could split the rattan and draw out the reed, it too was used. Manufacturers liked reed because it was more pliable

LEFT: Reproduction wicker furniture includes chairs with rolled backs and armrests and pineapple feet.

and easier to handle, and the public adored it because, unlike cane, it could be painted.

Most of the wicker made before 1880 was intended for indoor use. Pieces included an extraordinary array of chairs, settees, tables, stands, and rockers. Designs featured scrolling, curlicues, and serpentine shapes, and the exuberant eclecticism spoke to the Victorian imagination. The furniture was both safe and mysterious: it was airy and open, which was considered sanitary and healthful, but the exotic patterns suggested faraway, forbidden places. Early twentieth-century wicker was more simply designed, both to follow the style of the day and to cut down on manufacturing costs. Most of the wicker made today is in this plainer style and is intended for both indoor and outdoor porch use.

RECOGNIZING WICKER STYLES

Not all wicker is from the Victorian era. The following are some of the various styles the collector may encounter:

American Victorian era wicker is best recognized by its exuberance and vitality. Some identifying characteristics to look for are a variety of materials and design motifs, curved or serpentine shaping, close tight

weaving in ornate shapes, and asymmetrical design. Key manufacturer's labels are Wakefield and Heywood.

English cane furniture of the early twentieth century has an overall sculpted look. It is characterized by fluid lines, full to-the-floor skirts, and rounded backs. Strong ash frames are woven with unbleached willow, and nails and tacks are conspicuously absent. Key manufacturer's labels are Dryad, Ellmore, Angraves, and Casdons.

Austrian and German wicker of the early twentieth century features straight, severe, geometric silhouettes. The seats may be hard and require cushions. The ivory white willow will have aged to a soft golden glow. Key

QUALITY CHECKLIST

- Natural wicker is a rare find and should not be painted. If you really want a painted piece, keep shopping and leave the natural wicker to another buyer.

- Don't reject an old wicker piece that needs minor repairs. Replacing broken spokes and reweaving small areas are not difficult for the novice. There are many excellent, illustrated sources that can walk you through the steps and suggest sources for supplies.

CARE TIPS

- Wicker made of reed and willow can be safely washed with warm soapy water and a soft brush, then rinsed off with a garden hose. If the wicker is especially brittle, the water will help to restore moisture.

- Wicker made of paper fiber, such as Lloyd loom wicker, can be vacuumed or sponged clean. Avoid getting it soaking wet as this will weaken or even destroy the fibers.

manufacturer's labels are Prag-Rudmiker, Ludwig Sild, Julius Moser, Derichs + Saverteig, and Theodor Reimann.

American "Bar Harbor" wicker mimics the straightforward lines of Mission-style furniture, though it does incorporate softer features, like softly rounded corners, built-in magazine pockets, and pineapple feet. Large-diameter reed is used for a symmetrical, open, and diamondlike weave. Armrests are broad and flat, and the wood seats require cushions.

American Lloyd loom wicker has a generally boxy silhouette that is softened by gentle curves. The weave is plain and even, with woven-in diamond patterns in chair and settee backs. Nails are visible where the machine-woven paper fiber is attached to the frame.

Far East wicker is lightweight because it has a bamboo or rattan framework instead of a heavier hardwood frame. Seats are typically circular and woven of reed. The reeds tend to be fibrous and brittle.

WINDSOR CHAIRS

The spindle-back Windsor chair is the most popular hand-built chair ever known. It is a true country chair, made in the tradition of English wheelwrights. It was a natural product of the American colonies with their rich forests of green wood waiting to be cleared for farming. The many diverse forms of the Windsor spread throughout the British Empire. In the nineteenth century, the familiar, sturdy construction was echoed in factory-made chairs sold worldwide.

OPPOSITE PAGE: New wicker furniture made for the contemporary market revives yesteryear's signature features: rolled arms and backrests, sturdy hardwood frames, and open, airy filigree insets. *ABOVE:* Two American sack-back Windsor chairs feature sloping arms and H-shaped stretchers.

A BRIEF HISTORY

As early as the sixteenth century, wheelwrights in England's Berkshire district may have begun their experimental chair making. They coped out chair spindles in the same way they made wheel spokes. Hard, flexible woods like ash were soaked and bent into rounded chair backs. By the early eighteenth century, steam bending and peg boards were in use. A length of wood could be repeatedly steamed, bent, and held in shape on a peg board until dry. After each steaming, the wood was coaxed to bend a bit further and the pegs were moved to their new position on the board. The first chairs made this way were shipped from the town of Windsor to London in 1724, offering one theory as to how the chair got its name.

Windsor chairs were traditionally inexpensive—just a few shillings in eighteenth-century America—because they were so readily constructed from surplus woods. The Windsor chair appealed to people of every social class and marked the final transition to a period when everyone, not only the wealthy, could enjoy the ease of sitting in a chair.

Windsors were good-looking, sturdy, and comfortable. The splayed legs made them virtually tip-free, and the H- and crinoline stretcher configurations allowed people to bend their knees and tuck their feet under the chair. Seats were wide or had arms reaching just halfway around, to accommodate ample skirts and coats. In England, arms were flat on top and wide enough to hold

a tankard of ale. Since each spindle and turning was made as thin as possible, Windsors were light in weight and easy to lift. In pre- and post-Revolutionary America, Windsors were used in gardens, porches, townhomes, and farmhouses and were exported to the West Indies. Records show that chair maker Frances Trumble supplied the Pennsylvania State House (now Independence Hall) with 114 Windsors between 1776 and 1778. Settees as well as individual chairs were ordered for courthouses and public buildings.

By the early nineteenth century, as craftsmen migrated to new areas, American regional styles became less clear-cut and the chairs became heavier and less graceful. They soon lost favor to decoratively painted factory-made chairs. In England, the Windsor lingered a bit longer. Green- and white-painted Windsors dotted England's parks through the mid-1800s, and wheelback and yew tree Windsors continued to be made in huge dining rooms sets of up to twelve chairs.

DESIGN AND CONSTRUCTION

The method of making a Windsor chair is called "stick construction" because all the parts, except for the seat, are sticks. The legs and stretchers can be decoratively turned, but the sticks forming the backrest of the chair are smooth and plain. They were cut from dense, springy hardwoods, such as hickory, that could be shaved without splintering. The thin, green sticks were held in one hand and trimmed and shaped with the

other using a knife. They could also be secured in a clamp and trimmed with a drawshave. It was nearly impossible to use a lathe as the thin, flexible sticks would spin about like a whip.

The backrests of American Windsors almost always have an odd number of spindles—a center spindle with an equal number on each side. Up to eleven spindles can be found on eighteenth-century side chairs, though a count of nine is acceptable to most collectors. Generally, the thinner and more numerous the spindles, the older the chair. Sometimes the two outer spindles are thicker and turned instead of slender and straight. English-made Windsors feature a center cutwork splat flanked by spindles on either side.

The seat was hewn from soft, knot-free pine or poplar, then hollowed out into a comfortable contour for sitting. Soft woods were chosen because they were easier to work and did not warp. Legs and stretchers were turned from harder, stronger woods, including maple, birch, ash, chestnut, and cherry. To attach the legs, the chair maker bored angled holes in the seat underside. Using green wood for both seat and legs and dry seasoned wood for the wedges and stretchers ensured a good, tight join as the new wood shrank. Later, in the nineteenth century, glue was applied to strengthen these joins.

The finished chairs were painted rather than stained to conceal the fact that they were constructed from several different woods. Dark green and white were the most popular colors, but red, brown, black, and yellow were also used.

AMERICAN WINDSORS

Eighteenth-century American Windsors chairs were characterized by their lightweight look, delicate spindles, and different backrest configurations. The basic styles are low-back, loop-back, and fan-back. Other variations included long Windsor settees and writing armchairs, complete with small drawers built in under the seat or desk. They became the prototype for the writing desks used today in schools worldwide.

LOW-BACK VARIATIONS

The low-back Windsor was first made in Philadelphia around 1740 and had become popular with New Jersey and New York chair makers by 1780. It is recognized by the low semicircular rail that serves as both chair back and arms. This rail was supported by vertical spindles arranged in a U shape around the edge of the seat.

To give the low-back chair a headrest, the chair maker cut the center spindles longer and let them extend up beyond the rail. Capping them with a horizontal crest created the comb-back Windsor. In another style, called the sack back, the spindles were cut in an arc and a bowed piece was fitted over them. The ends of this bowed piece were socketed into the main rail, which gave the chair back a lovely graceful arch.

OPPOSITE PAGE: American comb-back rocker, high comb-back, and fan-back Windsor chairs. *ABOVE:* American continuous arm, sack-back, and loop-back Windsor chairs.

LOOP BACK VARIATIONS

The loop-back Windsor first appeared in England in the 1780s. It was the next logical chairmaking attempt after the sack back. Here, the arch was radically bent in a deep U shape that joins directly into the chair seat. The continuous arm style was a variation on this idea. It featured an arched back and arms steam-bent from one piece of wood. The method was perfected by a New York chair maker in the 1780s and continued in production in New England through 1810. The style was very popular despite the fact that the double curve created unusual stress on the wood, causing breakage. Interestingly, Philadelphia chair makers, guardians of the Windsor tradition, never picked up on this style.

THE FAN BACK

The fan-back Windsor gets its name from the tall spindles that splay out from the chair seat in a fan shape. They join into a crest rail that is shaped like a cupid's bow. The seat of the fan-back chair is often narrower with a slight wedge shape, and the legs have a

pronounced splay. Two diagonal bracing sticks often were built in to give extra support when a person leaned back against the spindles. The fan back is the forerunner of rod back, arrow-back, and other nineteenth-century wooden kitchen chairs.

ENGLISH WINDSORS

English Windsor chairs often were made from yew. This flexible wood was used in the Middle Ages for England's famous longbows. Although the Windsor chair originated in England, the chairs built there never attained the grace and lightness of the American chairs. Instead, they were stronger and heftier-looking, with center splats, turned legs, and crinoline stretchers.

The center splat was wide and decorated with cutout designs near the top. The most popular was a wheel cutout. Other motifs included gothic arches, Prince of

---

ABOVE LEFT: A sack-back English Windsor armchair with cutwork splat. The turned legs are joined by a U-shaped crinoline stretcher. *ABOVE RIGHT:* A comb-back English Windsor with graceful cabriole front legs.

Wales feathers, tulips, and vases. Some chairs used three narrow splats instead of one large splat. Yew tree Windsors had cabriole or turned legs and a high hoop back.

Early in the nineteenth century, a totally new stick Windsor appeared. It was called the rod-back or birdcage Windsor. All the back posts, crest rails, legs, and spindles were shaped to resemble rods of bamboo and were joined at right angles. This style also appeared in America, where it was painted and striped.

NINETEENTH-CENTURY WINDSOR STYLES

In the nineteenth century, American factories began to produce Windsor-style chairs. Machine lathes turned thicker, uniform spindles, and steam-bending produced curved crest rails and rolled-down arms with ease. These new Windsors were thicker and chunkier all around, with far fewer spindles, but their origins were clear.

Factory variations of the low-back Windsor all featured a deep crest with center cutout handhold. They included the Douglas chair, used in western states in mid-century, the firehouse Windsor, which had a crinoline stretcher, and the late Victorian era captain's chair, which could have a caned or saddled seat. The captain's chair was frequently used in offices and pubs and today is seen in informal restaurants.

Another factory-made Windsor is the lath-back chair. Instead of shaved or turned spindles, this Windsor variation uses flat laths, about 1 inch (2.5cm) wide. The laths are cut from a flexible wood, such as beech, and are gently steam-shaped to conform to the user's back. This style continued to appear on porch rockers and settees into the early twentieth century.

See also Arrow-Back Chair. See also under Australia—Stick and Slab Furniture, Peddle Chair; The British Isles—Ireland.

WOODS

Country furniture makers used both hardwoods and softwoods. They almost always used woods that were available locally. Hardwoods were chosen for their strength, carving possibilities, and sometimes even their flexibility. Pine is an abundant softwood and was often chosen for furniture to be painted. The following chart provides an overview of the various woods country furniture makers have favored over the centuries. It describes the color and grain of each wood and where the wood was found. The chart is a beginner's guide to recognizing and appreciating the many woods encountered in antique as well as reproduction country furniture.

QUALITY CHECKLIST

- Examine the spindles of hand-built American Windsor chairs carefully. Thinner spindles show greater craftsmanship. The spindles should appear to be of uniform width upon first glance but should also reveal the irregularities of hand shaving upon close inspection. They may be slightly thicker at the bottom where the woodworker held the stick for shaving.

- American regional variations can be picked out in the legs and seat. Legs ending in a small ball foot are in the Philadelphia and New York style. Tapered legs without a foot are in the New England style. Round seat hollows were made in Connecticut. A U-shaped saddle seat shows northern New England origins.

- English yew tree Windsors often were made in large sets, though these are difficult to assemble today. Affordable substitutes are twentieth-century wheel-back look-alikes, manufactured in quantity between 1920 and 1935 for tearooms and restaurants.

COUNTRY FURNITURE WOODS

HARDWOODS

WOOD	COLOR	GRAIN	WHERE FOUND
ALDER	Pinkish brown; darkens upon exposure to golden or reddish tan.	Straight, smooth textured; can be knotted or figured.	Northern Europe, including British Isles, Scandinavia.
ALPINE ASH	Pinkish to yellowish brown.	Straight, dense, oaklike.	Tasmanian mountains, eastern Victoria, south-eastern New South Wales.
APPLE	Pinkish to reddish tan.	Fine, almost invisible grain.	Europe, North America.
ASH	Pale creamy white to light honey to pinkish brown.	Straight, dense, oaklike; can be wavy and irregular; unpronounced pores.	Europe, North America. European ash exported to Australia.
BASSWOOD	Pale and creamy to brownish yellow.	Straight, even-textured; rarely figured.	North America.
BEECH	Pale white to light brown; occasionally pink.	Straight, dense, even-textured, with characteristic brown flecks.	Europe. Exported to Australia.
BIRCH	Pale cream to light yellowish brown tinged with pink or red.	Close-grained, well-figured, varies from straight to undulating (flame birch). Curly grain easily mistaken for maple.	Europe, North America, Asia. American birch exported to England in late 18th century.
BLACKWOOD	Golden brown with dark streaks and black flecks.	Straight with occasional knots.	Australia.
BOTANY BAY WOOD	Deep pink to rich red-brown with darker flecks, so wood resembles salted beef.	Fine, uniform grain.	Australia, especially New South Wales.
BUTTERNUT	Very light brown.	Open-grained with large pores.	North America, especially Ontario to Maryland and west.
CAMPHOR-WOOD	Grayish yellow to brown.	Close, even grain.	Southeast Asia, northern New South Wales, southern Queensland rain forests.

TYPICAL USES

SPECIAL NOTES

Chairs, table legs, small cabinets.

Good for turning. Impervious to damp.

Australian settlers' primitive and country pieces.

Also called Tasmanian oak. Belongs to Eucalyptus genus.

Chair stretchers, legs, spindles; small boxes; tables; stools. Occasionally for case pieces, e.g., slant-front desks and French provincial armoires. Given natural finish when used for Boston rocker arms.

Too hard for carving though good for turning. Wood obtained mostly when old apple trees or limbs are cut down. Wax or linseed oil finish brings out beauty.

Spindle-, banister-, and slat-back chairs; straight "broomstick" chair legs; Windsor chair legs, sticks, hoops, and seats; stools and tabletops; bedposts; rustic furniture; turned legs for cottage chairs; late Victorian cottage bedroom suites; Golden Oak furniture.

Very strong yet lightweight, supple, and springy. Bends well when steamed; easy to cut. Pleasant smell for drawer and wardrobe interiors.

Chair seats, painted chests and desks, Victorian era drawer bottoms and backboards.

Soft, but harder than pine. Resembles poplar. Takes stain well.

Chair legs, Windsor chair hoops, Scandinavian painted furniture, Thonet bentwood furniture. In Australia, stained or painted to imitate expensive woods.

Moderately hard and strong, lightweight, springy, difficult to split. Excellent for turning. Takes a water-base stain without raising grain.

Turnings, chair legs, painted furniture. Curly grained variety used for colonial American and Canadian tabletops, drawer fronts, and skirts on all-birch pieces. In North America, stained to resemble mahogany and walnut. Bark used as veneer on rustic furniture.

"Poor man's walnut." Preferred in Maine and New Hampshire over maple. Excellent for imitating cherry. Stain brings out curly figure.

Chair legs, spindles, fiddleback splats; supports for pedestal and conventional dining tables.

Turns well. Takes an excellent polish.

Table legs and chests.

Also called beefwood, forest oak, river oak, she-oak, and swamp oak. One of the most important woods used by Australian colonial cabinetmakers.

Used by pioneer settlers in America and Canada for chests of drawers, tables, desks, cupboards. Used in combination with figured maple.

Also called white walnut. Favored by Norwegian immigrants to America.

Clothes chests and trunks used by Australian colonists.

Also called black sassafras. Species of cinnamon with distinctive moth-repellent odor.

WOOD	COLOR	GRAIN	WHERE FOUND
CHERRY	Attractive reddish or pinkish brown.	Close-grained, even-textured.	Europe, North America.
CHESTNUT	Warm, mellow yellowish brown, aging to medium brown.	Straight, oaklike, though more even, open-pored.	Europe, North America.
ELM	Pale reddish brown that darkens with age; similar to oak.	Handsome, broad, coarse grain with dark figuring.	Europe, North America, Asia. Great Britain exported to Australia.
FRUITWOOD	See Apple, Cherry, Pear.		
GUMWOOD	Rich, deep red-brown.	Coarse texture with figures and curls.	Australia.
HICKORY	White to cream with inconspicuous fine brown lines, tan heartwood.	Straight, open grain with long pores.	North America.
MAPLE	White or light brownish yellow aging to a rich honey amber.	Close, handsome grain; can be straight, curly (tiger striping), bird's-eye, blistered, or quilted.	North America, especially New England. A favorite in Massachusetts.
OAK	When freshly cut, color varies from pale cream or grayish white to dark pinkish brown; upon exposure, darkens to warm brown.	Coarse-grained, open-pored; quarter sawing produces distinctive tiger stripe pattern.	Europe, North America. Used widely in England, northern France.
PEAR	Pinkish with darker flecks; lighter than cherry.	Fine-grained.	Cultivated in France, Germany, Switzerland, the Tyrol.
POPLAR	Canary-colored with a slight greenish gray cast.	Close-grained,	North America.
SYCAMORE	Light in color; called harewood when stained gray.	Fine, even-textured; quarter cut produces iridescent sheen.	Europe.
WALNUT	Rich, golden brown with darker figure.	Straight grain, medium-coarse, uniform texture.	Europe, North America. France banned exports after 1720.
WILLOW	Pinkish white to reddish tan.	Straight, fine-textured.	Europe, North America.

TYPICAL USES

French provincial armoires and buffets. American butterfly tables, chests of drawers, tables, Boston rocker arms. Often substituted for mahogany, especially in Connecticut but also in Pennsylvania, Virginia, Kentucky, New York.

French provincial armoires, buffets, and chairs; tables, stool tops; also concealed structural elements in chests of drawers, beds, sofas in 19th-century America.

Dressers, tabletops, stool tops, Windsor chair seats, rustic furniture, coffins. Used in combination with oak in case furniture.

Settlers' rough hewn slab stools and tables, primitive stick chairs; slabs are hollowed out on underside to lighten weight. Also, straight tapered legs of more refined furniture.

Spindles for American Windsor chairs and Boston rockers, bent parts of Windsor chairs, rustic furniture.

Banister-back chairs, cupboards, cradles, four-poster beds, gateleg tables, also underframing.

Armoires and buffets in northern France. Tables and tabletops, stool tops, trestle table bases, four-poster beds, chests, dressers, settles, cupboards, chair spindles in Great Britain and North America. Regained popularity in late 19th–early 20th centuries in Golden Oak and Mission Oak furniture.

Small pieces of country furniture. Carving on armoires, picture and mirror frames, clock brackets.

Windsor chair seats, dressers, cupboards, blanket chests, backboards, chairs in Connecticut. In 20th century, used for inexpensive cupboards, William and Mary revival furniture with walnut stain.

Kitchen tabletops, dairy furniture, kitchen and dairy utensils.

French provincial armoires, buffets, and chairs, especially in southern provinces. Also early Victorian furniture.

Turnings, steam-bent chair backs, bentwood furniture, rustic twig furniture.

SPECIAL NOTES

Hard, strong, ideal for carving and turning. Sometimes confused with mahogany. Does not warp.

Similar in appearance to oak but not as strong or hard-wearing.

Susceptible to worm. Does not split or crack but tends to warp with changes in humidity. In England, as popular as oak for country furniture.

Also called bloodwood. Splinters easily, difficult to turn on lathe, so generally avoided by fine cabinetmakers. Surface rubs to smooth, mellow finish.

Tough and springy. Used for furniture parts needing strength without heaviness. A bit splintery.

Hard, strong, tough, difficult to cut. Doesn't readily warp. Used as an inexpensive substitute for walnut and mahogany. Maple furniture by anonymous rural cabinetmakers is highly valued today.

Difficult to carve. English oak trees took 150–200 years to mature. Felled trees were left in streams to season for one to two years before milling.

Can be stained black to imitate ebony.

Also called yellow poplar, whitewood, and tulip tree. Inexpensive alternative to beech and maple.

Same genus (Acer) as North American maple. Heavy scrubbing does not raise grain.

Easily worked and carved; readily available and inexpensive until 20th century. Replaced by oak in popularity during late Victorian period.

Steam-bends well.

COUNTRY FURNITURE WOODS

SOFTWOODS

WOOD	COLOR	GRAIN	WHERE FOUND
CEDAR	Reddish brown to creamy white, depending on variety.	Moderately coarse, uneven.	Europe, North America.
HOOP PINE	Pale, creamy yellow.	Straight; fine, close texture; growth rings not conspicuous.	Australia. Grows to 200 feet in Queensland rain forests.
HUON PINE	Pale, creamy yellow, darkens to rich honey color.	Generally straight with very fine, close growth rings; small bird's-eye knots.	Tasmania. Shipped to Australia.
KAURI PINE	Cream-colored.	Straight, compressed, without visible growth rings.	New Zealand. Grows to 120 feet with trunks up to 15 feet in diameter; heavily harvested for importation by Australia during 19th-century boom years.
PONDEROSA PINE	Nearly white to pale yellowish.	Straight grain, evenly or unevenly spaced, with distinct growth rings.	Western North America, especially Rocky Mountains from Canada to Mexico.
SCOTCH PINE	Soft white to creamy yellow tinged with pink.	Broad, open, with prominent growth rings.	Northern Europe. Packed as ballast in ships bound for Australia, where it was salvaged for furniture making.
WESTERN RED CEDAR	Soft, pinkish brown.	Straight with prominent dark growth rings.	Western seaboard of North America.
WHITE PINE	Pale cream darkens with age to honey.	No visible grain or pores. Some characteristic knots.	Eastern North America, especially New England.
YELLOW PINE	Yellow with black.	Prominent grain.	Short-leaf varieties found in New Jersey, Pennsylvania, Virginia; long-leaf in American South.
YEW	Reddish golden brown heartwood with nearly white sapwood that darkens after exposure.	Close, fine, somewhat wavy, even-textured, with natural knots and whorls.	Europe; especially valued in England.

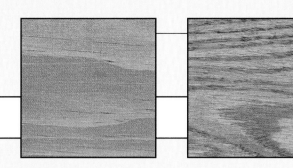

TYPICAL USES

Chests, small boxes, rustic furniture. Most often set aside for chest and drawer linings.

Kitchen dressers, sideboards, tables, meat safes, inexpensive utilitarian furniture, linings, skirtings; also flooring, doors.

Wardrobes, chests of drawers, bedroom furniture.

Cottage and kitchen furniture.

New Mexico *carpintero*-built furniture, 16th–19th centuries.

Used in 18th century for wall paneling, carcases of veneered or lacquered furniture, painted furniture, mirror frames, drawer linings. Used in 19th century for cottage and kitchen furniture: dressers, cupboards, corner cupboards, tables, chests of drawers, beds, wardrobes, mirror frames.

Australian kitchen dressers, cupboards, tables, backboards; also used for garden furniture, shingles, windows, doors.

All kinds of American country furniture: Windsor and Boston rocker seats, four-poster bed headboards, tabletops, cupboards, Pennsylvania Dutch painted furniture, cottage furniture; also backboards, drawer sides, backs and bottoms of case pieces, unseen structural pieces.

Secondary wood for furniture making (white pine preferred).

English Windsor chairs, especially for cutwork splats, hoops, and turnings. Also a carcase timber; used in combination with other woods.

SPECIAL NOTES

Easily worked; a bit harder than pine. Strong aromatic scent said to repel moth larvae, act as a preservative. Oils should be sealed in with coat of shellac.

Second most important softwood used in Australia after kauri pine, which it resembles. Named for distinctive bands on trunk.

Distinctive odor with insect-repellant qualities due to presence of methyl eugenol oil in wood.

Most widely used softwood in Australia.

Lightweight, not very strong, average nail-holding ability. Easy to work. Dries quickly.

Also called Baltic pine. Known in England as "deal."

Exported along with large quantities of California redwood to Australia.

Most common American softwood. Knotty pine was originally considered a second best plank and was always painted. Stains and finishes beautifully.

A "hard" softwood. Long leaf variety does not make good furniture.

Celebrated wood of the medieval English longbow. Resists decay. Takes a high polish.

GLOSSARY

ACANTHUS — A multilobed leaf used in classical and Renaissance architecture and adopted later for rococo furniture design.

ADZE — Tool for smoothing wood surfaces. Similar to an ax, except that the blade is set perpendicular to the handle.

ALLIGATORED — Allover crackled or blistered effect on surface paint or varnish that resembles alligator hide.

ANILINE DYE — A synthetic organic dye.

APRON — A decorative piece of wood that hangs below a chest of drawers, tabletop, or stool or chair seat. Also called a skirt.

ARKWRIGHT — A woodworker who made arks or chests.

BAROQUE — Elaborate, ornate, flamboyant style originating in the late Renaissance and continuing through the eighteenth century. French Louis XIV and English William and Mary are examples of baroque furniture.

BEADING — In woodwork, a decorative molding with small, round bumps resembling a string of pearls. In canework, the finished edge on a woven-on cane seat.

BIBELOT — A small household ornament or decorative object valued for its curiosity, beauty, sentimental associations, or rarity.

BIEDERMEIER FURNITURE (GERMANY: 1815–1850) — A sturdily made, conservative, bourgeois interpretation of French Empire furniture. Extremely popular with middle classes throughout central Europe and Scandinavia.

BRACKET FOOT — A low L-shaped support made of two pieces of wood and joined to case furniture at the lower corner.

BREAKFRONT — A large formal cabinet, such as a library bookcase, with a rectangular midsection that juts out.

BUN FOOT — A large globe-shaped foot that is slightly flattened at the top and bottom.

BUTTRESS HINGE — A projecting cylindrical hinge that extends the length of the door. Used on armoires; also called a pin hinge.

CABRIOLE LEG — A strong, curved furniture leg inspired by animal legs. It is thick and curves out at the knee, becomes thin and tapered at the ankle, and ends in an ornamental foot.

CANTED CORNER — A flat 45-degree angling of the corner of cabinet furniture.

CANTERBURY — A floor stand with partitions for organizing and holding magazines, sheet music, and books.

CARCASE — The framework of cabinet furniture before decorative elements, such as veneer, are applied.

CASE FURNITURE — Cabinets and other boxlike or enclosed furniture, as opposed to chairs.

CHAMFERED — Angle-cut so as to remove wood equally from each plane surface. Typically applies to table legs.

CHIFFONIER — A Victorian era buffet with chest or cupboard below and open shelves above. Also refers to a high chest of drawers, often with attached swiveling mirror.

CHIPPENDALE FURNITURE
    (ENGLAND: 1749–1779; AMERICA: 1755–1790).
        A formal rococo style, named after English cabinetmaker Thomas Chippendale, that featured mahogany furniture with curvilinear design, detailed carved ornamentation, cabriole legs, ball and claw feet, delicate pierce-carved splat backs, and Chinese-inspired crest rails with ears. Late Chippendale was less ornamental and more rectilinear.

CHISEL   A wedgelike tool used for cutting and shaping.

CLEAT   A batten or piece of wood used to brace or strengthen.

CORNICE   A deep molding enclosing or crowning the top edge of a cabinet. May be a detachable frame, as on *kasten* and *Schränke.*

CREST   The topmost rail on a chair, settee, or cabinet.

CRINOLINE STRETCHER
        A chair stretcher in which an inward-curving piece joins the front legs and two short, straight pieces connect it to the back legs. Used on Windsor chairs.

CUPID'S BOW   A crest rail that is symmetrically wave-shaped, dipping in at the center and curving up at the ends.

CYMA CURVE   A double S-shaped curve. See Ogee.

DOVETAILING   A wood joining method using interlocking cutout wedges.

DOWEL   A round wooden peg used in furniture construction.

DRAWSHAVE   A woodworking tool consisting of a blade with a handle at each end.

EMPIRE FURNITURE (EUROPE: 1804–1815)
        A formal French style celebrating the Napoleonic Empire. Inspired by classical architecture, it introduced deeply scrolled sofa arms and backs, saber-shaped backswept chair legs, lyre motifs, sphinx feet, and cyma curves. The Empire influence continued in America, Australia, and Europe into the mid-1800s.

ESCUTCHEON   The decorative plate, usually metal, that protects a keyhole.

FIELDED PANEL   A wood panel with chamfered or bevelled edges and a raised center section, called a field, that is set into a mortised framework.

FINIAL   An ornamental projecting knob, as on the top of a bedpost.

FLUTING   Concave, parallel, shallow grooves inspired by classical Corinthian columns.

FOX WEDGE   A hidden wedge. The wedge is partially inserted into the tenon, then concealed as the tenon is tapped into the mortise.

FRAME   The heavy wooden skeleton of joined case furniture, into which panels are slotted.

FRENCH FOOT   Slightly outswept foot that continues directly from leg.

FRIEZE   The horizontal border directly below the cornice. Also the rectangular framework supporting a tabletop.

GILDING   A decorative surface finish of gold leaf.

GOUGE   A specialized chisel used for circular shaping.

H-HINGE   A hinge made up of two symmetrical metal parts that together resemble the letter H. Also called parliament hinge.

HASP-AND-STAPLE LOCK
        A hasp is a hinged link or plate that fits over an iron loop or staple. The hasp is secured with a separate padlock.

HEPPLEWHITE FURNITURE
    (ENGLAND: 1750–1790; AMERICA: 1785–1810)
        A formal neoclassical style named after English cabinetmaker Thomas Hepplewhite that introduced light, delicate mahogany furniture with straight lines, French feet, backswept legs, inlaid veneer, glazed doors, and other refinements.

HIGHBOY   A tall chest of drawers that is raised up on high legs.

JACOBEAN FURNITURE
  (ENGLAND: 1600–1690)
    A late medieval style, named after James I of England, featuring oak wainscot and turned armchairs, court and press cupboards, dower chests, joint stools, turned chairs with rush or splint seats. Also called Stuart furniture and, in America, Puritan furniture.

KNEE The upper rounded section of a cabriole leg.

LATH A thin, flat strip of wood.

LATHE A machine that rotates a block of wood for shaping with other tools.

LISTING The hand- or machine-woven wool tape used by the Shakers to weave two-tone chair seats.

LOPER One of a pair of pull-out slides for supporting the drop lid of a desk.

MARQUETRY Decorative inlaid veneering using different wood grains and colors to create patterns.

MARRIAGE A two- or three-stage piece of furniture in which the individual sections originally came from different sources.

MORTISE-AND-TENON JOIN
    A common wood joining method in which a projecting arm locks into a corresponding hole.

MUNTINS The horizontal and vertical wood divisions that hold panes of glass in a window.

OGEE An S-shaped decorative molding.

ONION FOOT See Bun foot.

ORMOLU Ornate cast brass or bronze decoration applied to furniture, mirrors, sconces, and other objects to resemble gold.

PAD FOOT The slightly flattened end on a cabriole leg that resembles an animal's paw.

PATINA The rich depth of color and texture that wood acquires over years of natural oxidation and normal use. Patina is a valuable quality of antique furniture and is not readily simulated.

PEDIMENT A triangular crest that rises to a center point.

PINTLE HINGE A rod or dowel that joins a cabinet door or chest lid to the framework and allows it to swing open.

PLINTH BASE A low floor-hugging framework, often separate, that supports cabinet furniture.

QUEEN ANNE FURNITURE
  (ENGLAND: 1702–1749; AMERICA: 1720–1760)
    An English early rococo style that introduced lightweight construction, smooth surfaces, delicate cabriole legs with no stretchers, Dutch pad feet, vase-shaped chair splats, curved chair rails, the H-hinge, and fan, sunburst, and scallop shell carvings. Preferred woods were walnut, maple, cherry, and mahogany.

RAIL A horizontal support in a chair or chest frame.

REEDING Smooth, curved, convex ridges; the reverse effect of fluting.

ROCOCO Elaborate formal style originating in the eighteenth century that stylized the baroque flamboyance by emphasizing asymmetry, S-curves, carving, and natural motifs including shells, rocks, and foliage. French Louis XV and English Chippendale are examples of rococo furniture.

ROLLING PIN The Australian name for the cylindrical molding with end finials applied to the backs of miner's couches and the head-boards and footboards of four-poster beds.

SADDLED SEAT A softwood seat, as on a Windsor chair, that is gently shaped to resemble the seat of a saddle.

SERPENTINE A three-part curve that is convex in the center and concave at each end.

SETTEE A seat with an open back and arms for two or more persons.

SHERATON FURNITURE
   (ENGLAND: 1790–1810; AMERICA: 1790–1815).
      A formal neoclassical style named after English cabinetmaker Thomas Sheraton that featured delicate carving, straight lines, rectangular chair backs, slender turned and reeded legs, paw feet, urn-shaped splats, lyre motifs.

SKIRT   See Apron.

SPANISH FOOT   A ribbed outward-curving foot that curls in at the base.

SPINDLE   A shaved or lathe-turned rod, stick, or dowel.

SPLAT   The vertical center piece, often decoratively shaped, in a chair back.

SQUAB   A padded cushion shaped to fit a chair or couch seat.

STILE   A vertical support in a chair or chest frame.

STRAP HINGE   A hinge with a long extending arm that is bolted or screwed to the wood.

STRETCHER   A turned or squared rail connecting and thereby strengthening chair or table legs.

TACK CLOTH   Cheesecloth impregnated with a resinous substance so that it picks up small pieces of lint and dust.

TAMBOUR DOOR   A flexible sliding door made of thin strips of wood glued to a fabric backing.

TESTER   The framework on a high four-poster bed for holding a canopy; also the canopy and fabric hangings themselves.

THROUGH TENON   A tenon that is even with or protrudes from the opposite side of its entry in the case that the mortise was cut clear through the wood.

TONGUE-AND-GROOVE JOIN
    A method of joining the long edges of wood boards together by slotting long tenons into chiseled-out channels.

TRUMPET LEG   A turned, cone-shaped leg that is narrow at the bottom and flares out at the top.

TURNING   The process of decoratively shaping wood blanks on a lathe.

VENEER   Thin slices of well-figured, decoratively grained wood glued to a carcase frame.

WAINSCOT   The lower paneled section of a wall.

WILLIAM AND MARY FURNITURE
   (ENGLAND AND HOLLAND: 1689–1702;
   AMERICA: 1700–1725)
      A baroque style that featured tall, heavily turned trumpet legs, double-curved legs and stretchers, low-hanging aprons, ball, onion, and Spanish feet, and tear-drop drawer pulls. Furniture included walnut and oak slant-top desks, gateleg, butterfly and tavern tables, highboys, lowboys, high-backed chairs with caned panels, and upholstered easy chairs.

SOURCES

ANTIQUES

THE FOLLOWING AUCTION HOUSES, SOCIETIES, AND DIRECTORIES CAN OFFER INFORMATION ON ANTIQUE COUNTRY FURNITURE.

AUSTRALIA

The Australiana Society
P.O. Box 322
Roseville, NSW 2069

Christie's Australia Pty. Ltd.
1 Darling Street
South Yarra
Melbourne, VIC 3141
613 820 4311.
Regional representatives are located in Adelaide and Sydney.

Sotheby's
Robert Bleakley
13 Gurner Street, Paddington
Sydney, NSW 2021
61 (2) 332 3500

Sotheby's
Ann Roberts
926 High Street
Armadale
Melbourne, VIC 8143
61 (3) 509-2900

CANADA

Christie, Manson & Woods Canada
170 Bloor Street West, Suite 210
Toronto, ON M5S 1T9
(416) 960-2063

Sotheby's
9 Hazelton Avenue
Toronto, ON M5R 2E1
(416) 926-1774
Regional Canadian associates are located in Montreal, Vancouver, and Victoria.

UNITED KINGDOM AND IRELAND

Christie, Manson & Woods Ltd.
8 King Street, St. James's
London SW1Y 6QT
England
071 859 9060
Regional representatives are located throughout the United Kingdom and Ireland.

Christie's Scotland Ltd.
164-166 Bath Street
Glasgow G2 4TG
Scotland
041 332 8134

Christie's South Kensington Ltd.
85 Old Brompton Road
London SW7 3LD
England
071 581 7611

Guide to Antique Shops of Britain
Antique Collector's Club
5 Church Street
Woodbridge, Suffolk IP12 1DS
England
39 438 5501
Annual, about 1,000 pages, lists about 7,000 antique shops in Great Britain. To order in North America, write or call:
Antique Collector's Club
Market Street Industrial Park
Wappinger's Falls, NY 12590
(914) 297-0003

Robson Lowe at Christie's
8 King Street, St. James's
London SW1Y 6QT
England
071 839 9060

Sotheby's
34-35 New Bond Street
London W1A 2AA
England
071 493 8080
Regional representatives are located throughout the United Kingdom.

UNITED STATES

Antiques Directory and Traveller's Guide
Abbotsford Press
63 Hillside Avenue
Melrose, MA 02176
1-800-347-8838
Guide to more than 2,000 antique shops in New England and New York's Hudson Valley. Updated annually.

AntiqueWeek [weekly]
AntiqueWeek Antique Shop Guide [annual]
Mayhill Publications, Inc.
P.O. Box 90
Knightstown, IN 46148
1-800-876-5133
Each publication is available in two regional editions covering central and eastern United States. *AntiqueWeek* includes auction calendar listings as well as antique shop information. In continuous publication since 1967.

Christie, Manson & Woods International, Inc.
502 Park Avenue
New York, NY 10022
(212) 546-1000; American furniture and decorative art, (212) 546-1181; European furniture, 212-546-1151. Regional U.S. offices are located in Baltimore, Boston, Chicago, Dallas, Los Angeles, Miami, New Orleans, Newport, New York, Palm Beach, Philadelphia, San Francisco, and Washington.

Sotheby's
1334 York Avenue
New York, NY 10021
(212) 606-7000
Regional U.S. representatives and associates are located in Atlanta, Baltimore, Beverly Hills, Boston, Chicago, Dallas, Hawaii, New Orleans, New York, Palm Beach, Philadelphia, Rancho Santa Fe, St. Louis, San Francisco, Seattle, and Washington, D.C.

REPRODUCTION FURNITURE

*WRITE OR CALL FOR INFORMATION ON RETAIL STORES IN YOUR AREA.

AUSTRALIA

Crafts Council of New South Wales
88 George Street
The Rocks
Sydney, NSW 2000
(02) 247 9126

Melchair Furniture Pty Ltd*
65-69 Killara Road
Campbellfield, VIC 3061
(03) 357 8033
Pressed wood kangaroo back chairs.

UNITED KINGDOM

TO LOCATE SMALL AND MEDIUM-SIZED BRITISH FIRMS MAKING REPRODUCTION FURNITURE AND FITTED FURNITURE FOR KITCHENS, BATHS, AND BEDROOMS, CONSULT THE ADVERTISEMENTS IN THE HOME DECORATING MAGAZINES LISTED UNDER PERIODICALS. THE FOLLOWING ORGANIZATIONS ARE DEVOTED TO PROMOTING THE WORK OF INDIVIDUAL ARTISANS:

Made in Scotland Ltd
The Craft Centre
Station Road
Beauly, Inverness-shire IV4 7EH
Scotland
(0463) 782578

Rural Development Commission
141 Castle Street
Salisbury, Wiltshire SP1 3TP
England
(0722) 336255

UNITED STATES:

Century Furniture Industries*
401 11 Street, NW
Hickory, NC 28601
(704) 328-1851
Licensed reproductions from the Henry Ford Museum & Greenfield Village Collection

Cohasset Colonials
533 Ship Street
Cohasset, MA 02025-2096
(617) 383-0110
Reproduction furniture to build from kits.

Colonial Williamsburg Craft House*
P.O. Box 3532, Dept. 023
Williamsburg, VA 23187-3532
Catalog available; call 1-800-446-9240.

The Harden Furniture Company*
Mill Pond Way
McConnellsville, NY 13401-1844

Henredon Furniture Industries,
Incorporated*
P.O. Box 70
Morganton, NC 28655

The Lane Company, Inc.*
Box 151, E. Franklin Avenue
Altavista, VA 24517-0151
Licensed reproductions from the
Museum of American Folk Art

Lexington Furniture Industries*
Lexington, NC 27293

Shaker Workshops
P.O. Box 1028
Concord, MA 01742
(617) 646-8985
Reproduction furniture to build from
kits. Catalog available.

TO LOCATE SMALLER CABINETMAKING
SHOPS AND ARTISANS SPECIALIZING IN
AMERICAN REPRODUCTIONS, CONSULT
THE JURY-SELECTED DIRECTORY
PUBLISHED ANNUALLY IN THE AUGUST
ISSUE OF *EARLY AMERICAN LIFE*
MAGAZINE AND THE ADVERTISEMENTS
IN *THE MAGAZINE ANTIQUES* AND
MAINE ANTIQUES DIGEST. THE
FOLLOWING ORGANIZATIONS WILL
ALSO BE OF HELP:

Pennsylvania Guild of Craftsmen
P.O. Box 820
Richboro, PA 18954

Society of Workers in Early Arts and
Trades (SWEAT)
606 Lake Lena Blvd.
Auburndale, FL 33823
Annual directory of U.S. and
Canadian craftspersons, a quarterly
newsletter, and computer database
listings.

MUSEUMS

THE MUSEUMS LISTED BELOW
REPRESENT A SMALL SAMPLING OF THE
MANY EXHIBITS AND COLLECTIONS
FEATURING COUNTRY FURNITURE.
WRITE OR CALL AHEAD FOR
INFORMATION REGARDING DAYS AND
HOURS OPEN, ADMISSION FEES, AND
SPECIAL EXHIBITS AND EVENTS. FOR
FURTHER SOURCES, CONSULT A LOCAL
MUSEUM GUIDE FOR YOUR AREA OR
DESTINATION, IF YOU ARE TRAVELING.

AUSTRALIA

Art Gallery of South Australia
North Terrace
Adelaide, SA 5000
(08) 207-7200
Comprehensive collection of
Australian works of art, English and
European furniture.

Art Gallery of Western Australia
Perth Cultural Center
James Street
Perth, WA 6000
(09) 328 7233

Australian National Gallery
Parkes Place
Parkes, ACT 2601
(06) 271 2411
Collection includes Australian fine
and decorative arts, folk art.

Jam Factory Craft & Design Centre
1 Morphett Street
Adelaide, SA 5000
(08) 410 0727

National Gallery of Victoria
180 St. Kilda Road
Melbourne, VIC 3004
(03) 685 0222

Powerhouse Museum of Applied Arts
& Sciences
659 Harris Street
Ultimo, NSW 2007
217-0111
Extensive collection, including
Australian decorative arts, bush
furniture.

Queensland Art Gallery
Queensland Cultural Centre
South Bank
South Brisbane, QLD 4101
(07) 840 7333

Tasmanian Museum & Art Gallery
40 Macquarie Street
Hobart, TAS 7000
(002) 23 1422

CANADA

McCord Museum of Canadian
History/Musée McCord d'Histoire
Canadienne
690 rue Sherbrooke ouest
Montreal, Quebec H3A 1E9
Large, comprehensive collection
includes eighteenth- to twentieth-
century furniture.

Ukrainian Cultural Heritage Village
c/o 8820-112 Street
Edmonton, Alberta T6G 2P8
Over thirty restored and furnished
structures reflecting Ukrainian
settlement in Canada, 1892-1930.

Upper Canada Village
R.R. #1
Morrisburg, Ontario K0C 1X0
(613) 543-3704
Open-air museum with forty-five
restored buildings portraying rural
community, c. 1865.

IRELAND

Bunratty Castle and Folk Park
Bunratty, Co. Clare
Adjoining Folk Park features replicas
of rural and town homes, furnishings
representing many different regions of
nineteenth-century Ireland.

UNITED KINGDOM

The American Museum in Britain
Claverton Manor
Bath, Avon BA2 7BD
(0225) 460503
Includes seventeenth- through
nineteenth-century American
furnishings; special galleries devoted
to Shakers, Pennsylvania Germans,
New Mexico colonists.

Museum of East Anglian Life
Abbot's Hall
Stowmarket, Suffolk IP14 1DL
Open-air seventy-acre site including
historic buildings, domestic and
industrial displays, craft
demonstrations.

Victoria and Albert Museum—The
National Museum of Art and Design
Cromwell Road
South Kensington, London SW7 2RL
(071) 938-8500
The United Kingdom's largest and
most well-known museum.

The White House Museum of
Buildings and Country Life
Aston Munslow, nr. Craven Arms,
Shropshire SY7 9ER
A true English country house and
farm; home of the Stedman family
from 1332 until 1946.

Wycombe Chair Museum
Castle Hill House
Priory Avenue
High Wycombe, Buckinghamshire
HP13 6PX
Exhibits on Windsor chair making,
cane and rush seating, country
furniture history.

UNITED STATES:

Adirondack Museum
Routes 28N and 30
Blue Mountain Lake, NY 12812
(518) 352-7311
Indoor and outdoor exhibits,
including rustic furniture.

American Swedish Institute
2600 Park Avenue
Minneapolis, MN 55407
(612) 871-4907
Collection documenting Swedish
pioneer and immigrant life in
America; also seventeenth- to
eighteenth-century Swedish
furnishings.

Colonial Williamsburg Foundation
P.O. Box 1776
Williamsburg, VA 23187-1776
(804) 229-1000
Re-creation of the eighteenth-century
town of Williamsburg; 173-acre site
with nearly five hundred preserved,
restored, or reconstructed buildings
open to the public.

Hancock Shaker Village
P.O. Box 898
Junction of Route 20 and 41
Pittsfield, MA 01202
(413) 443-0188

Henry Ford Museum and Greenfield
Village
20900 Oakwood Blvd.
P.O. Box 1970
Dearborn, MI 48121-1970
(313) 271-1620
Indoor/outdoor museum of American
cultural and material history; 260-acre
site with approximately one hundred
historic houses and craft workshops.

Hitchcock Museum
Riverton, CT 06065
(203) 379-1003
Site of the reopened and operating
Hitchcock chair factory. Lambert
House, factory store, and village
gardens are open for display.

Museum of American Folk Art
Two Lincoln Square
(Columbus Avenue between 65th and
66th)
New York, NY 10023
Mailing address:
61 W 62nd Street
New York, NY 10023-7015
(212) 977-7170
American eighteenth- through
twentieth-century folk and decorative
art. Licensed reproduction furniture
through The Lane Company.

Museum of New Mexico
Palace of the Governor
P.O. Box 2087
Sante Fe, NM 87504-2087
(505) 827-6450
History and folk art of New Mexico,
including colonial period.

Old Sturbridge Village
1 Old Sturbridge Village Road
Sturbridge, MA 01566
(508) 347-3362
Re-created New England village,
1790–1840, over forty historic homes,
workshops, other buildings; craft
demonstrations.

Shaker Village of Pleasant Hill
3500 Lexington Road
Harrodsburg, KY 40330
(606) 734-5411
Furniture and thirty buildings from
original Shaker community, early
1800s.

Vesterheim, The Norwegian-American
Museum
502 W. Water Street
Decorah, IA 52101
(319) 382-9681
Norwegian and Norwegian-American
material culture. One of the largest
and oldest ethnic musuems in the
United States.

Winterthur Museum and Gardens
Winterthur, DE 19735
(302) 888-4600
Early American furniture and
domestic objects arranged in nearly
two hundred period rooms,
seventeenth century through 1860.

PERIODICALS

THE FOLLOWING PUBLICATIONS
INCLUDE ARTICLES, CALENDAR
LISTINGS, AND ADVERTISEMENTS OF
INTEREST TO THOSE COLLECTING OR
DECORATING WITH ANTIQUE OR
REPRODUCTION COUNTRY FURNITURE.
WRITE FOR SUBSCRIPTION INFOR-
MATION, INCLUDING FOREIGN RATES.

AUSTRALIA

Australiana
The Australiana Society
P.O. Box 322
Roseville, NSW 2069
560 6022
Quarterly journal of The Australiana
Society.

Australian House Beautiful
Southdown Press
32 Walsh Street
W. Melbourne, VIC 3000

Australian House & Garden
Australian Consolidated Press
Box 5252
Sydney, NSW 2000

Heritage Australia
Australian Council of National Trusts
P.O. Box 1002
Civic Square, ACT 2608
062-476766

National Trust Magazine
Observatory Hill
Sydney, NSW 2000
Subscription inquiries:
G.P.O. Box 518
Sydney, NSW 2001
Official publication of the National
Trust of Australia, which seeks to
conserve Australia's heritage of historic
buildings and natural beauty.

CANADA

Canadian House & Home
Canadian Home Publishers
511 King Street West, Suite 120
Toronto, Ontario M5V 2Z4
(416) 593-0666

Century Home
Bluestone House, Inc.
12 Mill Street South
Port Hope, Ontario L1A 2S5
(416) 885-2449

City & Country Home
Canadian Home Decor Magazines
277 Front Street East, Suite 100
Toronto, Ontario M5A 1E8
(416) 368-7889

UNITED KINGDOM

Country Homes & Interiors
Homes & Gardens
The SouthBank Publishing Group
IPC Magazines Ltd.
King's Reach Tower
Stamford Street
London SE1 9LS
England
01 261 5000
Subscription inquiries:
Quadrant Subscription Services Ltd.
Oakfield House
Perrymount Road
Haywards Heath, West Sussex RH16
3DH
(0789) 200289

Period Living
EMAP Elan
Victory House
14 Leicester Place
London WC2H 7BP
England
(0908) 371981

WoodTurning
Woodworking Today
Guild of Master Craftsman
Publications Ltd
Castle Place
166 High Street
Lewes, East Sussex BN7 1XU
England
(0273) 477374

The World of Interiors
The Condé Nast Publications Ltd.
234 King's Road
London SW3 5UA
England
071 351 5177

UNITED STATES:

House Beautiful
Hearst Corporation
1700 Broadway
New York, NY 10019-5905
(212) 903-5000

Country Home
Traditional Home
Meredith Corporation
1716 Locust Street
Des Moines, IA 50380-0635

Country Living
250 W. 55th Street,
New York, NY 10019
Subscription inquiries:
P.O. Box 7136
Red Oak, IA 51591-2136

Early American Life
6405 Flank Drive
Harrisburg, PA 17112
Subscription inquiries:
P.O. Box 1620
Mt. Morris, IL 61054

Elle Decor
Elle Publishing
1633 Broadway
New York, NY 10019
(212) 767-5800
International decorating styles.

The Magazine Antiques
Brant Publications
575 Broadway
New York, NY 10012
(212) 941-2800
Covers all antiques, with emphasis on
furniture.

Maine Antiques Digest
Box 1429
Waldoboro, ME 04572-0645
(207) 832-7534
Covers United States art and antiques
market (not just Maine)

BIBLIOGRAPHY

Barwick, JoAnn. *Scandinavian Country.* New York: Clarkson Potter Publishers, 1991.

Blanchard, Robert Ray. *How to Restore and Decorate Chairs in Early American Styles.* New York: Dover Publications, Inc., 1980.

Boger, Louise Ade. *The Complete Guide to Furniture Styles.* New York: Charles Scribner's Sons, 1969.

Buchanan, George. *The Illustrated Handbook of Furniture Restoration.* New York: Harper & Row, Publishers, 1985.

Butler, Joseph T. *Field Guide to American Antique Furniture.* New York: Facts on File, 1985.

Claret Rubira, José. *Encyclopedia of Spanish Period Furniture Designs.* New York: Sterling Publishing Co., Inc., 1984.

Country Furniture: America's Rich Legacy of Design and Craftsmanship. Time-Life Books, Inc., 1989.

Craig, Clifford, Kevin Fahy, and E. Graeme Robertson. *Early Colonial Furniture in New South Wales and Van Diemen's Land.* Melbourne: Georgian House, 1972.

Csilléry, Klára K. *Hungarian Village Furniture.* Corvina, Budapest: Kossuth Printing House, 1972.

Dannenberg, Linda, Pierre Levec, and Pierre Moulin. *Pierre Deux's Brittany.* New York: Clarkson Potter Publishers, 1989.

Dannenberg, Linda, Pierre Levec, and Pierre Moulin. *Pierre Deux's Normandy.* New York: Clarkson Potter Publishers, 1988.

Davidson, Alan, ed. *The Cook's Room.* New York: HarperCollins Publishers, 1991.

Denker, Ellen, and Bert Denker. *The Rocking Chair Book.* New York: Mayflower Books, Inc., 1979.

Emmerling, Mary. *American Country Classics.* New York: Clarkson Potter Publishers, 1990.

Emmerling, Mary. *American Country South.* New York: Clarkson Potter Publishers, 1989.

Fairbanks, Jonathan L., and Elizabeth Bidwell Bates. *American Furniture 1620 to the Present.* New York: Richard Marek Publishers, 1981.

Fales, Dean A., Jr. *American Painted Furniture, 1660–1880.* New York: Bonanza Books, 1886.

Filbee, Marjorie. *Dictionary of Country Furniture.* London: The Connoisseur, 1977.

Gaynor, Elizabeth. *Finland: Living Design.* New York: Rizzoli, 1984.

Gilbert, Christopher. *English Vernacular Furniture, 1750–1900.* New Haven: Yale University Press, 1991.

Gilborn, Craig. *Adirondack Furniture and the Rustic Tradition.* New York: Harry N. Abrams, Inc., Publishers, 1987.

Hill, Anthony. *Antique Furniture in Australia: Finding, Identifying, Restoring and Enjoying It.* Ringwood, Victoria, Australia: Viking Penguin Books Australia Ltd. 1985.

Hinckley, F. Lewis. *Directory of the Historic Cabinet Woods.* New York: Crown Publishers, Inc., 1960.

Hooper, Toby, and Juliana Hooper. *Australian Country Furniture.* Ringwood, Victoria, Australia: Viking Penguin Books, Australia Ltd, 1988.

Innes, Jocasta. *Decorators' Directory of Style.* New York: Gallery Books, 1987.

Jackson, Albert, and David Day. *The Antiques Care & Repair Handbook.* New York: Alfred A. Knopf, 1984.

Johnson, Edwin. *Restoring Antique Furniture.* New York: Sterling Publishing Co., Inc., 1982.

Katz, Sali Barnett. *Hispanic Furniture.* Stamford, Conn. Architectural Book Publishing Co., 1986.

Keijser, Hans, and Lars Sjöberg, adapted by Ron Willick. *Making Swedish Country Furniture and Household Things.* Point Roberts, Wash.: Hartley & Marks, Inc., 1990.

Kettell, Russell Hawes. *Pine Furniture of Early New England.* Garden City, New York: Doubleday, Doran & Company, 1929.

King, Constance. *Country Pine Furniture.* Secaucus, N. J.: Chartwell Books, 1989.

Kovel, Ralph, and Terry Kovel. *American Country Furniture 1780–1875.* New York: Crown Publishers, Inc., 1965.

Larsson, Carl. *A Home.* New York: G. P. Putnam's Sons, 1974.

Madigan, Mary Jean, and Susan Colgan, eds. *Early American Furniture from Settlement to City.* New York: Billboard Publications, Inc., 1983.

Martin, Philip. *Rosemaling in the Upper Midwest.* Mount Horeb, Wis.: Wisconsin Folk Museum, 1989.

Oglesby, Catharine. *French Provincial Decorative Art.* New York: Charles Scribner's Sons, 1951.

Ormsbee, Thomas H. *Field Guide to American Victorian Furniture.* New York: Bonanza Books, 1952.

Pain, Howard. *The Heritage of Country Furniture.* Toronto: Van Nostrand Reinhold Ltd., 1978.

Plath, Iona. *The Decorative Arts of Sweden.* New York: Dover Publications, Inc., 1966.

Plowden, Anna, and Frances Halahan. *Looking After Antiques.* New York: Harper & Row Publishers, 1988.

Quimby, Ian M. G., and Scott T. Swank, ed. *Perspectives on American Folk Art.* New York: W. W. Norton & Company, 1980.

Ramsey, L. G., and Helen Comstock, eds. *Antique Furniture: The Guide for Collectors, Investors and Dealers.* New York: Hawthorn Books Inc., 1969.

Saunders, Richard. *Wicker Furniture: A Guide to Restoring and Collecting.* New York: Crown Publishers, Inc., 1990.

Saunders, Richard, and Paula Olsson. *Living With Wicker.* New York: Crown Publishers, Inc., 1992.

Seebohm, Carol. *English Country.* New York: Clarkson Potter Publishers, 1987.

Shackleton, Philip. *The Furniture of Old Ontario.* Toronto: Macmillan of Canada, 1978.

Shipway, Verna Cook, and Warren Shipway. *Mexican Interiors.* New York: Architectural Book Publishing Co., Inc., 1965.

Sloane, Eric. *A Museum of Early American Tools.* New York: Henry Holt and Company, Inc., 1990.

Taylor, Lonn, and Dessa Bokides. *New Mexican Furniture 1600–1940.* Sante Fe, N. Mex.: Museum of New Mexico Press, 1987.

Toller, Jane. *English Country Furniture.* South Brunswick and New York: A. S. Barnes and Company, 1973.

Vedder, Alan C. *Furniture of Spanish New Mexico.* Sante Fe, N. Mex.: Sunstone Press, 1982.

Viel, Lyndon C. *Antique Ethnic Furniture.* Des Moines, Iowa: Wallace Homestead, 1983.

Ward, Gerald W. R., ed. *Perspectives on American Furniture.* New York: W. W. Norton & Company, 1988.

Williams, A. D. *Spanish Colonial Furniture.* Salt Lake City: Gibbs M. Smith, Inc., 1982.

INDEX

ENCYCLOPEDIA OF COUNTRY FURNITURE

PHOTO CREDITS

ILLUSTRATIONS BY STEVEN ARCELLA: PP. 20 (TOP), 26 (TOP), 47, 72 (TOP), 82 (ALL)83 (ALL), 84, 87, 145 (ALL),

© MARK BENNET: PP. 75, 78, 125 (TOP)

COURTESY OF BUFFALO BILL HISTORICAL CENTER, CODY, WY: P. 81 (ALL)

COURTESY OF COHASSET COLONIALS, MASSACHUSETTS: PP. 115 (BOTTOM), 116

© GRAHAM CORNALL/CORNALL ANTIQUES, VICTORIA, AUSTRALIA: PP. 12 (BOTTOM), 13 (ALL), 14 (BOTTOM), 15 (ALL), 20 (MIDDLE), 44 (BOTTOM LEFT AND BOTTOM RIGHT), 49 (LEFT), 52 (TOP), 53, 54, 58–59, 77 (RIGHT), 86 (BOTTOM), 88, 123, 127 (ALL), 128, 152

© RICHARD DAY: PP. 56 (BOTTOM), 77 (LEFT), 114 (RIGHT), 143 (BOTTOM), 144

© DICK DIETRICH: P. 20 (BOTTOM)

COURTESY OF ERCOL FURNITURE LTD.,BUCKINGHAMSHIRE, ENGLAND: P. 25

© DANIEL EIFERT; DESIGN: MARCIA GEWANTER: P. 57

© ESTO PHOTOGRAPHICS: P. 12 (TOP)

© TIMOTHY FULLER: P. 109

© A. GURMANKIN/UNICORN STOCK PHOTOS: P. 148

© KARI HAAVISTO: PP. 113, 130, 131, 136, 138, 139 (RIGHT), 140, 146 (BOTTOM), 154 (TOP)

COURTESY OF CHRIS HARTER, NEW YORK: PP. 37 (TOP LEFT AND RIGHT), 115 (TOP)

© JIM HAYS/UNICORN STOCK PHOTOS: P. 33

COURTESY OF KENNETH HEISER, PENNSYLVANIA: PP. 30, 38 (BOTTOM)

COURTESY OF HENKEL HARRIS, VIRGINIA: PP. 118, 119

COURTESY OF HITCHCOCK CHAIR COMPANY, CONNECTICUT: PP. 79 (ALL), 80

© IPC MAGAZINES 1992 LTD./ROBERT HARDING SYNDICATION; PHOTOGRAPHY BY TONY TIMMINGTON: PP. 26 (BOTTOM), 29

COURTESY OF JC PENNEY: P. 162

© JOHN KANE: P. 37 (BOTTOM): DESIGN BY JIM SCHRIBER; PP. 52 (BOTTOM), 117, 124

© LYNN KARLIN: PP. 44 (TOP), 142 (RIGHT)

© BALTHAZAR KORAB: PP. 35 (RIGHT), 100

© IMAGE/DENNIS KRUKOWSKI; PP. 3, 6 (TOP); ALL PICTURES AS SEEN IN THE FARMHOUSE, BANTAM DELL DOUBLEDAY, 1987: PP. 11, 163: BILLYEU FARM; 17: FARAWAY RANCH; 22 (TOP): DESIGN/BRENDA SPEIGHT; PP. 85, 114 (TOP): DESIGN/DAVID WEBSTER AND ASSOCIATES, THE HOUSE ON FREER TATENT; P. 122 : GREENWOOD FARM

COURTESY OF LA BARGE ALEXANDRINE COLLECTION: P.70 (BOTTOM)

© CHUN Y. LAI/ ESTO PHOTOGRAPHICS: PP. 16 (TOP), 74, 86 TOP, 89 (TOP), 90, 111, 125 (BOTTOM), 146 TOP, 149 (LEFT)

© TIM LEE: PP. 6 (BOTTOM), 174

© ERICH LESSING/ART RESOURCE, NEW YORK: PP. 35 (LEFT), 36, 50 (BOTTOM)

© E. A. McGEE/FPG INTERNATIONAL: P. 50 (LEFT)

COURTESY OF MELCHAIR INC. CAMPBELLFIELD, AUSTRALIA: P. 14 (TOP)

COURTESY OF MINWAX: PP. 168 (ALL), 169 (ALL), 172 (ALL), 173 (ALL)

METROPOLITAN MUSEUM OF ART: GIFT OF MRS. RUSSEL SAGE: P.142 (LEFT)

© THE MONTREAL MUSEUM OF FINE ARTS COLLECTION: P. 31: PHOTOGPRAPHY BY CHRISTINE GUEST; PP. 32, 69: PHOTOGRAPHY BY MARILYN AITKEN

NEW YORK PUBLIC LIBRARY PICTURE COLLECTION: P. 45

COURTESY OF THE MUSEUM OF INTERNATIONAL FOLK ART, SANTA FE, NEW MEXICO; PHOTOGRAPHY BY BLAIR CLARK: PP. 101, 104 (LEFT), 108 (BOTTOM)

© KENT OPPENHEIMER: P. 156

COURTESY OF PARKS OF THE ST. LAWRENCE, UPPER CANADA VILLAGE, ONTARIO: PP. 141, 150

© ROBERT PERRON: PP. 16 (RIGHT), 51 (BOTTOM), 76, 112, 150, 153, 155, 158; P. 92 (RIGHT): COURTESY OF HOUSE BEAUTIFUL

COURTESY OF PIER 1 IMPORTS, TEXAS: P. 160

© ROBERT RECK: P. 102

© ERIC ROTH: 19, 38 (TOP), 89 (BOTTOM), 93, 110

© EDE ROTHAUS: PP. 10, 99 (TOP LEFT), 99 (TOP RIGHT)

© BILL ROTHSCHILD: PP. 18, 43; FURNITURE COURTESY OF WENDOVERS, N. Y. C.: PP. 22 (BOTTOM), 27, 28 (ALL), 92 (LEFT), 151

© NICOLAS SAPIEHA/ART RESOURCE, NEW YORK: PP. 97, 98 (ALL), 99 (BOTTOM)

© SHELLEY SECCOMBE: PP. 56 (TOP), 64, 149 (RIGHT)

© WILLIAM B. SEITZ: PP. 8,91

© SHELBURNE MUSEUM, SHELBURNE, VERMONT: PP. 39, 42 (ALL), 48, 51 (TOP)

COURTESY OF THE SOUTHAMPTON COMPANY INC., NORTH CAROLINA: P. 166 (ALL)

COURTESY OF JOHN SPICER, OHIO: PP. 61 (ALL), 96

COURTESY OF TAOS FURNITURE, NEW MEXICO: PP. 103, 104 (RIGHT), 104 (BOTTOM), 106

COURTESY OF THONET, NORTH CAROLINA: PP. 23 (ALL), 24 (ALL), 34 (BOTTOM)

COURTESY OF TRADITION FRANCE: PP.66, 70(TOP)

COURTESY OF GREG VASILEFF, CONNECTICUTT: P. 40: PHOTOGRAPHY BY JOHN SCHNEFKE

© VESTERHEIM NORWEGIAN MUSEUM: PP. 49 (RIGHT), 63, 132, 133 (ALL), 134 (ALL), 135 (ALL),137, 139 (LEFT), 154 (BOTTOM)

© JONATHAN WALLEN: PP. 34 (TOP), 55, 67, 94, 108 (TOP)

COURTESY OF WATCH HILL ANTIQUES, MICHIGAN: PP. 72 (BOTTOM), 73 (ALL)

© TERRY WILD STUDIO: PP. 62, 126, 129